David McKittrick, who was born in Belfast, has been Ireland correspondent for the *Independent* since 1986. He has reported on Northern Ireland and Anglo-Irish relations since the early 1970s. He is a regular broadcaster on British and Irish television and radio. A previous collection of his work, *Despatches from Belfast*, was published by Blackstaff Press in 1989.

ENDGAME

The Search for Peace in Northern Ireland

DAVID McKITTRICK

THE
BLACKSTAFF
PRESS

BELFAST

First published in 1994 by
The Blackstaff Press Limited
3 Galway Park, Dundonald, Belfast BT16 0AN, Northern Ireland
with the assistance of the Joseph Rowntree Charitable Trust
© This collection, David McKittrick, 1994
© Photographs, the *Independent*, 1994
Typeset by Paragon Typesetters, Queensferry, Clywd
Printed in England by the Cromwell Press Limited
A CIP catalogue record for this book
is available from the British Library
ISBN 0-85640-530-2

CONTENTS

PART TWO
THE PEACE PROCESS

for
Granny McKittrick

PREFACE

This book covers Northern Ireland events and Anglo-Irish relations in the eventful period from 1989 till mid-1994. It was a time filled with violence and conflict, but also a period of fundamental underlying changes in society. Above all, it witnessed the emergence of the "peace process" – the idea that, after 25 years of killing, the republican movement might at last be seriously contemplating a move away from violence.

At the time of writing, much of the original hope for an early end to the IRA campaign has faded. But the idea has not vanished completely, and it has left an important residue: a sense in many quarters that the Troubles are at last entering their final phase. The notion has taken root that while the violence may continue for months and possibly for years, the search has begun for a formula which could represent, for all concerned, honourable peace terms. This is in itself an advance on the previously widely held belief that Northern Ireland was locked into an endless war. Whatever happens, disagreements and conflicts between the various elements will continue. The hope is that some day in the not too distant future they will be conducted through argument and debate rather than at the point of a gun.

This material first appeared in the *Independent* and the *Independent on Sunday*. The articles have been tidied, edited, and in some cases shortened, in order to fit into thematic chapters. As will be evident, the paper has always been concerned not only to cover the events of the day but also to look behind the news at trends and developments which, though less obvious, are nonetheless of great significance.

Much thanks is due to the many sources who regularly helped with information, analysis and insight. My thanks go to my colleagues in various departments of the *Independent*, in particular to David Felton and the home desk team. Our picture desk and graphics department were especially helpful in supplying the illustrations.

Many journalists have been of great help, in different ways, over the years. I am particularly indebted to Deric Henderson, Tom Kelly, Ed Moloney, Eamonn Mallie, Fionnuala O Connor, Brian Rowan and John Ware. Fionnuala O Connor and Tom Kelly spent much time reading various drafts of this book and offered much useful advice and suggestions on its content and structure. Steve Bruce, Seamus Kelters and another friend who must remain nameless were also helpful. It has, I hope, been much improved by their efforts; any remaining shortcomings and errors are all my own work.

The team at Blackstaff Press who guided me through my first collection (*Despatches from Belfast*, 1989) were as patient, understanding and supportive as ever.

Finally, thanks to the family, Pat, Kerry and Julie, for putting up with it all during times which were often fraught and full of tension.

DAVID MCKITTRICK
BELFAST
AUGUST 1994

PART
ONE

•

POLITICAL STASIS,
SOCIAL FLUX

1
TWENTY YEARS
OF CONFLICT

The twentieth anniversary of the arrival of British soldiers on the streets of Northern Ireland brought a moment to consider what had gone wrong over all those years, and whether the future held the promise of anything better. The sobering assessment was that, two decades on, no political breakthrough or end to the violence seemed in sight.

Decades of violence
in a world of stalemate

The observation is as true today as when Edmund Burke first made it: most Englishmen have only one ambition about Ireland, and that is to hear no more about it. Implicit in that observation is one of the central problems of the Troubles, which is that successive British governments have never given the question their full and sustained attention.

There have been nine Northern Ireland Secretaries of State since 1972. The quality of the ministers sent to Belfast has, with a couple of exceptions, varied from the average to the frankly inferior. Prime Ministers have devoted little time and thought to the question: this most intractable of problems has usually been left to undistinguished minds. Their approach has almost always been governed by the notion of containment. The assumption is that Northern Ireland is, for the foreseeable future, to remain as part of the United Kingdom, while the hope is that violence can be kept to bearable levels.

Clearly, sights have been lowered a great deal in two decades. Twenty years ago the general view was that the issue was reasonably straightforward, with the problem defined as one of helping the Catholics who had suffered for decades under a discriminatory Protestant government. British policy then focused on ways of securing Catholic participation in government – first in the old Stormont parliament and, when that proved hopeless, in the powersharing executive that came into being in 1974. At the same time, however, the question became much more complicated as violence steadily increased, reaching its peak with a death toll of almost 500 in 1972.

The IRA campaign reduced British and international sympathy for the Irish nationalist point of view, leading many observers to redefine the problem as one of terrorism rather than civil rights. The authorities found themselves attempting to deal with two major factions on the Catholic side, one prepared to participate in the state, the other aiming to overthrow it by violent means.

When a loyalist general strike brought down the powersharing executive after only five months, disillusion developed in many quarters. It seemed a truism that Catholics could only be brought fully into the political processes by

4

offering them participation in government; yet the Protestant community consistently made clear its determination, and its ability, to frustrate any attempt to do so. It was at this point that most British politicians concluded that nothing could be done and lost interest.

The decline in sympathy for the Catholics continued, largely because the IRA kept up its campaign while loyalist killings – which have always received less publicity than republican violence – decreased sharply after 1977. The political leaders of Unionism failed, however, to take advantage of this trend to engineer a consequent increase in support for their cause. The result was a stalemate which lasted for many years. Little political progress was made, while recurring security crises buffeted Northern Ireland, and occasionally Britain and the Republic.

Then in the early 1980s the idea grew that containment was not working. The fact that support for the IRA's political wing, Sinn Féin, reached a peak of 102,000 votes in 1983 was viewed as evidence of a dangerous deterioration in the political fabric. Extreme republicanism seemed to be thriving in the political vacuum. This led to one of those rare episodes when senior figures of the British establishment devoted serious attention to the issue: the Whitehall committee concerned was chaired by Lord Armstrong, who was then cabinet secretary. The outcome of the endeavour was the Anglo-Irish agreement of 1985, which was hailed on all sides as a momentous development.

The agreement, which promised a consultative role for Dublin, aligned Britain with constitutional nationalism as led by Garret FitzGerald in the south and Social Democratic and Labour party leader John Hume in the north. It held out the prospect of closer security co-operation against the IRA, together with a programme of reforms to tackle Catholic grievances. In short, it defined the IRA, and Unionist attitudes in general, as the chief obstacles to progress. Dr FitzGerald and Mr Hume were delighted, Sinn Féin and the IRA apprehensive, and Unionism appalled. The government realised that Protestants would be outraged, but proceeded nonetheless. It seemed the antithesis of containment.

The agreement was without doubt a major departure, but its long-term significance is as yet unclear. It has certainly driven a wedge between Britain and Unionism by conceding the principle that the south has a legitimate say in the north. But the close London–Dublin partnership which nationalists had hoped for, and Unionists feared, has yet to materialise. Tom King, the Northern Ireland Secretary who administered the accord for its first three years of life, sought to downgrade it. Reforms tended to be delayed and diluted, and Dublin has often not been consulted on important issues. The question for the future is whether the government will return to the original concept of the accord or continue to play it down, perhaps to a point where it may eventually become all but meaningless.

5

Unionism failed to stop the agreement being signed, and all its efforts have failed to bring it down. Unionism deals in the politics of absolutes, and the existence of the agreement is a standing affront to its basic tenets. The accord – whatever its limitations in practice – concedes, and in fact enshrines, a principle which Unionism has found impossible to accept: that the Republic has a legitimate interest in the affairs of Northern Ireland.

In other senses, however, it can be argued that Unionists have had their victories in the past two decades. There has been no perceptible progress towards Irish unity and no real advance towards powersharing, which they suspect is a Trojan horse. A return of devolved power has been on offer ever since Stormont fell, but the single condition attached – that Catholics must be in government – has been unacceptable to Unionists. They have preferred no bread to half a loaf. It has meant 20 years of playing a surly, unattractive defensive game which has won their cause no new converts and alienated many. It is an isolated and xenophobic community, relying on obstinacy and strength of numbers rather than political argument.

The sterile years of Stormont robbed the Protestant community of much of its political skill, to the point where its leaders have come to regard even the idea of discussions as dangerous. This perspective is a function of the nature of Unionism in that it is defined essentially by a negation, a refusal not only to contemplate Irish unity but also to recognise the validity of the nationalist tradition within Northern Ireland. Unionist objections to unity are not irrational. Their fear is that in a united Ireland, as traditionally understood, they would be worse off financially, would be governed by Catholics who have little regard for their Protestantism, and would lose their British citizenship. This part of the Unionist case is strong; the weak point, in the eyes of most outside observers, is that Unionists behave so badly when themselves in power.

The most able in the Protestant community have tended to steer away from politics, viewing it as a slightly disreputable activity with sectarian overtones. The resulting degeneration of the political art was most clearly seen when its leaders failed to prevent the signing of the agreement.

Twenty years on, no consensus has developed within Unionism on what its objectives should be, beyond the tearing down of the Anglo-Irish agreement. The Protestant community contains a wide range of opinion, stretching from those who place heavy emphasis on the British link to those who regard England with deep suspicion as a godless and untrustworthy place. James Molyneaux and Ian Paisley may be political partners, but the former's emphasis on the British link sits uneasily with the latter's independent streak.

The British idiom becomes more perceptible towards the east of Northern Ireland. It reaches a high point in north Down, where there are demands for the Conservative party to set up shop. But while some press for closer links with the rest of the United Kingdom, others have been prepared to pass on British defence secrets to South Africa in exchange for arms – arms which would be used to intimidate Britain. The only common thread visible in this confusion of approaches is the desire to outflank Catholic neighbours rather than come to terms with them.

Some opinion polls have found many Protestants expressing a willingness to share power, but in the polling booths they vote overwhelmingly for Mr Molyneaux and Mr Paisley, leaders who will brook no such compromise. The first regards negotiation as weakness while the second has built a career on articulating, as profoundly as anyone can, the nightmares of Unionists. The agreement shook Protestants; it taught them some harsh lessons; but it shows no sign of bringing them to the negotiating table. Three centuries after the Protestants of Londonderry held out against the forces of James II, the siege mentality remains intact. Unionists are a community which has too many frontiers; which will never find security because the simple fact of its location in Ireland renders it chronically insecure; and which continues to define politics as a matter not of consensus but of resistance.

A degree of movement has, by contrast, been visible on the nationalist side. The factor which in the late 1960s threw the Unionist government into such disarray was the shift in Catholic political demands: the call was not for Irish unity but for equal rights. Some of those who made that call did so merely to wrong-foot Stormont, but many were motivated by an urge to participate in the business of the state. The civil rights campaign was a major departure from old-style nationalist politics, which were characterised by boycott and doleful complaint. It was, in fact, the first tangible sign of a new definition of Irish nationalism, which appeared in the 1960s and gradually gained ground over the past two decades. Traditional nationalism held that the heart of the problem was the British presence, which was said to have deliberately divided Ireland in order to control it. The conventional nationalist recipe for solving the problem was, therefore, to persuade – or force – the British to leave. The assumption was that Unionists, faced with an imminent British withdrawal, would embrace a new destiny as a minority in a united Ireland. Some of them might fight and some might leave for Scotland or England, but after a time the majority of Protestants would settle down and become reconciled to their new circumstance.

The new nationalist theory, as evolved by Mr Hume, Dr FitzGerald and others, rejected many of the old assumptions. In the revised view the key to the problem was not Britain but the Protestant community. The import was that the British presence was not imperialist but neutral, that the border was maintained not by Britain but by Unionism, and that Irish unity could only come about with Protestant consent. The real border, it was now said, was not geographical but in people's minds. Though very different from conventional

7

Irish nationalism, this doctrine by no means jettisoned the idea that a united Ireland was the ultimate solution. It saw unity as coming about not through compulsion but almost naturally, after a long period in which Protestant and Catholic would gradually learn to live with each other. Unity, the rhetoric had it, would come through reconciliation rather than coercion. This approach has now become the new orthodoxy, all major nationalist parties north and south – with the single exception of Sinn Féin – subscribing to it. It was resisted for some time by Charles Haughey's Fianna Fáil, but has now reluctantly been accepted.

In the early days of the Troubles the hope was that ancient suspicions would be eroded by the experience of the two traditions working together in government. Since 1974, however, no Unionists have been willing to share power – few, indeed, have even acknowledged that the new nationalism might be preferable to the old. The prevailing Protestant view is that the new line is simply the old one presented in a subtler and more sophisticated way.

But if Unionism was not persuaded that the switch was both genuine and significant, Britain was. The new approach provided the foundation for the Anglo-Irish agreement, which was an acknowledgement by nonviolent nationalists that the British presence would remain for the foreseeable future. The nationalist emphasis is increasingly on improving the lot of northern Catholics rather than persuading the British to leave.

Withdrawal has quietly slipped off the agenda of all nationalist parties except Sinn Féin. Irish governments do not – publicly or privately – advocate disengagement. This is due not so much to a concern for Unionist rights as to an appreciation of the risks involved. These were spelled out unusually frankly recently by Garret FitzGerald when he wrote: "The reason why I and many others in Irish politics are opposed to British withdrawal in advance of arriving at an agreed resolution of the north–south problem is the evident danger that such a departure, or indeed even the announcement of the intention to depart, could unleash violence on a scale hitherto unknown in Northern Ireland, and lead eventually to the repartition of the area by force. Of course, no one can say with certainty that this is what would happen in such an event, but the danger is seen by most of us as sufficiently grave – the loss of life that might take place could be on a far greater scale than anything that has happened hitherto, or is likely to happen for many years ahead, and the situation left by a repartition would be far worse and less capable of ultimate resolution than the present situation – to preclude taking this risk."

Dr FitzGerald and Dr Conor Cruise O'Brien, his one-time colleague in coalition, agree on scarcely anything concerning Northern Ireland, but they hold strikingly similar opinions on the likelihood of a large-scale escalation of violence and repartition in the event of withdrawal. This view, reluctantly arrived at and rarely set out so starkly in public, is now the position of the leaders of constitutional nationalism.

The Republic is a settled, comfortable state which would be appalled by the prospect of having to accommodate the supporters not only of Ian Paisley but also of Sinn Féin, and which, indeed, has engaged in no serious planning on how such a thing might be achieved. Its principal concern is to stop violence from spreading south – a policy that might, only slightly mischievously, be characterised as containment.

So the Anglo-Irish agreement is viewed in Dublin not as a move towards Irish unity but rather as an attempt to set up a more efficient system of management within Northern Ireland – as a device, in fact, for keeping the north at bay. Such interest as there is in the Republic now tends to take the form of hoping that Catholics and Protestants can learn to live peacefully together. Certainly there has been no enthusiasm, as the half-hearted response to Dr FitzGerald's unsuccessful constitutional crusade showed, for turning the Republic into the type of secular state which might in the long term render the Republic less objectionable to northern Unionists.

Whenever Dublin complains to London today, it is not about the principle of the British presence but rather about incidents or actions where it considers the northern authorities have acted in an unjust or counterproductive way. Thus serious disputes arose from the Stalker affair, the Birmingham Six case and the Gibraltar shootings.

The tone of Dublin's objections to such episodes was very well illustrated last year by, unusually, the wife of a former British ambassador to the Republic. Writing in the *Irish Times*, Lady Rosemary Goodison referred to these three incidents and commented: "To compromise in this way the moral integrity of the forces of law and order is to play straight into the hands of the terrorists who already hold so many cards. Everyone knows that, and spells it out often and often. Why then are there so many appallingly insensitive decisions? I am desperately concerned with the moral issues, but I am also horrified at the lack of common sense and foresight on the part of the authorities. Looked at in the coolest light, all the moral advantage to Britain and the forces of law and order in Northern Ireland which accrued after the Enniskillen massacre was squandered."

The criticism is that British security policy, when ineptly formulated or clumsily implemented, can help Sinn Féin and the IRA; and it is certainly true that the two organisations can receive a substantial boost when the authorities or the security forces get it wrong.

Sinn Féin represents the last expression of the failure of Irish nationalism to come to terms with Unionism. In its philosophy, only the British matter: the Protestants are simply a sideshow which will collapse once imperialism is smashed. In this world of absolutes, Britain is dishonourable, the use of force

9

is justified and necessary, and Unionists have no national rights. A complex problem is said to have a simple solution, since the problem is defined as a war and as such will end not in compromise but in either victory or defeat.

The Sinn Féin vote in the Republic is derisory, but in a series of elections in the north it has secured more than one-third of the nationalist vote. Clearly there is still a market for old-style nationalism. Its support comes from a variety of roots including traditional republicanism, urban deprivation, loyalty to imprisoned family members, the perception that Northern Ireland is an unreformable sectarian state, and the experience of clashes with the security forces or with extreme loyalists. All these factors come together in Catholic west Belfast, which supplies a large proportion of the Sinn Féin vote. Parts of this poverty-stricken district are probably the most run-down places in these islands. Its young people suffer from unemployment which may well be the highest in Europe, and suffer, too, from heavy and unwelcome security force attention. They regard the army, not the IRA, as the aggressor.

Five minutes amid the squalor in Divis Flats is enough to impress on visitors the depth of alienation from the rest of society. [The flats, which contained some of the worst housing in Northern Ireland, were largely demolished by early 1994.] There have been reforms in the past 20 years, but most of the benefit has gone to the Catholic middle class. That class has grown fast and has prospered in the past two decades. But large sections of the working class have been left behind and still have poor housing, poor health and poor prospects. Catholic male unemployment is still more than double the Protestant rate. There is argument, within government, about whether or not such deeply disaffected people might ever be brought into the political processes. Any attempt to do so would require not only political change but also efforts at economic betterment and new measures to begin the long process of making the security forces more accountable and more acceptable. Such a programme was envisaged in the Anglo-Irish agreement but was not followed through. In the meantime, the material is there to supply Sinn Féin votes for years ahead, and to supply recruits to use the IRA's formidable stockpile of weaponry.

Twenty years on, the two communities are as divided as ever, though the two governments have drawn closer. In the end, almost everyone involved in the conflict is trapped. Britain is trapped because withdrawal could mean conflagration and reinvolvement. The Republic is trapped next door to an unruly and potentially dangerous entity. Nationalists are stuck in the Northern Ireland state; and Unionists are stuck in Ireland. Unionists have not been able to contemplate the sharing of power; nationalist rhetoric has yet to catch up with reality; and Britain has yet to give its wholehearted attention to the problem. It has been a dreadful 20 years, and there are few optimistic enough to believe that the conflict will soon end.

2
CHANGE,
AND NO CHANGE

Anti-Catholic discrimination was the central issue that brought the civil rights movement onto the streets in the late 1960s, provoked a loyalist reaction, and led to the turmoil of the Troubles. In the 1990s the key questions were: What has changed? And what has not?

Although Northern Ireland is often viewed as a society in stasis, major changes have taken place under cover of the Troubles, and these have had major political consequences. One of the most significant of these changes is the rapid growth of the Catholic middle class.

11

Catholics find
a middle-class oasis

Malone is Belfast's most exclusive and most expensive suburb. Its broad tree-lined avenues feature substantial Victorian semis and detached homes set in generous gardens, their driveways strewn with leaves and BMWs. Executives, lawyers, doctors and other professionals live here. They commute to the city centre, only ten minutes' drive away; they take their children to the excellent local grammar schools; they walk in the nearby country park. They buy paintings, they have holiday homes in Donegal, Dublin or France, they give to charity.

There are no army patrols to disturb this opulent oasis, few outward signs of the political unrest. The Troubles are only a few miles away, but they are light years distant psychologically and sociologically. The residents of Malone have largely escaped the effects of the violence, and some of them have profited from it.

Although this was traditionally a predominantly Protestant enclave, it has now ceased to be a bastion of Unionist privilege. Today Catholics make up nearly half the population, with the percentage growing all the time. The local Catholic church, St Brigid's, was built a century ago for the maids and domestics who serviced the big houses: now the parish has 5,000 members who are in Malone not as servants but as home-owners. The church is too small and a bigger one is being built alongside. Disgruntled Protestants who disapprove of the trend have been known to refer to the district as "Vatican City". The rapidly expanding Catholic middle class, here and elsewhere in Northern Ireland, is upwardly mobile and is moving fast. Its members have been the beneficiaries of two decades of reforms which have effected fundamental, if uneven, change in the old patterns.

The Catholic middle class, previously artificially small in a state once largely run by Protestants, is now getting its place in the sun. And a quirk of the economy means that the well-off in Northern Ireland are actually much better off than their counterparts in either London or Dublin. Because house prices are comparatively low, mortgage repayments are much smaller than, for example, in London. In Malone a newly built luxury flat may cost £50,000, while a detached Victorian villa can be had for £100,000 or less. This means many in Northern Ireland have a great deal more spending cash than their English counterparts, and hence a noticeably more comfortable life style.

The story of the growth of this relatively new phenomenon illustrates how change can come about within a society which, to the outside eye, can appear fossilised. Those changes had their roots in education. There had always been a small Catholic middle class which tended to serve the Catholic community in areas such as the law, medicine, construction, shops and pubs. It has now become much larger and has diversified into areas which traditionally were Protestant preserves. The process began when education reforms in the late 1940's brought third-level education within the grasp of working-class students, both Catholic and Protestant. The 1960s saw an overall growth in higher education and a steady increase in the number of Catholics going to university. Thus while Queen's University in Belfast had fewer than 500 Catholic students in 1953, it had more than 1,400 by 1968, just before the Troubles began.

The importance of this was noted by the late Captain Terence O'Neill, who as Prime Minister of Northern Ireland in the 1960s made some ultimately unsuccessful attempts towards accommodating this new phenomenon into the system. As he explained his rationale: "It was quite obvious that a new generation of Catholics were going to grow up, educated in a way that their parents hadn't been, and they would be totally dissatisfied with the deprived status which their parents and grandparents had taken for granted. Anybody with any intelligence could see that this was going to happen."

Many more Catholic undergraduates were thus coming through. But the advent of the political unrest in the late 1960s had a striking side effect – what one observer has described as "democratisation wrought willy-nilly by the Troubles". What happened was that even more university places became available to Catholics for two reasons: first, many more Protestant students – very often the most talented – abandoned unsettled Belfast to attend universities in Britain; and second, the flow of foreign students to Northern Ireland all but ceased. The net result was a remarkable change. The student body at Queen's University, which at the beginning of the Troubles was more than 70 per cent Protestant, is today 50 per cent Catholic. Catholics are now in a majority in a number of faculties, reaching 60 per cent representation in law and economics. Furthermore, a very high proportion of Catholics reaching Queen's come from working-class backgrounds: it has been described, in fact, as the most working-class university in the United Kingdom. It should be noted, however, that a degree is not an infallible ticket to a job, for statistics show that Catholic graduates are more likely to be unemployed.

Almost 40 per cent of Northern Ireland university entrants go to Britain rather than to local universities, and of those who go across the water more than two-thirds are Protestant. In addition, the Protestants who go abroad are more likely to stay away: about half the Catholics return, but closer to one-third of Protestants. This Protestant brain drain has meant greater Catholic access to university and to the job market afterwards. It represents a reversal of previous patterns, in which, traditionally, more Catholics than Protestants emigrated from Northern Ireland. The exodus of able Protestants has actually increased in the past four or five years. Some would say this is merely because Protestant grammar schools encourage their pupils to seek third-level education in Britain. Others give a more political explanation, theorising that the Anglo-Irish agreement is having a psychological effect on Protestants, who believe their community is losing out in terms of jobs and position.

Whatever the reasons, the education system is now providing more and more qualified Catholics to compete for jobs. The pool of graduates continues to become increasingly Catholic, which means that the Catholic middle class can be expected to continue to grow.

The past two decades have seen significant, though somewhat patchy, advances for Catholics in the job market. They have traditionally had a lower social class profile than Protestants, being well represented in a number of comparatively low-status occupations. These include hairdressers, waiters and bar staff, nurses and catering supervisors. They have been underrepresented in various higher-status jobs, including engineers, senior government officials, senior police and prison officers, scientists and draughtsmen. Many of these stereotypes still hold good, but research shows Catholic numbers growing in such occupations as economists and statisticians, personnel and industrial relations managers, scientists and engineers. The general expansion in education, health and welfare has provided new jobs for Catholics while the law has become an increasingly Catholic profession due to a particularly large influx of young working-class Catholics.

But it is in the public sector, which makes up a large part of the economy, that the most striking advances have taken place. Before London took over direct responsibility for running Northern Ireland in 1972, there were many complaints that the Unionist-dominated Stormont parliament actively discriminated against Catholics. The Northern Ireland civil service, Northern Ireland's largest single employer, was widely held to be biased in favour of Protestant recruitment and promotion, with Catholics rare in its upper reaches. Over the years, however, the proportion employed has risen markedly – from 27 per cent in 1983 to 34 per cent today. One reason for this was the investigation launched into the civil service some years ago by the Fair Employment Agency (now Commission). The civil service originally reacted in a most defensive manner, but came

14

to acknowledge that there were inequities in its ranks and took a series of steps aimed at redressing them.

Most of its former critics now acknowledge that real progress has been made. Examples of this were provided in the last few months, when two of the most senior posts – permanent secretaries in charge of key government departments – were both filled by Catholics. According to one observer: "They have certainly made their efforts. At the start some people in the civil service didn't like it but now it's accepted that things have to be put right."

The story is a similar one in the major boards that administer functions such as health, education and housing. The pattern in these quangos is again one of growing Catholic representation, with complaints of discrimination now rarer. Many chief executives and senior officers are Catholic.

Such a pattern of change is, however, by no means universal. There are still large areas of business and commercial life that are still very substantially Protestant, with continuing discrepancies in areas such as some banks and building societies.

In the one small area of public life still partly controlled by Unionists, the largely powerless district councils, Catholics are generally underrepresented. A survey of nine Unionist-controlled councils found that of one hundred senior officers only four were Catholic. Several councils stridently oppose, and have repeatedly clashed with, the Fair Employment Commission, which monitors employment patterns. Even in less contentious areas, few Protestants have been actively enthusiastic about improving opportunities for Catholics. No Unionist politician has ever commended the work of the commission, and many routinely denounce it as being biased in favour of Catholics.

The picture, then, is a patchy one. There are firms, councils and even large sections of the economy which Catholics still tend to shy away from, on the assumption that they would still not receive a fair deal. As the years pass, however, the number of openings has grown steadily: many bastions of privilege have fallen, though a good few remain. Astute parents know which occupations to steer their children toward, and which ones to avoid. The situation is clearly imperfect but improvements there have been, and it is the growing Catholic middle class that has benefited from them.

> Don't talk to me of nationality, outmoded and long-finished,
> For we in Northern Ireland are both Irish and we're British.
> And as for us the privileged class, we're truly cosmopolitan,
> We go to mass with Catholic and our golf we play with Protestant.

Those lines, from a poem entitled "Song of the middle-class Catholic", were actually written two decades ago, but the sentiment they express – working-class bitterness at middle-class advancement – is even stronger today. Although nobody planned it that way, the rise of the Catholic middle class has brought into being a new fissure in an already divided community – the very large gap between the Catholic haves and have-nots. Thousands of Catholics are now doing conspicuously well, but the other side of the coin is that substantial section of the working class which is either unemployed or in low-paid jobs. For many at the lower end of the scale the past two decades have been years not of progress but of increasing disadvantage. The number of Catholic unemployed, for instance, has risen sharply over the past 20 years as joblessness has generally increased. Catholic male unemployment remains two and a half times higher than Protestant unemployment. In particular, unemployment has risen steeply in the construction industry, where many Catholics work. Today more than 30,000 Catholic men are out of work.

There has been a cushioning effect for many Protestants who, on losing manufacturing jobs, have found alternative work in policing and other security-related occupations. Catholics have not been protected in the same way, and in some pockets unemployment reaches 50 per cent and more. The position has, in fact, come to mirror that of blacks in the United States, where the reforms of the American civil rights movement helped create a new black middle class, but have brought about little improvement in the position of the black unemployed.

In Northern Ireland a significant extra social irritant exists in the almost inevitable friction between the security forces and residents of republican areas, which are very often those of high unemployment. The lawyer in Malone would be startled to see a soldier in his avenue, but the unemployed labourer in west Belfast may open his door to find a dozen troops in his street. The owner of an older car will often receive attention at RUC roadblocks. But police, in Northern Ireland as elsewhere, are highly sensitive to indicators of class, and the driver of a larger, more expensive car will in general be waved through without a search. Such factors mean that the life experiences of the two classes can be completely different. A Sinn Féin leader was scathing about the differing perspectives: "Middle-class Catholics have got their civil rights. It's a different world, a different reality. For them the civil rights struggle is over; it's a question of building their businesses."

The differences are accentuated by the particular characteristics of the education system, where continuing selection at the age of 11 works in favour of the brighter and more highly motivated children. Well-respected grammar schools provide excellent education, generally for free, achieving examination results well above the United Kingdom average. The unfortunate corollary, however, is that non-grammar secondary schools deliver onto the streets at 16 a high percentage of children who have passed no examinations.

A Catholic teacher remarked: "Anybody who can get a mortgage now gets out of west Belfast. What you're left with is seething masses who are not going to get jobs and as far as can be seen are unemployable. Most of the kids leave schools with no qualifications at all – no exams passed, no skills. The middle-class Catholics have really slammed the door and forgotten where they came from." This sentiment was echoed by another woman teacher: "The ones who leave don't want to know what's back there. And there's a lot of antagonism and envy about that."

The argument can be made that the progress of the middle class has increased the sense of isolation of the disadvantaged. According to a Belfast councillor: "The people left behind, the ones who vote for Sinn Féin, feel they have been completely alienated, isolated and marginalised, that everybody's down on them. It's a classic example of blaming the victim."

The changing social structures have important political consequences. Movement into the middle class brings with it middle-class values, centring on stability. As one politician put it: "They're interested in progress and stability and development for their kids and their property. They're not going to pull down the pillars."

The class divisions are reflected in the political parties which represent Catholics. Sinn Féin, the political wing of the IRA, takes up to 40 per cent of the nationalist vote, winning support almost exclusively from the working class. The SDLP takes the major slice of the Catholic vote, with the support of a large proportion of the working class together with the bulk of the middle class. The SDLP and Sinn Féin are fierce rivals, the former opposing violence and advocating accommodation rather than forcing Britain out of Ireland. There is only a very limited floating vote between the two parties: the supporters of both regard their interests as inimical.

A common complaint levelled against the middle class, however, is one of a generalised political apathy. According to a law lecturer: "Inside the Catholic middle class there is an increasing apoliticisation as they simply pursue wealth." Another observer said: "They're card-carrying members of the Apathy party." Some of this apparent indifference undoubtedly comes from a sense of the intractability of the Irish problem; but another part arises from a feeling that real gains have been made. For one thing, the system of government, which under Unionism Catholics regarded as actively biased against them, now has an entirely different character. The British administration which runs Northern Ireland under direct rule from Westminster is not viewed as discriminatory but as nonsectarian. According to one Catholic professional: "Many middle-class Catholics are perfectly happy with direct rule. It has provided opportunities for growth and for participation. They're broadly content with the institutions and they want to get on with their lives. I don't know if the Unionist establishment has changed all that much, but of course they no longer rule the place."

One source of satisfaction is the sizeable political influence which the new middle class wields, largely through John Hume and his party. For half a century the Catholic community was notoriously ill-organised politically, exercising little influence either within Northern Ireland or outside it. Today, by contrast, the SDLP carries a great deal of clout in London, Dublin, America and Europe. A Sinn Féin leader recently referred, with evident envy, to the SDLP's "apparent access to decision-making".

The most striking evidence of SDLP influence was the 1985 Anglo-Irish agreement between London and Dublin. The accord gave Irish nationalists a say in the formulation of British policy, formally acknowledging that their tradition was a legitimate one. According to one of its British negotiators: "One of the main points of the agreement was to enable the Catholic population to participate in the instruments of government and the general fabric of society."

One of those involved on the Irish side made the same point in a different way: "The agreement was about the politics of accommodation. A lot of it was inspired by the sense that there was a new constituency emerging in the Catholic middle class. The philosophy of the thing is essentially to neutralise, as much as possible, the colour of the institutions in Northern Ireland. It's a question of trying to take the hurt out of the institutions of state. What they're looking for is fair-mindedness, tact with the symbols, a feeling of not having their noses rubbed in the symbolism of the thing."

In other words, much of the thrust today is not towards separatism but towards accommodation. The agreement remains highly popular with the Catholic middle class. As one Catholic teacher put it: "If ever a political arrangement had support, it was that. It recognised our sense of identity. It may be intangible but it's a real gain."

This sense of the agreement as a real achievement helps to explain the less than wholehearted nationalist support for the continuing attempts of the Northern Ireland Secretary, Peter Brooke, to assemble the parties for talks on a new devolution initiative. There is, on the one hand, the common middle-class instinct to participate in the management of society. But there is also ambiguity, springing partly from a widespread sense that the agreement should not be placed in any jeopardy for the sake of uncertain gains. There is a Catholic suspicion that most Unionist politicians are not serious about offering a share of real power to nationalists. At the same time there is also a concern that a new measure of devolution might unhelpfully repoliticise questions which, under direct rule, have been reasonably fairly administered. Issues such as housing policy, once highly contentious, have been successfully removed from the

18

political arena. The fear is that the devolution of such powers to local politicians could reopen old wounds in such areas. As one Catholic businessman put it: "A lot of us aren't all that interested in this talk about a devolved government. People don't see what they could possibly have to gain from it, apart from maybe a hell of a lot more hassle and agitation. It could simply be an opportunity once again to highlight differences in divisive ways."

There are signs that Mr Brooke and some of his advisers may have under-estimated Catholic middle-class reservations about devolution when he launched his devolution initiative almost a year ago. Any analysis of the prospects for a new devolved scheme of government has to take account of the fact that nationalists are no longer automatically in favour of devolution, since among other things they are concerned to conserve those advances made under direct rule, and to protect the Anglo-Irish agreement.

One mistake that direct rulers can make is to assume that members of the Catholic middle class have in effect ceased to be Irish nationalists and are there-fore ripe for inclusion in a new internal settlement. It is true that their nationalism is very different from that of the IRA and Sinn Féin; for one thing, there is a marked new sense of Europeanism evident. Nationalists – both north and south of the border – are markedly more pro-European than, for example, most sections of opinion in Britain. Many middle-class Catholics now speak of traditional Irish nationalism being transcended by the development of a new cosmopolitan European identity. The error is to assume that such new thinking, together with an improvement in material conditions, necessarily means that Irish nationalism is on the wane. It is certainly changing, but what is happening is in the nature of a refinement rather than an abandonment. Some layers of alienation have been peeled away, but its members continue to regard themselves as Irish rather than British. The Catholic middle class may have joined the economic élite; it may indeed be more flexible and amenable to negotiation than in the past. But that does not mean it has been fully integrated into Northern Ireland's political systems.

The Malone Road is less than a mile away from the public housing estates of west Belfast, but in many ways the two districts are worlds apart. The fortunes of the Catholic middle class may have improved dramatically, but much of the Catholic working class faces continuing deprivation.

The combined effects of history, continuing mistrust and other factors mean that despite two decades of government hopes of constructing a more equitable society, much of the Catholic community remains seriously disadvantaged. This is particularly so in unemployment, where Catholic men are still more likely to be without jobs than their Protestant counterparts.

By contrast, Protestants have one of the UK's lowest jobless rates, an illustration that the two communities have very different economic experiences and life chances. Such inequity has deep political, social and economic consequences, since there is evidence of connections between unemployment, religious separation and violence.

Jobless figures highlight stark inequality

On the dole: the Falls Road social security office

A n outspoken loyalist woman from the Shankill Road summed up a firm perception among many Protestants: "We've seen the nationalist community crying out for years for things and now they're getting them. They've better housing than us now. They get all the jobs they want now and it's all turning full circle. We're ending up with nothing." A number of Protestant politicians and clergy are now making similar points. As a rising Catholic middle class makes advances and becomes more visible, the impression is widespread that the Catholic community as a whole is now winning out. There is certainly

21

Protestant poverty and unemployment, yet almost every objective measurement of disadvantage indicates that after more than two decades of direct rule from London, the Catholic community remains far behind.

The scale of Catholic disadvantage is most starkly laid out as follows in a confidential government document: "On all the major social and economic indicators Catholics are worse off than Protestants. They are more likely to be unemployed, more likely to experience long-term unemployment and significantly less likely to hold professional, managerial or other non-manual positions. More Catholics than Protestants leave school lacking any formal educational qualifications. There is a greater provision of grammar school places for Protestant than Catholic children. Significantly more Catholics than Protestants live in public sector housing and experience overcrowding. Catholic households have a lower income than Protestant households. Almost double the proportion of Catholic households are dependent on social security. Catholics suffer from higher levels of disability and ill-health."

Other elements can be added to this stark assessment. Catholics are more likely to be found in industries such as construction, which have lower status and higher unemployment. Sixty-eight per cent of the long-term unemployed are Catholic. In some Catholic wards up to 89 per cent of families have no car. The Catholic community has a higher rate of premature live births and a lower vaccination uptake. The worst Catholic ghettos are marked out by low skill levels, a weak private sector, depressing physical environment, low morale and job expectations, high levels of criminal and paramilitary activity, inter-community conflict, and friction with the security forces.

In recent years attention has focused on political alienation from authority, but it is clear that much of the Catholic and nationalist dissatisfaction is based on economic as well as political alienation. One survey found that 31 per cent of Catholics and 19 per cent of Protestants cited unemployment as the biggest problem, rather than any constitutional or political issue. Asked which single change was most needed to end the Troubles, one-third of Catholics chose "equal opportunities for Protestants and Catholics", compared to only 13 per cent who gave a united Ireland as their answer.

As the following table illustrates, Catholics and Protestants have radically different employment experiences. The Catholic male unemployment rate is double that of anywhere else, while Protestant unemployment, by contrast, is among the lowest. One slightly encouraging sign is that by one measurement the differential has narrowed. Catholic men used to be 2.5 times more likely to be jobless than their Protestant counterparts: this ratio has now dropped to 2.2:1. The figure for women, which stands at 1.8:1, has actually risen slightly.

Analysis of the latest census data shows that the disparity remains striking. It reveals that 28.4 per cent of all Catholic economically active men are

MALE UNEMPLOYMENT BY UK REGION

	%
Northern Ireland Catholics	**24.2**
Northern Ireland	**13.9**
North-west	12.6
West Midlands	12.5
Yorks and Humberside	12.0
Wales	11.7
Scotland	11.1
South-east	10.9
East Midlands	10.5
South-west	10.4
Northern Ireland Protestants	**10.1**
East Anglia	8.2

(Source: official labour force surveys. These figures differ slightly from census data.)

unemployed, compared with 12.7 per cent of Protestant men. Of the 50 local government wards with the highest unemployment rates, 45 are exclusively or predominantly Catholic. In striking contrast, the 80 wards with lowest unemployment are exclusively or predominantly Protestant.

Most of the worst blackspots are almost entirely Catholic, as shown by the eight top jobless areas.

WARD	% MALE UNEMPLOYMENT	% OF CATHOLICS IN WARD
Brandywell (Londonderry)	60	99
Falls (west Belfast)	58	97
Whiterock (west Belfast)	58	100
New Lodge (north Belfast)	56	95
Ardoyne (north Belfast)	53	99
Creggan Central (Londonderry)	52	99
Crossmaglen (south Armagh)	51	98
Upper Springfield (west Belfast)	51	100
Shantallow West (Londonderry)	50	97

The most concentrated problem lies in the Catholic areas of west and north Belfast, where more than 11,000 people in the cramped and deprived ghettos have no jobs. Here, overall unemployment touches 50 per cent, with male unemployment reaching 58 per cent in some wards. Within these wards there are further blackspots. In six areas of west and north Belfast, for example, male joblessness in public housing estates reaches almost two-thirds of all men. And within these estates are pockets where, according to local politicians and community activists, almost no one has a job. Many of those who do have work are among the lowest-paid in society. For example, some agencies who supply women to clean city-centre offices at night pay their staff as little as £1.05 an hour.

The contrast with the expanding Catholic middle class could not be more striking. While many Catholics are now making progress, especially in the abnormally large public sector, considerable sections of the working class are barely connected to the labour market and have been economically and socially left behind.

The association between high unemployment, divided communities and violence is plain. The New Lodge district of north Belfast, for example, has 56 per cent male unemployment, almost complete Catholic–Protestant segregation, and the highest level of killings in Northern Ireland. It also has a high Sinn Féin vote. The same picture may be seen in the Falls Road and adjoining districts in the west of the city, in the Bogside and Creggan areas of Londonderry, and in Crossmaglen in south Armagh. Studies show that the cities and towns with large Catholic ghetto populations have the highest rates of violence. The pattern also holds good on the Protestant side, where the Shankill and Crumlin areas of west and north Belfast are the heartlands of both Protestant unemployment and loyalist paramilitarism. All this suggests that attempts to deal with loyalist and, more particularly, republican violence are unlikely to succeed unless they take account of economic conditions as well as political and purely security factors.

One striking feature of republican activity is that Sinn Féin does not as a rule lose votes when its military wing, the IRA, carries out bombings which destroy jobs. This is partly because the major bombings take place outside the republican ghettos, where few Sinn Féin sympathisers are employed. Sinn Féin is frequently accused of hypocrisy, in that its representatives support, and indeed sometimes launch, job creation initiatives within their own areas. Its supporters, however, clearly see no conflict in this approach, viewing their districts as being systematically discriminated against and deliberately starved of jobs. IRA bombing clearly reduces the chances of outside investment in such areas, but the terrorists escape local censure for this. A recent west Belfast survey showed that Sinn Féin support is concentrated among the unemployed and those living at subsistence levels.

One member of the SDLP said: "The employed working class tends to vote for us, but Sinn Féin have a near-monopoly of the inner-city poverty vote. They have managed to politicise those people, presenting a vote for Sinn Féin as a way of striking back." A Sinn Féin leader said simply: "Our people understand."

Eamon Hanna, chief executive of Phoenix Trust, a voluntary economic development organisation in west Belfast, said the majority of the unemployed had no sympathy for violence, but that it formed a background against which violence could flourish. He added: "Some families are now going into their fourth generation of unemployment. They have a large sense of despair and a belief that they are never going to get any meaningful employment at all. Jobs would make a tremendous contribution to bringing a sense of stability to the place. People would have a stake in the community. I'm not arguing that they should get concessions because of the violence: they are unemployed and they deserve jobs. They have a right to expect that the government should actually do the maximum possible for them."

For more than 20 years the government has been committed to remedying the imbalances in a society shaped by half a century of one-party Unionist rule and institutionalised favouritism towards Protestants. Anti-discrimination agencies have been in place since the mid-1970s, and anti-discrimination laws were substantially strengthened in 1990. Considerable strides have been made in finding jobs for Catholics, especially in the civil service and the public sector.

But a combination of factors has meant that most of the advances hoped for in the 1970s have not come about, and in some ways conditions have worsened. The fact that the unemployment rate for Catholic men has risen from 17 per cent in 1971 to 28 per cent today is just one of many indicators that much of the Catholic population remains caught fast in a poverty trap. In the last few years in particular, many millions of pounds have been diverted towards the most disadvantaged areas, and a major five-year review is under way. But the economic difficulties of the last two decades, in combination with the violence and other factors, mean that Catholics remain a seriously disadvantaged minority.

It is clear that factors other than present-day discrimination play an important part in maintaining inequality. Many Catholics live in areas of high unemployment, particularly the west, and work in industries with high unemployment. Weaknesses in the Catholic school system mean it produces fewer science specialists. Catholics are reluctant to join the security forces and often unwilling to work in Protestant areas where over the years many Catholic workers have been shot dead by loyalists. And the Catholic population is younger, and therefore more subject to high jobless rates, than Protestants.

Within Northern Ireland opinions vary widely on the causes of the disparity. One commentator noted: "In the minds of many people disadvantage and discrimination are one and the same." But some sections of Unionist political and academic opinion deny that discrimination is – or indeed ever was – a significant problem. In this argument, perception is all. When one opinion poll asked, "Do Protestants and Catholics have the same chance of a job?", two-thirds of Catholics said they did not, while two-thirds of Protestants said they did.

While this debate continues, so too does Catholic unemployment and poverty, along with the firm belief that disadvantage is sustained by deliberate discrimination. Taken together these are among the most potent factors in maintaining alienation and thus ensuring continuing support for terrorism.

Many members of the expanding Catholic middle class are graduates of Queen's University Belfast. For most of the Troubles academic institutions were regarded as ivory towers, aloof from the political and sectarian fray, but in 1989 the university found itself plunged into controversy.

A three-year investigation concluded that Catholics were seriously underrepresented among its 3,000-strong staff. The Fair Employment Agency (forerunner of the Fair Employment Commission) revealed the university employed four times as many Protestants as Catholics in its locally recruited staff.

A university learns about discrimination

A minor storm erupted in Belfast in 1986 when publicity was given to a researcher's Ph.D. thesis which concluded that Queen's University employed only a small minority of Catholics on its teaching staff. The conclusion was angrily attacked as a slur on Northern Ireland's premier seat of learning. Defenders of Queen's said the statistics assembled in support of this contention were misleading, easily explained, or just plain wrong.

Queen's itself responded loftily: "We do not keep any record of the religious affiliation of staff or students. We have no way of checking the claims made, nor do we intend to do so. The only criteria for education and employment at Queen's University are those of academic and professional ability, potential and achievement." The hint of disdain has, however, been replaced by a rather different posture as the university sought to explain the statistics compiled by the Fair Employment Agency. Professor Sean Fulton, senior pro-vice-chancellor, assured the media that in his 10 years at Queen's he had seen no evidence of active discrimination. But he conceded that there was imbalance, which the university had discovered with "disappointment".

Queen's is the older and larger of Northern Ireland's two universities, with more than 6,000 students and a workforce of almost 3,000. It is thus a major employer and, with its long-established links with government, industry and the professions, occupies a key position in many aspects of Northern Ireland life.

The figures were there to provide evidence of imbalance in almost every part of the university. When employees from abroad and "doubtfuls" are put to the side, the statistics show that 79 per cent of employees are Protestant and 21 per cent Catholic. In only one of eight employment categories – computers, the second smallest – do Catholics exceed 30 per cent. The academic staff is no exception: here 82 per cent of the staff recruited from Northern Ireland are Protestants. Indeed, the presence of imbalance is uniform almost throughout, stretching from one end of the scale of salary and prestige to the other: thus there are few Catholic medical professors and few Catholic boilermen.

Professor Fulton produced figures to demonstrate that advances had been

27

made in the last few years: the Catholic percentage was up by 5 per cent in some areas, and among academics had risen by 2 per cent. Progress had been made, he argued, after the agency had provided the first hard evidence of Catholic underrepresentation. It has always been widely known, however, that Catholics were underrepresented in many areas of university employment. Exact statistics may not have been available, but the facts of life were obvious enough: 12 Catholics among 111 administrative and executive staff; 9 Catholics out of 62 staff in the economics faculty; 6 Catholics among 82 boilermen and tradesmen. The top jobs were known to be held largely by Protestants: of the 95 best-paid jobs, only 10 per cent were held by Catholics. Such things do not go unnoticed.

The question is why the academic authorities did not, before official agencies began to take an interest in 1986, apply their minds to the question of imbalance. A cynical answer was provided by the *Irish News*, Belfast's Catholic newspaper, which headlined its report "Queen's bigotry" and quoted a Catholic politician who claimed the situation was "the direct result of a bloody-minded conspiracy on the part of supposedly intelligent and intellectual people". Parts of Queen's were "more like a Masonic lodge", the politician alleged.

The other, more charitable, perspective was provided by Bob Cooper, the agency's chairman, who said he could not possibly say whether there had been direct discrimination in recent years. His attitude is that direct, deliberate discrimination was once widespread, but is not now the major issue: the problem lies with long-established patterns that are proving most difficult to eradicate. The past, in his words, casts a very long shadow.

The great irony in the Queen's case is that while the university's staff has remained predominantly Protestant, the percentage of Catholics in the student body has increased dramatically. In 1908 less than 10 per cent of students were Catholic; in 1960 the figure rose to 22 per cent; today the figure stands at 50 per cent. In some faculties, such as law and arts, Catholic students are now in a majority. Areas once regarded as Protestant preserves now have a large Catholic representation: the agriculture department, for example, which 20 years ago had less than 10 per cent of Catholic students, now has 43 per cent. The most striking discrepancy of all occurs in the economics and social sciences faculty, where a student body which is 69 per cent Catholic is looked after by a staff whose locally recruited members are 85 per cent Protestant.

The increase in Catholic students is in large measure indirectly due to the Troubles, with the exodus of Protestant students to Britain creating more places for Catholics. This has been particularly true for middle- and upper-class Protestants. As a result, the student body at Queen's has become, as a whole, much more Catholic and much more working-class. This fact, the Fair Employment Agency would argue, counters the argument that Catholics might be underrepresented on the staff of Queen's because they lack the necessary skills and qualifications. The agency also believes that the large number of Catholic graduates augurs well, in the long run, for the creation of a more equal society.

When the agency was established in the mid-1970s its hope was that companies and industries would observe it carrying out investigations into a few firms, and then be spurred into cleaning up their own patch. That did not happen: almost all concerned simply kept their heads down and hoped the agency would not pick on them. Queen's was a classic example of this attitude. Founded in 1845, its charter specifically forbids discrimination on grounds of political or religious belief. The university was one of the first employers to sign the agency's Declaration of Principle and Intent in 1976. It was in the habit of dismissing any allegations of imbalance among its staff. Like most employers, it resisted the notion of monitoring the religious composition of its workforce. The idea of carrying out a deliberate sectarian head count of employees is genuinely offensive to many people, including both employers and employees, Catholic as well as Protestant. It introduces a contentious issue into the work place and may create ill-feeling. The common procedure has therefore been to let sleeping dogs lie.

Yet the fact is that unless religious monitoring is carried out, the lack of accurate statistical information means that serious imbalances can go unacknowledged for years. The Queen's case shows how an unfair situation can persist when firms simply sit tight and do nothing, for inactivity alone can perpetuate imbalance. Thus it is that Bob Cooper had to admit that after more than a decade of government commitment to equal opportunity in employment, the deep division in Northern Ireland society is reflected in the labour forces of most employers.

The government's concern with equality has itself increased sharply in the last few years due to pressure from a variety of sources, principally Irish-America. This has led to new legislation, which has now made its way through Westminster. The new fair employment measure, in addition to renaming the agency and doubling its size, will require all major employers to monitor their workforces and make the figures available. The act marks the abandonment of the notion that employers will voluntarily put their house in order: from now on the onus will be on them to establish patterns in their workforces and, if necessary, take action designed to combat imbalances.

The next point is whether the strengthened legislation will be effective enough to make a real difference against practices and attitudes which have become ingrained over centuries. It will probably take years for the answer to that question to become clear. In the meantime, attempts go on to deal with a problem built up by decades of discrimination and sustained by years of inaction. The issue is a difficult one, but it lies at the heart of the question of whether the state of Northern Ireland can be transformed into one where both sides have equal opportunity. The Catholic sense of alienation which can, in its extreme form, lead to a resort to terrorism, springs in large part from a perception that key institutions such as Queen's have unfairness built into them. All this is not, therefore, simply an academic issue.

REPRESENTATION OF CATHOLICS IN EACH DIVISION OF QUEEN'S UNIVERSITY

EMPLOYMENT CATEGORY	PROTESTANT	CATHOLIC	OTHERS	TOTAL
	%	%		
Academic	337 (82)	74 (18)	382	793
Administrative	99 (89)	12 (11)	27	138
Technical	299 (78)	82 (22)	45	426
Clerical	286 (81)	69 (19)	37	392
Computer	78 (64)	43 (36)	14	135
Miscellaneous	471 (80)	116 (20)	44	631
Research	159 (74)	56 (26)	83	298
Library	65 (73)	24 (27)	27	116
Total	1,794 (79)	476 (21)	659	2,929

("Others" refers mainly to staff from outside Northern Ireland. The figures in brackets show Protestant and Catholic employment as a percentage of locally recruited staff.)

POSTSCRIPT

Further problems and embarrassment followed for Queen's in 1992 as it struggled to cope with a series of cases of alleged discrimination. It settled two such cases at a cost of £40,000.

In February 1993 a 300-page report commissioned by the university from independent consultants concluded there was an "understandable lack of trust and confidence" in its fair employment record and made more than 200 recommendations for change. The university accepted the report.

The pro-chancellor, Catholic businessman John B. McGuckian, took a news conference by surprise when, with a candour in marked contrast to the university's traditional defensiveness, he declared: "There absolutely was discrimination in Queen's University. It is beyond question and a matter of public record.

"It is accepted that there was discrimination in Northern Ireland. Queen's was one of the major institutions, and it is a fact that institutionally there was discrimination. It was endemic in the structure of the society.

"There are something like 14,000 people involved in Queen's, between students and staff and administrators. I'm not going to sit here and say that they're 14,000 saints. You can make up your mind how many bad guys there were – we're not saints in here, but we're trying to do our absolute best to make sure we behave ourselves."

Mr McGuckian said he now really believed there was a serious commitment to make the university a model for the rest of the community, and he hoped this would be achieved as quickly as possible. The figures seemed to show that some movement was under way: in five years the percentage of Catholics in the workforce increased from 21 per cent to 28 per cent.

While many Catholics were finding new job opportunities, decisions in a series of fair employment cases gave ammunition to those who contended that anti-Catholic bias was endemic and possibly ineradicable. These rulings went against Unionist-controlled district councils, including one which concluded that Belfast City Council had discriminated against five of its Catholic employees.

Councils found guilty of discrimination

In the late 1960s the Catholic belief that Unionists were abusing power in local councils was one of the principal factors in bringing the civil rights movement onto the streets. Today, a quarter of a century later, a series of disclosures is leading to claims that little has changed. Under anti-discrimination legislation that was strengthened in 1990, fair employment tribunals have been handing down verdicts which are causing concern in government circles and elsewhere.

Since May of this year 5 of the 26 local councils have been found guilty of discriminating against Catholics. In addition, research by the Fair Employment Commission (FEC) shows that hardly any of the 26 local councils have equitably structured workforces. The wider political significance of this is that local councils are one of the last bastions of Unionist control and are thus closely watched by Catholics as an indicator of whether Protestant politicians are prepared to share power. Although the councils themselves have little power, they have considerable symbolic importance, since in the absence of a devolved administration they are the only local political forums. They also provide considerable employment.

The anti-Catholic image of some councils, in particular Belfast, is often cited by nationalists as evidence that Unionist politicians think in terms of domination rather than partnership. This has an impact on the larger scene. Nationalist representatives suspect that council records express the real face of Unionism. One senior Catholic politician said: "Unionists may say they'll treat us as equals, but we look and see councils actively discriminating against Catholics. We see bigotry and sectarianism, and that makes it very hard to build trust."

As the table opposite shows, councils employ a smaller percentage of Catholics than other areas of the public sector. One of the key reasons for this is that the government exercises close supervision in the other areas listed, while most councils are under direct Unionist control.

Unionist politicians resent the existence of the FEC and often attack the concept as unnecessary. The FEC has complained that some councils adopt a negative and uncooperative attitude towards its investigations. Two years ago

RELIGIOUS REPRESENTATION IN
NORTHERN IRELAND PUBLIC BODIES

	CATHOLICS %	PROTESTANTS %
Housing Executive	46	54
Health boards	44	56
Education boards	42	58
Northern Ireland civil service	37	63
District councils	33	67

two Unionist councillors ripped up copies of the Fair Employment Act at a council meeting.

A series of FEC investigations into councils has revealed patterns of inequity. In two councils with nationalist majorities Protestants are underrepresented, but Catholics are underrepresented on many more. In some cases the percentage of Catholics is broadly in line with the local population, but in almost every instance Catholics are underrepresented in senior jobs within the council. Thus in one batch of five councils only five of forty-five senior officers were Catholic, while in another batch there were only two Catholics among sixty-six senior staff. The FEC concluded that at least 16 councils should take action to promote equality of opportunity. A number of councils rejected its reports while three — Ballymena, Craigavon and Limavady — have refused to sign a declaration making a public commitment to the principle of equality of opportunity.

CASE HISTORIES

Belfast
The city council, the scene of many political and sectarian dogfights over recent years, was found guilty of religious discrimination in appointing a Protestant woman to a senior post in preference to five better-qualified Catholics. This case concerned the appointment of a senior community services officer in 1990. The applicants included five Catholics and a Protestant woman, who all already worked for the council. The Protestant woman was given the job. The previous occupant of the post was a Catholic woman who had been criticised by "very angry" Unionist councillors for writing a newspaper article said to be favourable

33

to people in Catholic west Belfast. The complainants alleged that the council official who chaired the interviews was intent on "making sure that he got someone safe to ensure an easier future relationship with his political masters".

The tribunal found that compared with the woman appointed, all five Catholics were better-qualified educationally and had more relevant experience. One of the Catholic applicants had a degree in education, a postgraduate diploma in education, a postgraduate certificate in youth and community studies, and a master's degree in social policy, planning and administration. The successful applicant, by contrast, had five Junior passes, one GCE O-level, typing qualifications, and a youth and community work diploma that had been awarded without an examination.

The selection procedure had been structured, however, so that education and qualifications made up only 7.5 per cent of possible marks, an allocation which the tribunal described as disturbing. It added that it was difficult to comprehend why the Protestant applicant had been given extra marks because she was a member of the Brownies as a child. The tribunal said it could not explain the marks allocated by the interview chairman, who had given higher marks for experience to the Protestant candidate than to two of the Catholic candidates who each had three times as much experience as she. The tribunal also said it found it odd that the one person in a group of six who had the least service should be given highest marks for displaying greatest knowledge of what was involved in community work. It concluded that the council's account of the interviews was not as full and frank as it claimed.

Each of the five Catholics who took the case was awarded compensation of £10,500.

Ballymena

The Co Antrim council was found guilty of discriminating against a Catholic in the appointment of a manager of its new abbatoir. The Catholic complainant had been manager of the old abbatoir for 17 years, during which time his work was acknowledged to have given no cause for concern. The successful Protestant applicant had four and a half years' experience as a part-time deputy abbatoir superintendent.

The appointment was made by a special meeting of all 22 Ballymena councillors. A tribunal was told that during refreshments after the interviews all 12 members of the Rev Ian Paisley's Democratic Unionist party had sat at a table on their own. The Protestant man was chosen by a vote of 12 to 10.

Limavady

The Co Londonderry council was found guilty of discriminating against a Catholic in the appointment of a technical officer. A tribunal heard that Unionist councillors had held a private meeting before the interviews to discuss the applicants. The appointment was made by eight votes to seven, eight Unionists voting in favour and seven nationalists against. The tribunal said council witnesses appearing before it had been evasive and inconsistent. One councillor, when asked for his notes, had destroyed them.

Discrimination cases also concerned other employers in the public and private sector. The Eastern Health and Social Services Board, Northern Ireland's largest employer, was ordered to pay a Catholic woman £25,000 in compensation for what was described as "one of the worst and most blatant cases of discrimination by a state authority". A tribunal accused the board of spinning a web of deceit in an attempt to defeat the woman's claim, describing the board's conduct as "outrageous" and "malicious". It ruled that the woman "suffered fear, humiliation, insult, stress and deep hurt" from discrimination and from subsequent victimisation.

The tribunal was told that the woman had been working on a temporary basis at Purdysburn mental hospital in south Belfast, and had applied for a permanent job in the laundry, which employed 23 Protestants and three Catholics. Fifteen Protestants and 17 Catholics had applied, and six Protestants and one Catholic had been appointed. Although the complainant had 12 years' experience as a cook supervisor, she was the only one of six internal candidates who was unsuccessful.

The tribunal was told that a Union Jack was displayed in the laundry together with pictures of the royal family and a photograph of an employee with a local politician, and that Protestant tunes were played there during the marching season. It said local management had lied and destroyed potential evidence about the case. The tribunal said that after winning her case the woman had returned to work to find that no one would talk to her and that an employee she had known for 20 years would not speak to her. A person who had always given her a lift home told her there would be no lift in future.

At a heated meeting of trade union members it was said she had told lies to the tribunal. When a union representative raised the case, he had been told by the board's director of personnel: "You opened a Pandora's box – you will just have to learn to live with the issues raised."

The tribunal said that the board had expressed no regret about the discrimination, and she had been placed under the managers who had discriminated against her and who had then lied to the tribunal. Its judgment went on: "She had been abandoned by management and she had been shunned by her colleagues. She was not sleeping and she needed tranquillisers." The board had a duty to promote a neutral environment and to protect employees against victimisation, the tribunal said, and it must accept the responsibility for the woman being subjected to a totally unacceptable form of stress.

Figures emerging from the 1991 census, together with other research, caused great interest when they revealed important changes in Northern Ireland's sectarian demography. After some statistical squabbling among the experts, it was established that Catholics now make up around 42 per cent of the population – a significant rise in a state whose very history is based on the numbers game.

1 NOVEMBER 1992   THE INDEPENDENT ON SUNDAY

The numbers that matter

The psyche of the Protestant community has always harboured the fear that the Catholic minority might come to outnumber them and thus win control of Northern Ireland. As a traditional Unionist saying has it: "Some day they'll breed us out." The latest census results will sharply increase that fear.

The preoccupation with numbers arises from the fact that Northern Ireland was set up in 1921 on the basis of a mathematical calculation. The Protestants of the north-east established a statelet of the largest possible size with a substantial Protestant majority. The result was Northern Ireland, consisting of six of Ireland's thirty-two counties. Many other Protestants who lived south of the border were reluctantly abandoned, since their inclusion would have brought too many Catholics into the new state and upset the population balance. That balance, which was almost exactly two-thirds Protestant and one-third Catholic, was maintained to within a couple of percentage points for 40 years. The importance of the mathematics was emphasised by a Unionist system of government which put heavy emphasis on majority rule – in effect, "winner takes all".

The fear of "out-breeding" was not heightened by the 1971 and 1981 censuses, whose results were generally interpreted to mean that a Catholic majority could only come about far into the 21st century, if at all. The results of the 1991 census, however, will necessitate a reassessment of that assumption. The two-thirds to one-third ratio, whose existence provided such a consistent backdrop to politics for so many decades, is now seen to have gone. Politicians, church leaders and others are faced with a new mathematical, and political, model.

There will be much argument about when a Catholic majority might come about, and what that could mean. There have been many indications that the terms "Catholic" and "nationalist" are not necessarily synonymous, and that a substantial number of Catholics would prefer to stay within the United Kingdom. But many Unionists are deeply worried. The 1985 Anglo-Irish agreement states that "if in the future a majority of the people of Northern Ireland clearly wish for and formally consent to the establishment of a united Ireland", the government will introduce and support legislation to give effect to that wish.

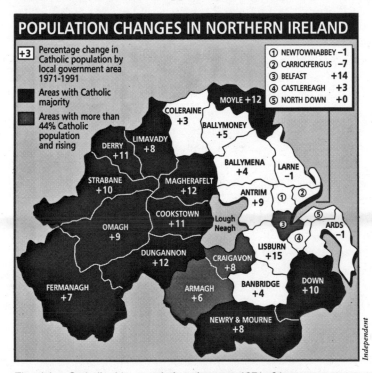

POPULATION CHANGES IN NORTHERN IRELAND

+3 Percentage change in Catholic population by local government area 1971-1991

Areas with Catholic majority

Areas with more than 44% Catholic population and rising

① NEWTOWNABBEY −1
② CARRICKFERGUS −7
③ BELFAST +14
④ CASTLEREAGH +3
⑤ NORTH DOWN +0

MOYLE +12
COLERAINE +3
BALLYMONEY +5
DERRY +11
LIMAVADY +8
BALLYMENA +4
LARNE −1
STRABANE +10
MAGHERAFELT +12
ANTRIM +9
COOKSTOWN +11
Lough Neagh
OMAGH +9
ARDS −1
LISBURN +15
DUNGANNON +12
CRAIGAVON +8
FERMANAGH +7
ARMAGH +6
BANBRIDGE +4
DOWN +10
NEWRY & MOURNE +8

Independent

The rising Catholic tide: population changes, 1971–91

The rise in the Catholic population will create unease in the Unionist community by adding a new element of uncertainty. Few expect a Catholic majority in the foreseeable future, and few believe that such a development would lead to instant Irish unity. But the fact that Catholic numbers have risen so significantly is bound to have a psychological effect on both sides of the sectarian divide and thus on political life. Already 11 of the 26 district councils have a Catholic majority while in 3 others the figure is above 40 per cent and rising. And a number of observers have already remarked on the increased sense of self-confidence within a Catholic community which is both growing numerically and rising socially.

Although it is impossible to foretell the future, the pattern is unlikely to be reversed. The school population of Belfast is around 50–50, but in the west Catholic schoolchildren outnumber Protestant pupils by three to one. A combination of reasons is thought to be responsible for the trends. The Catholic birth rate is higher than that of Protestants, but the emigration patterns that traditionally offset this, keeping Catholic numbers down, have been disrupted. In the 1960s around 60 per cent of those emigrating were Catholics, but Catholic emigration has fallen as it has become apparent that fewer jobs are now available in England. The Protestant departure rate, on the other hand, is believed to have risen.

Politically, two different Unionist responses have emerged to the changing demographic facts. One has been to become even more hardline, as in the case of Belfast council, where Unionist members run the show with little if any reference to the minority and simply shrug off the repeated accusations of discrimination. The second approach is to be seen in other councils, where a degree of powersharing between Unionists and the nationalist SDLP has already been unobtrusively introduced. A recent research project demonstrated that the five Unionist councils where a powersharing arrangement exists are all in places where the Unionist–nationalist balance is very close. According to one Belfast nationalist councillor: "Some of these guys are just nasty little bigots who will go right down to the wire. Others are more far-sighted: they know that it's the last ditch and the writing is on the wall, and they know they'll have to make a deal."

These two approaches in a sense represent the malign and benign scenarios for the future. In the first, fears and tensions increase, with a consequent rise in violence and instability; in the second, the feeling grows that accommodation is necessary and new working relationships are developed.

In the meantime, the population shifts are creating a number of what have been called, only slightly fancifully, fortress towns. These are redoubts where Protestants are retreating into tighter enclaves with something close to the mentality of the herd.

The census results reveal, or in some cases conceal, the effects that more than 20 years of violence have had on population distribution. The onset of the Troubles brought enormous upheavals, reversing what had been a gradual trend towards more integration of Protestants and Catholics. In the late 1960s and early 1970s widespread civil disturbances led to what has been described as the

38

largest enforced population movement in western Europe since the Second World War. Whole areas which had been mixed became segregated as one side or the other moved out, sometimes en masse. Most of the movement took place in Belfast and surrounding housing estates: no one knows how many people fled, but according to one official estimate between 8,000 and 15,000 families were forced to evacuate their homes in the three years from 1969 to 1972. Catholic families were particularly affected, as loyalist paramilitary groups organised campaigns of intimidation in an early example of ethnic cleansing. In east and north Belfast in particular, Catholic homes were systematically attacked and Catholic men shot.

One of the features of more recent times has been a less dramatic but still marked tendency for Protestants to move away from certain areas. In many instances an exodus has begun when members of the security forces, who are almost all Protestant, feel unsafe when the Catholic population begins to rise, fearing that some of the new arrivals may be IRA sympathisers. Security force members will often move to predominantly Protestant areas, and when they do they can begin a process which gathers momentum. In one part of Belfast, for example, two Protestant schools have closed because of a lack of pupils. Later they reopened, one as a Catholic school, the other as an integrated institution. Once Catholic school places become available, more Catholics tend to be attracted to the vicinity.

A Protestant clergyman whose flock is draining away said: "I ask them why they're moving but I've never yet got a satisfactory answer. They'll say, 'Well, a lot of our friends have moved.' The security aspect is part of it – an attack on a policeman living locally vibrates through the community."

In Londonderry, the second city, almost all Protestants have abandoned the city centre and moved across the river to the Waterside, or further away to the town of Limavady. In parts of Fermanagh such as Roslea, Protestant numbers have dwindled to almost zero, with families choosing to pull back from border areas into towns such as Lisnaskea and Lisbellaw. In Co Down, Protestants have moved back from Newry into Banbridge, one of the fortress towns.

In Belfast the Protestant middle class is gradually leaving the south of the city to upwardly mobile Catholics and opting for east Belfast or north Down, while from the north of the city there is steady movement to Newtownabbey and Carrickfergus. The net result is that most of the working class in Belfast is segregated in housing terms. More mixing takes place within the middle class, but with each passing year the contrast grows between the largely Protestant east and the predominantly Catholic west.

Another set of figures to emerge from the census showed a disconcerting picture of a society heading towards ever-starker religious segregation.

21 MARCH 1993   THE INDEPENDENT ON SUNDAY

Apartheid deepens on streets of Ulster

A detailed analysis of population trends shows that the degree of physical separation between Protestants and Catholics is increasing year by year, with the number of segregated areas more than doubling in the past two decades. Increasingly, large sections of the population are literally strangers to one another, a fact that has ominous implications for the government's hopes of finding political accommodation. These hopes rest on the assumption that the majority of people in the two communities share similar outlooks and interests, and are kept apart only by the actions of a few hundred gunmen – an assumption which now looks naïve. Community leaders also say that greater separation tends to lead to more violence.

An analysis of Northern Ireland's 566 district council wards shows that:

about half of the province's 1.5 million population live in areas which are more than 90 per cent Protestant or more than 90 per cent Catholic;

fewer than 110,000 people – around 7 per cent – live in areas with roughly equal numbers of Catholics and Protestants.

Close examination of the data often reveals that wards which are apparently mixed in fact contain two separate communities, sometimes physically parted by 20-foot-high reinforced walls known as "peace lines".

Over the last two decades, the number of predominantly Catholic wards has increased from 43 to 120. Areas which are almost exclusively Protestant have risen from 56 to 115.

A Belfast "peace line" – one of the walls separating the Falls from the Shankill

Of Belfast's 51 wards, 16 are over 95 per cent Protestant, 11 over 95 per cent Catholic. In all, 35 areas are at least 90 per cent of one religion or the other.

News of the survey took political leaders aback. John Alderdice, leader of the nonsectarian Alliance party, said: "It's an extraordinary mark of the polarisation, and most worrying. It's almost creating an apartheid situation."

Chris McGimpsey, a senior figure in the Ulster Unionist party, responded: "We're effectively splitting into two separate and distinct communities here. I see apartheid in Belfast. When a community turns in on itself, meeting less and less of the other community, they have less knowledge of them as human beings. That certainly increases the potential for sectarian violence."

Councillor Brian Feeney of the SDLP commented: "The figures demonstrate that there are going to be increasingly divisive politics in Belfast, if that is possible to imagine. There is also going to be an extension of the sectarian attrition: we have already seen the murders spread from north Belfast into south Belfast."

41

Even close observers have been surprised by the picture emerging from the research. Segregation has been a traditional feature of life, particularly in Belfast, but now a heightened herd instinct has led to greater division than ever. Gordon Moore, a trade union official since the 1940s, said: "I'm stunned by this, because I thought we had moved further on in the past 20 years. I'm saddened to hear that is the position, and I can see it might be a hopeless task to try to reverse this."

Jackie Hutchinson, a community worker in the Shankill district, which is 99 per cent Protestant, described the lives of teenagers in his area, where many become involved with loyalist paramilitary groups: "Young people start off in primary school: they are segregated. They go to secondary school: they are segregated. They leave school, no hope, probably, of getting a job because there's no inward investment, so they go to a Youth Training Programme [YTP]. There are separate YTPs for Catholics and Protestants. They go on to ACE [Action for Community Employment]: there are separate ACE schemes. Because they don't have any money they are stuck in their own areas, so they don't get to see other people with other religions or other cultures. That is their problem."

The new data show that segregation is widespread across both urban and rural areas, but at its worst in the two main cities, Londonderry and Belfast. In Belfast a substantial measure of religious integration exists in only two areas, middle-class pockets in the north and south. Even here, however, the mixing may only be temporary, in that these were once Protestant but are now, quietly but inexorably, becoming more and more Catholic. Thus the middle-class Malone district, which 10 years ago was three-quarters Protestant, is now more than 40 per cent Catholic, and local estate agents report that most homes are being bought by Catholic families. In effect, the developing Catholic middle class has been steadily displacing the Protestant middle class in the district.

Middle-class Protestants are in the process of gradually abandoning most of the north, west and south of the city and concentrating in the east. While divisions are most conspicuous in working-class parts of north and west Belfast, where the peace lines carve through streets, the east of the city is less obviously, but just as effectively, segregated, as it fills up with Protestant middle-class families. So wards in the plush areas around Stormont Castle, the seat of government, and the nearby police headquarters, are, in fact, up to 98 per cent Protestant. This has important implications for the administration, since many senior civil servants live in these areas and have only limited experience of life elsewhere in the city. A senior Catholic civil servant, asked whether his Protestant colleagues lacked insight into life in the Catholic areas, replied: "With some of them their ignorance is total, absolute and complete. You have people determining housing policy who have never been on the Shankill Road or the Falls Road."

On a human level, the geographical divisions mean that people can, in a fashion which seems quite natural to them, lead lives of near-apartheid. One Catholic woman who recently married an east Belfast Protestant says she realised, after spending an evening with his neighbours, that she was the first Catholic most of them had ever met socially. She commented: "They treat me so carefully, so cautiously, skirting round anything to do with the Troubles. More than once I've been asked, 'When did you come up here?' In other words, they assumed I was from the Republic – they just couldn't conceive I'd been born and brought up in Belfast."

A middle-class Protestant recalled playing with Catholic children when he was a boy: "We knew what religion we were all right, but we played, anyway. Now my kids don't really meet Catholics at all. In Belfast there's the odd pub where the two sides would drink together, but that's becoming more and more rare."

A Catholic woman from exclusively Catholic west Belfast said she made one Protestant friend at college but has now lost touch with her. When she visited a tiny Catholic enclave in east Belfast she felt uncomfortable and uneasy about "having them [Protestants] all round you".

While there are various social, sporting, cultural and other contacts across the divide, two decades of violence have served to deepen existing divisions. Almost all Protestant children continue to be educated in state schools while almost all Catholics go to schools run by the Catholic church. The mixed schools movement has received much attention in recent years, but fewer than 1 per cent of children attend integrated schools.

In terms of employment, some progress has been made towards establishing equal opportunity. But official statistics show that more than 250 sizeable firms still have workforces which are virtually or completely segregated. In addition to such obviously one-sided firms, experts in the field of fair employment say that more than half of all companies employing more than 25 people have discrepancies in the workforce which are substantially out of line with their catchment area.

In mixed work places people of different religions tend to insulate themselves from the other side by observing the unwritten but widespread rule that religion and politics are simply too sensitive to be discussed in mixed company. One well-known catch phrase is: "Whatever you say, say nothing."

Although segregation is recognised as a deeply unhealthy state of affairs, the government, housing authorities and security forces have been unable to reverse the trend towards greater and greater separation. One official said: "People do this for security, it's generally fear. And you can't insist to somebody that they live somewhere that's mixed, especially when they fear for their lives." A government source commented privately that there were two policy approaches which were, in fact, at variance with each other. He said: "On the one hand general

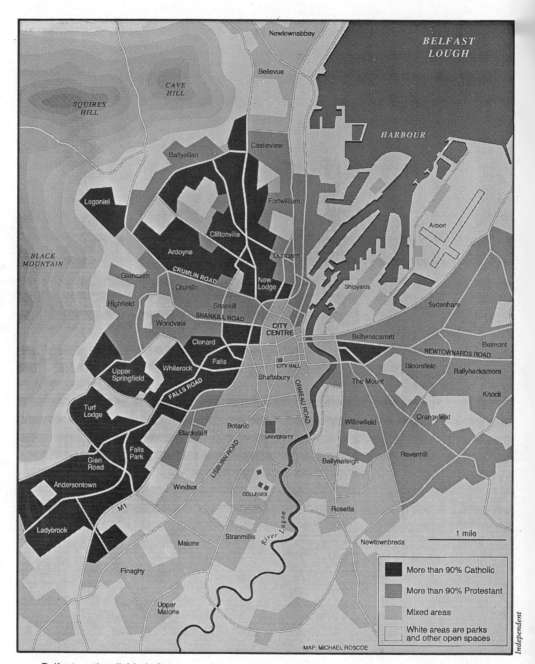

Belfast – the divided city

government social policy would theoretically favour a mix. But then security policy would probably favour a separation because it keeps things distinct and easier to control."

44

In the end, however, much of the segregation is voluntary and brought about by people who prefer to live with their co-religionists rather than go down the more difficult road of integration. Segregation is a symptom of the existing divisions, but its existence makes those divisions deeper than ever.

BELFAST – THE SEGREGATED CITY

WARD	PROTESTANTS %	CATHOLICS %
Woodvale	100	–
Island	99	1
Orangefield	99	1
Shankill	99	1
Sydenham	99	1
Ballysillan	99	1
Duncairn	99	1
The Mount	99	1
Crumlin Road	98	2
Bloomfield	98	2
Belmont	98	2
Woodstock	98	2
Highfield	98	2
Knock	98	2
Blackstaff	96	4
Cherryvalley	95	5
Stormont	94	6
Ballyhackamore	90	10
■ Glencairn	89	11
Ravenhill	82	18
Upper Malone	82	18
■ St Annes	79	21
□ Fortwilliam	76	24
□ Castleview	70	30
Windsor	69	31
Shaftesbury	65	35
□ Malone	64	36

Continued on next page

Continued

WARD	PROTESTANTS %	CATHOLICS %
Stranmillis	63	37
■ Ligoniel	62	38
☐ Cavehill	62	38
Rosetta	52	48
Ballymacarrett	51	49
Ballynafeigh	46	54
■ Cliftonville	43	57
☐ Bellevue	41	59
☐ Finaghy	37	63
☐ Chichester Park	31	69
Botanic	30	70
■ Ladybrook	13	87
Waterworks	7	93
New Lodge	5	95
Beechmount	3	97
Falls	3	97
Clonard	1	99
Ardoyne	1	99
Andersonstown	–	100
Falls Park	–	100
Glen Road	–	100
Glencolin	–	100
Upper Springfield	–	100
Whiterock	–	100

■ signifies wards which may seem to have some degree of integration, but which are in fact internally segregated, sometimes by peace lines.

☐ signifies those which are on the face of it integrated. Closer inspection shows, however, that they were once predominantly Protestant but that Protestants are steadily moving out.

High unemployment is one feature of a
traditionally weak local economy which has
suffered the ravages of terrorism and
political instability. As a result, increasingly
large sums of British public money are
needed to keep the economy afloat.

29 MAY 1991   THE INDEPENDENT

Subsidies create fear of dependency culture

The Exchequer subsidises the Northern Ireland economy to the tune of £2 billion annually, according to government figures. A large proportion of this sum goes on security costs, which are just under £1 billion a year and rising. But outside the security field, expenditure per head is well above the United Kingdom average in practically every area of government activity. Spending on industry and agriculture, for example, runs at almost five times the UK rate.

In all, public spending in the 1990 financial year was almost £6 billion, £2 billion of which was contributed from London. The figure is set to rise in 1991 to approaching £6.5 billion. Spending per head is running at 47 per cent higher than the UK average. The £2 billion is equivalent to a penny on income tax. Such costings rarely attract public notice, and spending levels form little or no part of political debate, which tends to concentrate on forms of government and only occasionally touches on economic matters.

The region's already weak private sector was affected by the violence and the difficulties of attracting new outside investment to a troubled area. A consequent increase in public expenditure means that 40 per cent of employees now work in the public sector. Such an economic structure has led some in government and some economists to express anxiety about the creation of a "dependency culture". According to one local economist: "We're very dependent in three ways. First, we depend on the public sector for employment, both

47

directly and indirectly. Four out of every ten people work for the government. And the expenditure of those people in the shops and restaurants and so on is very important for a lot of local services. Second, we've got the largest unemployment of any region, so those people are directly dependent on government expenditure. Then a third element is the manufacturing industry, together with agriculture, both of which have been very highly dependent on government grants – more so than other parts of the UK. So for one reason or another almost every part of Northern Ireland is very dependent on public money."

One former Northern Ireland Office minister, who did not wish to be named, said: "Local politicians don't agree on very much, but on one thing there's an absolutely total consensus – they argued they were short of money on every front. Actually, it was pouring out of everyone's ear holes. One of the sad things is that a lot of the enterprise and thrift seems to have gone. When I went round I'd ask little Protestant boys what they were going to do when they grew up, and they'd draw themselves up to attention and say, 'security'. And you could see why: that's where the jobs and uniforms and cars and mortgages are."

Annually, £440 per head is spent on law and order in Northern Ireland, compared with an overall UK figure of £145. In addition to this, the cost of maintaining the thousands of regular troops, together with the locally recruited Ulster Defence Regiment, is put at just over £200 million each year. There are various additional costs. In 1990, for example, the Ministry of Defence allocated an extra £126 million to tighten security at military bases in Britain and West Germany in the face of the continuing IRA campaign outside Ireland. No figures are available for the extra security precautions taken at nonmilitary potential targets, such as Whitehall and Westminster, or for the additional policing costs in Britain.

It is impossible to say how much of the expenditure is due to terrorism and how much to "ordinary" crime. There are also other costs which are impossible to calculate, such as the damage to tourism (in both parts of Ireland) and the extra money needed to attract industrial investment. The Irish government also spends a considerable amount of money on border security and other antiterrorist measures.

A breakdown of security expenditure shows that almost exactly half the total goes to the Royal Ulster Constabulary, reflecting the importance of the force in the security system. The RUC consists of 8,250 regulars, 3,000 full-time reservists, 1,650 part-time reservists and a further 3,050 civilians in backup roles. Wages account for a great deal of the £468 million spent in 1990–1, officers being comparatively well paid and working an estimated 13,500 hours of overtime daily.

Another significant item of expenditure is the large-scale police building programme which has already cost more than £100 million in the past seven years.

There are plans to spend a further £70 million in the next three years, with work scheduled to start on 86 new construction projects. According to government figures, 38 of these will cost more than half a million pounds each.

The additional cost of the army is not usually included in Northern Ireland figures, but the M.o.D. calculates the "Northern Ireland emergency factor" as £206 million for 1990–1. This figure does not cover the wages of the 10,000 troops, but does take accommodation costs into account. The M.o.D. says no separate figure is available to show the cost of the UDR.

The cost of prisons is particularly expensive, since the presence of large numbers of dangerous paramilitary inmates means security must be maintained at a high level. Last year's spending was £122 million. The average annual cost per inmate, depending on how the amount is calculated, lies somewhere between £65,000 and £80,000. The Maze jail outside Belfast, which houses hardline republicans and loyalists and has the highest security rating, cost £42 million in 1989–90. But 90 per cent of the total bill goes on wages and salaries, the prison service employing 3,200 officers plus 340 support staff.

An estimated £36 million was distributed in the 1990 financial year as compensation for deaths, injuries and damage to property, adding to the hundreds of millions paid out since the Troubles began. This figure had not been expected to rise significantly next year but recent IRA firebombing attacks may necessitate a recalculation, since according to one preliminary estimate, they inflicted £25 million worth of damage on major stores. Official statistics show that more than 27,000 claims are outstanding, while new claims are received at a rate of more than 13,000 annually.

Public expenditure has traditionally run at a high level in Northern Ireland, given that it is a relatively disadvantaged region on the periphery of both the United Kingdom and the European Community. But today it is heavily reliant on government spending, as its private sector remains weak, and many parts of industry receive substantial subsidies. Revenue raised in Northern Ireland covers some of this, but each year the Exchequer is required to make a contribution to meet the balance, which this year was in the region of £2 billion.

The authorities point to a number of factors to explain the high levels of expenditure. The continuing violence is an obvious major economic complicating factor, while various indicators show that the level of need is generally higher than in other regions.

Two versions of the approach to spending are available. According to the authorities, both the Treasury and the Northern Ireland Department of Finance do all they can to hold costs down. Another perspective, however, came from one former Northern Ireland minister, who said privately: "In general there was no pressure from Westminster over the money. There was a shrug of the shoulders, rather like saying it was like the civil list or something, something they just had to put up with. I didn't feel we got much scrutiny. What they tended to do was to pay the bills while the violence went on, and in a more immediate way the security expenses aren't skimped on. So a great deal of security money actually washed over into the general economy."

A different view came from an economist, who said: "Actually, Britain gets great value for the money it spends here, because it underpins a great many jobs in England, Scotland and Wales. We are a captive market, with very strong ties to British retailers and distributors, so a lot of what flows into here flows right back to British firms."

In the 1950s and 1960s, Northern Ireland was very much a political backwater which attracted little attention. When the Troubles broke out one of the by-products was to draw attention to areas of social provision, such as housing, which lagged well behind the rest of the UK. Public spending was increased to deal with this, while at the same time the civil unrest led to an increase of employment in the security field.

The oil crisis of 1973 and the continuing disturbances meant the inflow of capital virtually dried up as foreign firms shied away from what they regarded as an unstable area. As unemployment rose sharply, British governments stepped in and the public sector expanded rapidly during the 1970s, at a rate much above the UK average. According to one economist: "The beanfeast, the bonanza, really lasted essentially from 1971 to about 1980, but it has been very gently easing down since then."

The Northern Ireland economy has always been one of the weakest in the UK. Unemployment has persistently been above the UK average: even at its lowest ever point, in October last year, it stood at 94,000 – 13.7 per cent of the labour force – which was well above Britain's postwar peak of 11.5 per cent. In December last year unemployment stood at 14 per cent, more than double the national average of 6.5 per cent. Gross domestic product per head is significantly lower than in Britain. Although there is a lower proportion of elderly people, Northern Ireland has a much higher proportion of children. It actually has the lowest death rate in the UK, but when the age structure of the population is taken into account it has higher levels of morbidity.

Such factors are used to explain why public expenditure is higher per head in almost every sector of the economy than in England, Scotland or Wales. In trade, industry, energy and employment, money is spent on trying to attract new industry, in supporting existing companies and in training. This year's figure, showing spending at five times the national average, is somewhat higher than usual due to the inclusion of some of the cost of the privatisation of the Shorts aircraft and missile company. Privatising Shorts and the Belfast shipyard were both expensive operations, together costing at least £1 billion.

Agriculture is an important industry in Northern Ireland, employing around

10 per cent of the workforce, and is heavily subsidised. Housing was a particular priority in the 1970s and 1980s, with slum clearance schemes long overdue. Unfitness levels were as high as 14 per cent in 1979, but have been almost halved since then and now stand closer to the UK average.

Education is one of the major spending departments, the allocation of extra money being partly explained by the fact that the pupil population is proportionately higher by half than England and Wales. Extra need is also indicated by the fact that while grammar schools tend to achieve excellent results, more children leave school without any qualifications or examination passes.

In the field of health and personal social services, the higher spending is said to reflect higher levels of social deprivation, the greater number of low-income households, and differences in morbidity and mortality. In social security, payments to claimants are exactly the same as in Britain. Much of the extra money goes to the larger percentage of unemployed and in more child-benefit claims.

Only in the field of roads and transport are costs below the UK average, largely because of the building of a high-quality roads network in the 1960s. There is also the fact that no large-scale rail subsidies are required since Northern Ireland has few railway lines.

POSTSCRIPT

In 1992 the subvention had risen to £3.3 billion, with extra military costs adding a further £0.5 billion.

3

THE SOUTH

The years after 1989 brought change and even upheaval in southern Irish political and social affairs. After some years characterised by relatively little change, liberals secured a largely unexpected breakthrough in late 1990.

The office of president of Ireland had, throughout the Republic's history, been held by retired politicians, invariably from the Fianna Fáil party. In late 1990 the latest candidate to fit this bill, Brian Lenihan, appeared to be cantering to a comfortable victory, when suddenly everything went wrong for him. And everything started to go right for his main opponent, the feminist lawyer Mary Robinson.

Reformer takes on the old guard

"**Y**ou do realise," an Irish lawyer said in wonderment, "that we look like having, as president of Ireland, a radical feminist socialist woman who sympathises with the Unionists. The mind boggles." Minds all over Ireland have been boggling at the events of the presidential election campaign. What seemed to be a comfortable walkover for Brian Lenihan, deputy Prime Minister, defence minister and probably the most popular politician in the Republic, was suddenly transformed into a crisis which this week almost brought down the government.

Ireland has the youngest population in Europe, yet its party political structures have remained largely fossilised, reflecting as they do the politics of the 1920s. Mr Lenihan's party, Fianna Fáil, dominates the political landscape, drawing votes from left, right and centre. Its lack of a fixed economic ideology has helped prevent the emergence of class-based parties, and its general conservatism, much of it rural-based, has meant that social and legal reform comes at a snail's pace. The country's laws have therefore not kept up with the extent of demographic change. Mr Lenihan's personal catch phrase, "no problem", neatly encapsulates the general Fianna Fáil approach.

The other element in the Fianna Fáil make-up is the whiff of corruption that hangs over many parts of the party; allegations of cronyism and shady dealings have, of course, been plentiful during Charles Haughey's period as leader. An opponent talked of his "flawed pedigree"; a rival once spoke pointedly of "low standards in high places". One of Mr Lenihan's principal characteristics has been his almost unswerving personal loyalty to Mr Haughey. He himself has been regarded as a likeable, able and reasonably upright politician, but all at once the old allegations against Fianna Fáil – suspicions about its funding and links with big business, rumours of financial scandals – have come bubbling back to the surface.

The Lenihan campaign imploded when a tape recording emerged from his past. He had repeatedly insisted that he had not tried to speak on the telephone to the current president, Patrick Hillery, during a 1982 crisis. His denials were emphatic, unequivocal and televised. Then a tape appeared of an interview given by Mr Lenihan to a student last May. Had he, the student asked, rung the president? "Oh, I did," replied Mr Lenihan. "Oh yeah, I mean I got through to him. I remember talking to him and he wanted to lay off . . . Looking back on it, it was a mistake on our part because Paddy Hillery would be very strict or conventional in that way, you know . . . He was very annoyed about that. I know he was annoyed with the whole bloody lot of us."

Try though he might, Mr Lenihan could not explain why he had said one thing to the student and the opposite during the campaign. The interview with the student was just a mistake, he said; "on mature recollection" – he used the phrase eight times in one television interview – he was sure he had made no such calls. His party at first affected to believe him, but its coalition partners, the Progressive Democrats, made it clear they would not continue in government with him. The resignations of PD ministers would have brought down the administration.

Last week, therefore, Mr Lenihan's leader and close friend, Charles Haughey, sacked him from the cabinet: he remained in the presidential race because it was too late to nominate anyone else. At a stroke Mary Robinson was propelled from a respectable second place in the polls to the position of favourite. The only real danger to her now is that a sentimental electorate might decide to give Mr Lenihan the presidency as a consolation prize.

So an extraordinary campaign may well end with an extraordinary result: the election as president of Ireland of a formidable woman who is not only a human rights lawyer of distinction but also a strong feminist and champion of the underdog. All other presidents have been middle-aged or elderly conservative men. Furthermore, she will be elected on a mandate to change and expand the presidency's largely ceremonial role. The president, she has said, should be a voice for the disadvantaged and marginalised in Irish society. No one familiar with her record doubts she will proceed to redefine the office, attempting to create a whole new focal point of influence in Irish politics. "And the logic of that," according to one who knows her well, "is that within a few years Mary and the government could be heading for a constitutional crisis."

She already has an impressive record of achievement for a radical female functioning in a political culture controlled by conservative males. According to an *Irish Times* writer: "She has possibly done more, with words alone, to induce change in Ireland than any other single politician." Although she has been deeply involved in politics, her principal achievements have been through her legal work. As a distinguished constitutional lawyer, she has specialised in battles to modernise and liberalise Irish law on a host of controversial issues.

Unsurprisingly for a state whose population is well over 90 per cent Catholic,

President Mary Robinson

many of the Republic's laws and much of its constitution have been heavily influenced by Catholic doctrines. Reforms which would be relatively straight-forward in other countries can touch nerves deep in the national psyche and pose the most fundamental of questions. Should the Republic's laws reflect its Catholicism, or aim to be pluralist and secular? Should church and state be separate? It is a conservative country, and its legislators have often preferred to shy away from contentious issues. An added complication is that the 1937 constitution, which, for example, forbids divorce, can only be changed by referendums. These have often generated intense and emotional campaigns.

Where many politicians have run for the hills, Mary Robinson has been in the thick of battles on the most difficult and sensitive questions: divorce, contra-ception, the right to information on abortion, homosexuality, illegitimacy, adop-tion, family law, and questions of taxation and legal aid. Not all the battles

55

were won, but she has scored striking successes in a number of areas. In the process she has come to public attention as a clever, far-sighted lawyer who combines legal expertise with social concern, whose personal constituency is the disadvantaged and, in particular, women.

She is also very much a European, in a markedly pro-European country: many of Dublin's intelligentsia no longer look to traditional Irish nationalism, but to what one author, Conor Gearty, has described as "the new intoxicatingly cosmopolitan Europeanism". In Ireland she helped pioneer the practice of taking cases to the European Court of Human Rights, an approach which produced several famous victories.

Her social conscience came from her family. She was born Mary Bourke in Ballina, Co Mayo, in the far west of Ireland in 1944. Her father was the local GP and the family was comfortably off. Mary and two of her brothers became lawyers while another two brothers became doctors. According to her husband Nick, he and she both believe that "if you have had the privilege of a happy and well-educated background and are able to command a good income, you have to put something back into society".

At Trinity College Dublin she took a first in law and an honours degree in French, returning to a Trinity chair after a fellowship year at Harvard. In 1969 Trinity elected her to the Senate, the Irish parliament's upper chamber, as the first Catholic ever elected by the Protestant university. Describing herself as a socialist – a label she now shies away from – she hit the news almost immediately by introducing a family planning bill.

In the years that followed she continued to lecture at Trinity and became a senior counsel, the Irish equivalent of QC. She found time to marry and have three children. Her husband Nick, who is a Protestant, is also a lawyer; he runs the Irish Centre for European Law at Trinity, which the Robinsons jointly founded. He is an active conservationist in a country whose splendid architectural heritage is often undervalued and frequently vandalised.

She twice stood unsuccessfully for the Irish parliament's lower chamber, the Dáil. She stayed in the Senate, at first as an independent, but later joining the Irish Labour party. Thus, at the age of 46, she already has two decades of parliamentary experience. Mrs Robinson herself admits that she is not a natural politician in the Irish sense, lacking the traditional glad-handing skills so valued in the small world of Irish politics. She gained an unfortunate reputation as a Trinity intellectual with an upper-class accent, some people finding her reticent and reserved. According to one feminist: "It was always a limitation, politically, that she didn't have the stomach or personality for squeezing the palms and doing the rubber-chicken circuit." Until this campaign, she jealously guarded her family's privacy: Ireland has just seen the first-ever pictures of the Robinsons *en famille*. She has also responded to professional advice on her personal image. Her wardrobe, which one woman described as austere to the point of severity, has been softened with designer outfits.

She left the Labour party in 1985 when, amid the general welcome for the Anglo-Irish agreement, she alone took the view that it was unfair to northern Unionists. But it was at the invitation of the Labour party that she entered the presidential race.

She began her campaign well before the other candidates, intensively travelling the country with her message that change was needed. Many thought that the medium of the campaign was the message: she had little or no chance of winning, it was said, so the real purpose was to air the arguments. She herself described it as "a very serious opportunity to think about ourselves and our country, and face up to the need for change". That part actually worked well enough, for she has throughout held the candidate of Fine Gael, the main opposition party, to third place. In the process she appears to have connected well enough with the man and woman in the street. She has shaken so many hands by this stage, it is said, that she probably shakes Nick's hand when she wakes each morning.

The irony of it all is that her elevation would remove her legal skills and dedication from the courtroom. As one friend said: "Mary will be a loss. There aren't very many people who have the same eye for issues and the same commitment to take up the cudgels. People like her are rare. She has painted herself into a corner." As against that, she possesses the political experience and constitutional skills which could indeed turn the presidency into an activist office and an instrument of social justice. With her in office the presidency could become a focal point for progressive opinion, which could significantly alter the political agenda. In two decades she has already delivered a series of shocks to the system; a Robinson presidency would provide the biggest shock yet.

The wind of change in the south, coupled with the continuing Troubles and a growing sense that Unionists also had rights, brought a reappraisal of attitudes towards the north.

Unity slips from top of the Irish agenda

The north is a difficult issue for the Republic of Ireland. In republican theory and in the minds of many of its citizens, the country will not be complete until the six north-eastern counties are united with the twenty-six. But the grim realities of more than two decades of violence mean that this aspiration now co-exists with a strong measure of aversion. Few in the Republic can imagine how a united Ireland could cope successfully with elements such as the Rev Ian Paisley and Gerry Adams of Sinn Féin.

In the meantime, the violence which racks the north disrupts Anglo-Irish relations, costs the south a great deal of money, and makes Ireland synonymous with conflict. Few approve of the violence; fewer still relish the prospect of an Ireland united through IRA terrorism, a development regarded as a recipe for serious instability.

Dublin today is a cosmopolitan European city. The Republic has its economic problems – unemployment, emigration and taxation run at very high levels – but its people are proud of their achievements since independence. The question of the north is an unwelcome reminder of the state's shortcomings.

For a number of reasons the European vision means much more here than it does in Britain: the country has benefited economically from the European Community, and its people also have real faith in the idea of a united Europe. Irish politicians enjoy the European stage, and European unity is now spoken of more often than Irish unity. Ireland is fated always to have its most important relationship with Britain, its much larger and occasionally insensitive neighbour. But Europe offers an alternative focus, and an attractive means of demonstrating the fulfilment of Ireland's historic ambition to take its place among the nations of the world.

For a decade and more the south has grappled intermittently with the question of how to handle issues such as contraception and divorce. A liberal intelligentsia wants a less Catholic state, with changes to the numerous laws which presently reflect Catholic doctrine, but many attempts at reform have been defeated by the church and other conservative elements. At a number of points in the past decade Charles Haughey's Fianna Fáil party, a basically centrist institution, linked up with the hierarchy to dish other parties' proposals for modernisation.

But the liberals turned the tables last year with the election of Mary Robinson as president. The body politic has yet to recover from the shock of the election of a left-wing radical feminist to the highest office in the land. While the debate on the exact significance of the event is still going on, it is quite clear that nothing will be quite the same again. Mrs Robinson and her supporters are set on sweeping the cobwebs away; the hierarchy, headed by Cardinal Cahal Daly, is clearly intent on opposing her and preserving as much of the Catholic ethos as possible. The stage is set for years of polite but hard-fought running battles.

The fact is that such debates have to date been conducted with little reference to the north, which is a measure of its status as a place apart. The arguments have been largely confined to the southern nationalist family. In general, reforms have been proposed or resisted on the basis that they are right or wrong for southern society, and not in terms of whether they might make the Republic more attractive to northern Unionists. There has, however, been a growing awareness of the realities of Unionism, including a wider appreciation of the implacability of its opposition to unity. This has been part of the wider education provided by the Troubles.

On the north, in fact, the reforming president and the conservative cardinal have much in common. They are, for example, on the same side of the growing debate on Articles 2 and 3 of the Irish constitution, which lay formal claim to the territory of Northern Ireland. One side, which includes Fianna Fáil and the northern nationalists of the SDLP, holds that changing these articles should only be contemplated as part of a wide-ranging settlement. By contrast, Mrs Robinson, Cardinal Daly and most of the southern parties believe their wording should be altered to include an explicit statement that Irish unity could only come about by consent. This argument has already helped focus the minds of some politicians and others in the south to think again about Northern Ireland and re-examine their attitudes towards northern Protestants.

The Troubles have also led to a reassessment and redefinition of the wider Anglo-Irish relationship, leading to the emergence of a new perspective on the Northern Ireland problem. In the early part of the Troubles the perception was that the British and Irish governments were in conflict, and on many issues they were. As the violence has dragged on, however, there has been a steady convergence of opinions and of interests. The Republic no longer sees itself as warring with the British over the fate of the north: rather, the two governments have come to view it as a difficult and dangerous problem for both. The emphasis now is on joint management and containment, principally through the mechanism of the 1985 Anglo-Irish agreement.

Britain appears to have no great interest in holding on to Northern Ireland, while the Republic clearly has no immediate ambitions to assume responsibility for it. The traditional aspiration for unity has receded into the future, but the north has not quite been abandoned. Instead, the new southern ambition is to wield influence on the management of the north. Southern politicians are fiercely protective of the Anglo-Irish accord, which they welcome as a standing affirmation by Britain of the legitimacy of Irish nationalism, and a reassurance that the north is not, as Mrs Thatcher once asserted, as British as Finchley. Britain, for its part, is glad to have the south as an active ally in its running of the north. The agreement has greatly reduced the practice of megaphone diplomacy, and Irish politicians no longer stomp the US and Europe censuring Britain for its presence and its actions in the north.

The two governments still have different views on many issues, but a sense of partnership between them seems firmly established. The Anglo-Irish agreement has been a conspicuous success in fulfilling the nationalist aspiration, as it now exists in the Republic. The accord may not have solved the northern problem, but it has gone a long way to meeting the needs of the south.

The standard Irish nationalist version of the history of Northern Ireland from 1920 until 1968 is that Britain shamefully neglected the northern Catholic minority and left it to the tender mercies of the Unionists. This picture may be largely correct; but what is also true, though rarely highlighted, is that the southern state adopted a broadly similar attitude. Lip service was paid to the ideal of Irish unity, but the Catholics of the north received little beyond occasional rhetorical recognition from their co-religionists in Dublin. Instead, the southern state concentrated on building and defending its own independent status. The north was largely left to the side, as the business of another day. On those occasions when the IRA launched its campaigns – which, by comparison with the terrorism of today, were almost laughably amateurish and short-lived – the south's principal concern was to protect its own fledgling polity against instability.

Fianna Fáil, particularly under its longtime leader Eamon de Valera, complained vociferously against partition (especially while in opposition) but pragmatically recognised there was nothing it could do about the border. Its early militancy mellowed into what has been characterised as verbal republicanism.

When the civil rights movement emerged in the late 1960s, much interest and sympathy was awakened in the Republic, where the campaign was seen as a clear-cut issue of simple justice. But the degeneration into the violence of the 1970s alarmed and alienated many.

The establishment of a powersharing executive in Northern Ireland in 1974 won widespread support in the south, appearing as it did to signal the beginning

60

of a happy ending to the story. It seemed the traditionally sectarian north could be reshaped as a new partnership-based entity in which old divisions might gradually decline. The executive was, however, brought down after less than six months by a loyalist general strike which displayed the determination and the muscle of militant Unionism. According to one northern journalist then based in Dublin: "The 1974 strike was the first time people in the south actually realised that the northern Prods were real punters and not an abstraction. Mind you, many people still see them largely as an abstraction; but still, the strike took an awful lot of people aback. At some subconscious level the demonstration of the power of the Protestant community did shift attitudes, not just to the Prods but to the whole problem."

The episode caused many people, in the Republic as in Britain, to conclude that the problem was, for the moment at least, intractable. The idea that Ireland should be, and one day will be, a united country is an ineradicable part of the nationalist psyche; but few could see how this could be brought about.

Along the way there have been eruptions of nationalist (or perhaps more accurately, anti-British) sentiment. These included Bloody Sunday in 1972, when British troops shot dead 14 civilians in Londonderry; the 1981 prison hunger strikes; Mrs Thatcher's peremptory rejection of the New Ireland Forum report in 1984; the Guildford Four, Maguire Seven and Birmingham Six campaigns; and a number of extradition crises. The southern reactions to such incidents tend to be strong but short-lived. The other feature of such events is that many of them have primarily concerned, not northern issues, but relations between Dublin and London.

According to one senior administrator in the Republic: "There is a very deep, ingrained response when John Bull is seen to be bullying again – you know, ravishing the lovely maiden Ireland. Some of it is mythological; some of it is the normal nervousness about having a big powerful neighbour." A journalist added: "People are very willing and happy to stand up to Britain in defence of the integrity of their state when they feel they're being insulted, as in the Father Ryan extradition affair. That's what really gets them going."

The place where the issue of the north is usually dealt with, it seems, is in the psyche rather than on the immediate political agenda. Last month an opinion poll showed that voters place it at the very bottom of the list of important issues. Yet it is a question which, while invisible for much of the time, never quite goes away.

One long-running irritant in Anglo-Irish relations has been the operation of extradition arrangements. Britain made a series of requests to Dublin for republican suspects to be sent north, and many of these ended in controversy. The Irish government is now due, in 1994, to introduce measures to strengthen laws which have often operated in unpredictable ways.

7 APRIL 1990   THE INDEPENDENT

Controversial history of Irish extradition cases

One of the many ironies about the vexed question of extradition, which has given rise to so many recurring Anglo-Irish controversies, is that the Irish approach to the subject is rooted in British jurisprudence. Since the last century it has been a principle of British law that refugees from other countries should be able to resist extradition attempts on the grounds that their offence or offences were political. One attempt to define this, by John Stuart Mill, suggested that "any offence committed in the course of civil war, insurrection or commotion is a political offence". Britain offered shelter to a great many refugees fleeing from European states, among them Karl Marx. The tradition was legally established in the first British extradition act, which in 1870 declared: "No person is to be surrendered if his offence is one of a political character."

The question in Ireland is how the Republic should regard members of the IRA and similar organisations who flee to the south: whether the courts, and the state, should say that all IRA actions are political; or that none of them is; or that some of them are. Over the past two decades the courts have appeared, at different times, to hold each of those views.

Almost everyone regards IRA members as different from ordinary criminals:

where opinions differ is on the question of whether they are better or worse. A wide range of attitudes is to be found in the Republic. One Dublin lawyer who has handled a number of extradition cases said: "Half the people I meet think our extradition record is a wonderful vindication of personal liberty. The other half think my clients should be put up against a wall and shot, and they'd cheerfully take up the rifle."

The early 1970s brought a series of requests from Northern Ireland for the return of IRA suspects who had fled south. None was successful. The Irish High Court, in February 1974, handed down a judgment in an explosives case which clearly laid down that IRA offences were to be regarded as political. Mr Justice Finlay stated: "It seems to me impossible to categorise the existing situation in Northern Ireland as being otherwise than a political disturbance, part of and incidental to which is the keeping of explosives for the IRA."

The judgment was to go unchallenged for eight years. Although it displeased London it was, Irish lawyers are keen to point out, very much in line with the traditional British attitude. It was also in keeping with the general approach of Irish courts which, lawyers say, have a tendency to side with the underdog. According to one barrister with experience in both Dublin and London: "I looked into the Supreme Court lately and there before the court was a man – clearly a crook – arguing his case. A judge with the same accent as him was asking him questions, very politely. Then you look into the law courts in Britain and you see an entire system clearly designed to intimidate the people who appear before it. It's an entirely different philosophy."

A former senior Irish cabinet minister observed: "The British judiciary is establishment-orientated and its decisions reflect that very much. The Irish judiciary is quite differently orientated – the whole development of our jurisprudence has been towards developing human rights vis-à-vis the legislature. They will tend not to support the establishment, where human rights are concerned. Several times a year our Supreme Court rejects bills or parts of bills as unconstitutional. It's conservative in some matters but on human rights it's very radical."

Successive British governments argued that some mechanism should be found to allow IRA extraditions, but the two countries failed to agree. In 1974, for example, an Anglo-Irish Law Enforcement Commission, set up to look at the question of fugitive offenders, split exactly on national lines. The Irish members all took the view that the Irish constitution ruled out extradition for political offences. Their position, which their government shared, was that the constitution bound the Republic to observe generally recognised rules of international law, and that one such rule was the political offence exception. The British members all disagreed.

The Irish position meant that the Republic felt unable, in the late 1970s, to sign the European Convention on the Suppression of Terrorism, an instrument which ruled that a number of actions, such as the use of explosives or automatic weapons, should no longer qualify for the political offence exception. The resulting stalemate lasted for eight years. No IRA members or other paramilitants were extradited; Britain continued, unsuccessfully, to press for change; and Unionists pointed to the situation as evidence for their assertion that the south was a haven for terrorists.

But the pattern of nonextradition in terrorist-type cases was spectacularly broken in a landmark decision in December 1982, when the Supreme Court overturned years of precedent and ordered the handover of Irish National Liberation Army leader Dominic McGlinchey. [McGlinchey was killed in a republican feud in February 1994.] Although McGlinchey was reputed to have been involved in a great many killings, the Royal Ulster Constabulary sought his extradition on only one charge. This was the murder of an elderly grandmother, Hester McMullan, who was killed when an IRA gang opened fire on her house. Her son was a part-time RUC reservist.

In his judgment, the then Chief Justice, Thomas O'Higgins, said he was not prepared to assume that any charge associated with paramilitary groups in Northern Ireland should be regarded as political. He laid down the test that a political offence must be one committed in the course of "what reasonable civilised people would regard as political activity". The murder involved was that of "an elderly grandmother riddled with bullets", which he described as a revolting and cowardly crime which should shock the conscience of any normal person. Dealing with the political offence concept, the Chief Justice declared: "The judicial authorities on the scope of such offences have in many respects been rendered obsolete by the fact that modern terrorist violence is often the antithesis of what could reasonably be regarded as political. The excusing *per se* of murder done by self-ordained arbiters is the very antithesis of the ordinances of Christianity and civilisation."

The judgment, clearly a turning point in extradition cases, indicated that republicans would no longer automatically qualify for the political exemption. One legal observer described it as "not illuminated by a lot of legal principle, but it's got a lot of very high-sounding things in it". The decision swept away the deadlock of the 1970s and instituted a period of often unpredictable change in extradition practice. The Supreme Court's view of the political defence underwent a rapid, and not always consistent, evolution.

It was not until March 1984 that McGlinchey was arrested and became the first republican to be handed across the border. The case had a number of subsequent twists. He was tried and convicted of the murder in Belfast, but his conviction was quashed on appeal. He was then re-extradited to the Republic, where he was convicted of firearms offences.

Not long after the McGlinchey extradition another republican, Seamus Shannon, became the first alleged member of the IRA to be handed over. He was wanted for the murder of 86-year-old Sir Norman Stronge, the former speaker of the Stormont parliament, and his son. An IRA group shot them in their Co Armagh home, Tynan Abbey, and then burnt it down with the two bodies inside.

Rejecting Shannon's appeal in July 1984, Mr Justice O'Higgins followed the reasoning of his own McGlinchey decision. He declared: "Apart from the fact that the IRA have abjured normal political activity in favour of violence and terrorism, the circumstances disclosed as to the murders in question were so brutal, cowardly and callous that it would be a distortion of language if they were to be accorded the status of political offences."

The next major development came in March 1985, in what at first seemed to be an unimportant case involving an alleged INLA man, John Quinn. The Metropolitan police wanted him in connection with fraud charges involving £600 in traveller's cheques. The judgment handed down by the present Chief Justice, Thomas Finlay, broke a great deal of new ground. Not only was Quinn extradited, but the political offence exception was further undermined. Chief Justice Finlay ruled that since the aim of the INLA was to establish an all-Ireland workers' republic by force of arms, the group was therefore dedicated to overthrowing the constitution. Members of such a group, he concluded, could not claim the political offence exception. The clear implication was that membership of the INLA or IRA would, in effect, disqualify individuals from using the political offence exception. Thus paramilitary membership – which until 1982 had served as a guarantee against extradition – had within three years become something which would actually make it more likely.

(The case against Quinn, like those against McGlinchey and Shannon, did not stand up. Shannon was acquitted of murder, and all charges against Quinn were dropped in London.)

The McGlinchey, Shannon and Quinn cases also had an important political effect. In the light of these judgments, Dr Garret FitzGerald's administration felt that it was no longer barred from signing the European Convention on the Suppression of Terrorism, the instrument which itself further curtailed the political offence exception. The convention lays down that the political defence should not be available in a number of specified instances, including the use of explosives, automatic firearms, hijacking and kidnapping.

Complications arose in December 1986, however, when it became clear during the Dáil debates on ratifying the convention that politicians in a number of parties were uneasy about extraditions. Many raised the cases of the Birmingham Six, Guildford Four and Maguire Seven, criticising the quality of British justice. The

Irish government, under pressure, postponed the enactment of the measure for a year.

In late 1987 it seemed doubtful whether Charles Haughey's minority Fianna Fáil government could get the measure through, for the criticisms of British justice were still loud and frequent. Mr Haughey himself publicly expressed doubts: "To hand a citizen over to another jurisdiction is something that should only be undertaken with great care and scrupulous regard for the circumstances. It is clear that at present many Irish people are questioning whether Dáil Éireann should agree to submit Irish citizens to a system of justice in which a large section of the community in the north has not as yet been persuaded to place its confidence."

But three incidents in quick succession helped put the measure on the statute books: the IRA's Remembrance Day murders in Enniskillen; the discovery of more than 100 tons of arms *en route* to the IRA from Libya; and a particularly unpleasant kidnapping by an INLA gang who mutilated a hostage. Pushing the measure through the Dáil, Mr Haughey declared: "The convergence of these three major events in a short space of time has brought home dramatically to us all the reality of the terrorist violence which affects the whole of Ireland, north and south."

The British government was sceptical, and slightly resentful, about safeguards which were built into the new extradition act. Several months of stalemate followed because, according to the Irish, the British authorities were refusing to comply fully with the new safeguards.

During these years a number of extradition cases failed due to defects in warrants or other technicalities. But, especially in the light of the Quinn case, the political offence exemption seemed to pose no further barrier to the return of republicans to the RUC. This impression was reinforced by the decision to extradite Robert Russell, an IRA escaper from the Maze prison, in August 1988. Chief Justice Finlay, in a far-reaching judgment, said that decisions on how the north and south of Ireland were to be reintegrated were matters only for the government. Anyone else who attempted to carry out integration on his own was subverting the constitution and usurping the function of government. The political defence was not open to such people, he ruled. Taken in conjunction with the earlier judgments and the incorporation of the European convention into Irish law, it seemed that the political offence exception had all but disappeared as a means by which IRA and INLA members could avoid extradition.

In less than two years, however, this entire trend was to be reversed. It was the judgments handed down in March 1990 on two Maze escapers, Dermot Finucane and James Clarke, which dramatically changed the direction of extradition law. To almost universal surprise, Finucane and Clarke were freed – the former on two separate grounds.

First, the court's five judges unanimously agreed that the pair would probably suffer ill-treatment at the hands of prison officers if returned to the Maze. They had heard evidence that the authorities had taken no disciplinary action against warders who had ill-treated prisoners on the day of their escape in 1983. But in addition it was ruled in the Finucane case, by three votes to two, that the offence for which he had been jailed – possession of two rifles and ammunition – was one which would have qualified for the political exemption. This clearly went against the trend of the past eight years. The key to this part of the ruling lay not with Chief Justice Finlay but with another judge, Justice Brian Walsh, who wrote the leading judgment.

Mr Justice Walsh was, until his retirement in March 1990, one of Ireland's outstanding jurists. Liberal on some issues, conservative on others, he played, during almost three decades on the Supreme Court, a key part in building up the court's position as a defender of citizens' rights. He helped steer it into a role similar to that of the US Supreme Court. Yet right through the 1980s he was, mysteriously, excluded from all the key extradition cases. Many lawyers and politicians in Dublin believe the Walsh exclusion was no accident, since it was widely known that he was strongly opposed to the O'Higgins–Finlay approach, which was making extraditions much easier to achieve. His inclusion on the panel hearing the Finucane and Clarke cases transformed the court. He wrote a very strong judgment explicitly overturning the Russell judgment and, in the eyes of many legal sources, undermining other decisions that had led to extraditions.

At a stroke, the trend of the 1980s was reversed. The Walsh judgment re-examined the issue of the political defence, and sought to draw distinctions between different types of offences. The lawyers and politicians are still arguing about what exactly the judgment means, but in essence it seems to suggest that defendants who have indulged in terrorist activity of an indiscriminate nature – for example using machine guns and putting civilians at risk – cannot claim the political exemption. But other types of activity could qualify for the political defence. Finucane, for example, had been arrested with two other men in possession of two rifles, which the RUC said had 10 minutes earlier been used to shoot a soldier. Judge Walsh said this qualified for the political exemption.

His judgment, which was accepted by a majority of the Supreme Court, thus indicated a new approach. IRA and INLA members would not automatically qualify for the political offence exception; but nor would they be automatically disqualified from claiming it. Instead, each case would be judged in the light of its own particular circumstances.

According to legal sources, the Walsh judgment on Finucane, which is regarded as strong and well argued, will be the bench mark for future extradition cases. The sense in Dublin legal circles is that some previous judgments were founded on extremely dubious grounds. The Quinn and Russell judgments, in particular, are commonly described as "curious" and "extraordinary". As one barrister put it: "Most lawyers here would take the view that both Quinn and Russell were, in legal terms, wrongly decided. They represented efforts by the judiciary to move mountains when they couldn't do it, and they went out on a limb trying to force meanings which weren't available to them." Another said: "Russell and Quinn were both ripe to be picked off."

The widespread legal view is that the Supreme Court overreached itself in attempting to stipulate that republican paramilitants could not claim the political defence. Even lawyers who themselves approve of extraditions say that the Walsh judgment has come closest to reflecting what the extradition legislation actually lays down.

Most extradition warrants in future will be issued under the 1987 extradition act, which removes the political exception from certain cases. But it is not a catch-all measure: it will, for example, cover shootings carried out with machine guns but not those involving handguns or rifles. The prospect is that for some years the Supreme Court will be ruling that some IRA actions will be covered by the political defence, while others will not be. The potential for recurring controversies is obvious.

Extradition is a sensitive issue in Ireland: many people, including those with strong anti-IRA views, have reservations about it. A 1988 opinion poll indicated that only 31 per cent of the population approved of it. Irish legal and political attitudes are coloured by history, but also by a judgement on the quality of the system to which suspects are to be handed over. One British legal source acknowledged this: "There's an almost schizophrenic view among the Irish people on this. I think we have to be realists and say the courts are, ultimately, reflecting the fact that, in general, Irish people don't have much confidence in the British system of justice." An Irish civil rights specialist made exactly the same point: "Issues like the Birmingham Six and Stalker seep into the national consciousness, and they are reflected in things like extradition cases. That would be my political interpretation of it: it's not one I would ever dare to express in public."

As a society, the south seemed for years preoccupied with the question of abortion which, though illegal there, had an extraordinary capacity to rouse passions and emotions. Early in 1992 the country

came to terms, with a shock, with a law
which was so restrictive that it denied
an abortion to a 14-year-old pregnant
rape victim.

19 FEBRUARY 1992   THE INDEPENDENT

Painful human drama
may shape a nation

The abortion crisis which is having such a major impact in the Republic of Ireland is one of those rare moments when an entire nation is brought face to face with its own nature and its own shortcomings. In this case that unwelcome and intensely painful process has been heightened by the compelling human drama at its centre: the fact that at the heart of a nation's crisis of values is a frightened 14-year-old schoolgirl made pregnant by a rapist. It also involves concerned parents who, desperate to deal with the problem and at the same time anxious to bring the culprit to justice, voluntarily informed the Irish police that they were arranging an abortion. It was their action in doing so which has brought the full weight of the Irish legal system down on their family.

The issue has provoked an extraordinary national debate, which is seen as a severe test of the new Taoiseach, Albert Reynolds, and, indeed, of the entire political and legal system. Dublin newspapers have been devoting two or three pages to the issue each day, and the question has been dominating conversations all over the country.

The outcome will be an important pointer to the future shape of a society that has lived through what has been described as the most rapid social and cultural change that the Republic has seen since the 19th century. This experience has been summarised by a leading Dublin academic, Terence Brown: "A small, protected agricultural economy opened its markets to the forces of international capitalism, producing three decades of rapid and sometimes bewildering change. A settled, conservative, inward-looking, patriarchal, highly structured society found itself confronted by challenges in almost all spheres – to its sense of uniqueness as life became more and more modelled on the consumerist ideals

69

of the commercially advanced societies around it; to its moral code as consumerism made the pursuit of status and pleasure a kind of national imperative; to its family values, as social disruption and a changing ethos about the role of women in advanced societies placed strains on what were deemed traditional mores."

To this list can be added the issue of Northern Ireland which, flaring up in the late 1960s, posed profound questions: how the violence could be contained; whether Irish unity was a realistic option; and, indeed, whether the Irish nation was to be defined as 26 counties or 32. It has still not entirely adjusted itself to the gap between traditional rhetoric and the harsh realities of the north.

The Republic has had its successes in coping with the rate of change but it has fumbled some issues, including that of whether Catholic doctrine should be enshrined in its laws and constitution, or whether the aim should be a more pluralist state. In particular, liberals have been dismayed by the decisions, in two referendums, to maintain legal prohibitions on divorce and on abortion. These mean that Ireland is among the most backward nations in Europe, particularly in terms of the rights of women.

As a country it is often accused of hypocrisy, especially on the abortion issue, in that the vocal and well-organised anti-abortion lobbies took great satisfaction out of winning the 1983 referendum and thus inserting a ban in the constitution. At the same time more than 3,500 women, almost all of them Catholic, take the abortion trail to Britain each year. The figure has, in fact, gone up appreciably since the referendum, showing the huge gap that exists between ordinary women on the one hand, and the politicians, the churchmen and the Catholic fundamentalists on the other. Those fundamentalists achieved that win by hectoring politicians into holding a referendum based on dubious wording. Some of the politicians then sought to gain advantage from an episode which was in practical terms meaningless, since there was no legal abortion before it was held.

Before the referendum, the cynical joke went, there was no abortion at all; after it, there was no abortion at all, at all. But what has now emerged is that that episode was the start of a chain of legal precedents which has led to the spectacle of legal figures, the police and judges attempting to ensure that child rape victims are forced to give birth.

The entire country is now being compelled into confronting the fact that a blind eye could not forever be turned to a pressing social problem, and that years of embarrassment, opportunism and neglect have combined to endanger the welfare of a child in need. [The child was eventually permitted to have an abortion in England.]

January 1992 brought the departure from politics of Charles Haughey, who finally fell victim to one controversy too many. His successor as Fianna Fáil leader and Taoiseach was a Co Longford businessman, Albert Reynolds, a much lower-key figure. Mr Reynolds had a reputation as a safe pair of hands, but late 1992 brought an unexpected general election as he failed to hold together his coalition government.

9 NOVEMBER 1992   THE INDEPENDENT

Two words that could seal a Taoiseach's fate

Two words may set the tone for what promises to be a short, intense and ugly election campaign in the Irish Republic before its voters go to the polls on 25 November. The words are "dishonest" and "crap". The election has been thrust on the voters by the use of the first word by the Taoiseach, Albert Reynolds, about another minister in his coalition government. Nobody had expected an election before next year but, when the Taoiseach called one of his own ministers dishonest, a chain of events started that has propelled the country to the polls.

It was no secret that the coalition government had considerable internal tensions. But most of these seemed to arise from personality differences rather than fundamental policy disagreements, and as such it was assumed that personal dislikes, no matter how strong, would not be allowed to bring down the government. The fact that they have done so has raised serious doubts about Mr Reynolds's judgement. And more questions have been raised by his use of language, since in a recent broadcast interview he used the words: "That is crap,

71

pure crap." A large number of people have made it clear that this is not the language they expect from a Taoiseach.

Mr Reynolds came to that office just under a year ago after building a reputation as a sound, solid departmental minister. There is a growing suspicion, however, even in the ranks of his own party, that he may not be up to the top job. One former parliamentary representative of his party said: "He's a nice guy but he hasn't grown into the office. Whatever you'd say about Charlie Haughey, he could go up there and sound good. But Albert doesn't express himself in the way you would expect a Taoiseach to do, and he's produced this election out of thin air."

His performance, in fact, invites comparison with that of John Major. Both were chosen, in succession to charismatic and controversial leaders, to be safe pairs of hands. Both were expected to provide calm, competent, less exciting management, yet both plunged their parliaments into unexpected dramas.

If Mr Reynolds wins a majority in the election, he will be the hero of his Fianna Fáil party. If he does badly, however, the knives will be out, for he has many enemies in the party who are both powerful and bitter. Fianna Fáil is the largest party in the Republic, but its problem for many years has been that it almost, but not quite, managed to get an absolute majority. On five separate occasions Charles Haughey failed to do so: the task for Mr Reynolds is to get those vital extra percentage points.

He inherited a coalition arrangement between Fianna Fáil and the small but strategically placed Progressive Democrats, headed by Des O'Malley. It was Mr O'Malley whom Mr Reynolds branded as dishonest, apparently in the belief that the word was part of the normal vocabulary of political abuse. But Mr O'Malley's party was actually founded on the plank of raising standards of integrity and honesty in political life, and it was predictable that he would not accept the epithet. "It was the wrong word to use about Dessie," a Fianna Fáil source readily conceded. "Our party all hate him, all right, but dishonest is the last thing you'd say about him." Mr Reynolds would not withdraw the word or soften it, however, and so his government has collapsed.

People in Ireland have a great belief that there is more in any situation than meets the eye, and in many pubs they are saying the whole thing must have been a Machiavellian Reynolds ruse to force an election and get his majority. This theory does not stand up, partly because Irish elections are so unpredictable. Local factors count for much more than in Britain, partly because the country is divided into 41 multi-member constituencies, all of which, in effect, run their own little elections. Generalised political discussions very quickly come down to detailed consideration of the strength of transfer patterns in Cork South Central and who might take the fifth seat in Wicklow. The system means that a representative who may have a reasonable national profile can nonetheless

Taoiseach Albert Reynolds

be surgically removed by an electorate which is less than impressed with his constituency record. In addition, there is a feeling that independents could do well, given signs of a general disenchantment with politicians. Mr Reynolds has not enhanced the standing of politics, having caused a contest which many regard, in the words of one businessman, as "an election over name-calling, over their own egos".

All of this means that he cannot be certain of his majority and in fact most observers – including the bookies – reckon he is not going to make it. His big hope will be that the electorate responds to his argument that coalitions are intrinsically unstable, and produces an unexpected swing towards his party, as the only one large enough to provide one-party government. If he does not make it, many more possibilities would then come into play. He could try for a Fianna Fáil minority government; he could attempt to put together a coalition with Labour, a small party whose star is in the ascendant; or he could be removed by his enemies. When he became Taoiseach he ruthlessly axed a whole swathe of ministers, most of whom have not forgiven him and wish him ill. As one Fianna Fáil source put it: "They're seething away there, looking for any opportunity to do him down. They're lying in the long grass."

The only other realistic candidate for Taoiseach will be John Bruton, leader of Fine Gael. His problems are his own reputation for clumsiness – the joke goes that he is a bull who carries his own china shop around with him – and the fact that he will almost certainly need the help of two other parties to assemble a coalition. Since one of those parties is on the left and the other on the right, he faces a difficult task in persuading the electorate that it would not be a particularly rickety construction. At the moment the most likely outcome looks to be a Fianna Fáil–Labour team, but the campaign will be unpredictable as well as tough.

The election result was a shock to everyone. Dick Spring's Labour party vote shot up 10 percentage points while the two main parties, Fianna Fáil and Fine Gael, fared disastrously, each dropping around five points. It was another vote for change.

4 DECEMBER 1992   THE INDEPENDENT

Labour vote shakes Ireland

Although weeks of hard bargaining lie ahead before the next Irish government is formed, it is already clear that the general election result justifies the clichés: it really was a watershed, and nothing will ever be quite the same again. Sweeping changes in Irish society finally disrupted antiquated political structures, cracking old moulds which represent a hangover from the civil war of the 1920s. A new Ireland is emerging, leaving many of the old political figures shocked, dismayed and perplexed. The old structures no longer fit the new realities of a country whose young population has shrugged off much of the former deference to politician and bishop. Those parties which failed to keep up with the changing times suffered severe losses in the election, while those which caught the new mood prospered.

The Republic, that most conservative of countries, now faces a liberal agenda after decades in which change was fiercely, and in general successfully, resisted. The major parties and the Catholic church still have much power and influence, but from now on they will be fighting a rearguard action. Once before, in the late 1960s, it seemed that liberalism was about to make a breakthrough, with left-wing and feminist elements to the fore. The forces of reaction held the line, however, with the 1970s and much of the 1980s belonging to the conservatives. They triumphed in referendums on abortion and divorce and restricted the availability of contraceptives. The lid stayed on.

The two big parties, Fianna Fáil and Fine Gael, ruled the roost politically. Fianna Fáil successfully held together its traditional mix of small farmers, part of the middle class and a sizeable slice of the working class. With its watchwords of flexibility and pragmatism it was able to move about the political spectrum with great dexterity, casting itself in the guise of centre-left or centre-right as the occasion demanded. Fine Gael also covered a large expanse of territory, encompassing both a Thatcherite-style right and liberal social democrats. Its fortunes were particularly improved by Garret FitzGerald's spell as leader, when he built party support to new heights by emphasising its liberal face.

The fact that the two parties had opposed each other in the 1920s civil war became less and less relevant as the decades passed, but there was always a class element to their differences. Fine Gael tended to regard themselves as figures of rectitude and decency, looking down on Fianna Fáil as slightly untrustworthy upstarts. Each party was, therefore, made up of complex and sometimes incongruous internal coalitions of interest: both took votes from city, town and country, both attracting middle-class, working-class and farming support. Both contained liberal elements, but these tended to be in a minority and therefore somewhat isolated.

This untidy fracturing helped ensure that the Irish Labour party remained in a perennially poor third place. It was robbed of much of its natural working-class support by Fianna Fáil, while many liberal personalities despaired of its chances and, instead, either joined one of the other parties or simply opted out. The trade unions, while nominally pro-Labour, in practice often found it possible to make productive arrangements with Fianna Fáil governments.

Labour itself was a mixture of left, centre and some crusty old local barons. Its turning point came when Dick Spring, an initially unpromising leader, expelled the militant left, imposed discipline, and opted for social democracy. He bought double-breasted suits, apparently from the same tailor as Neil Kinnock. His buzz words were "modern", "reform" and, above all, "change". Mr Spring had correctly identified the new mood, but even he must be as startled as everyone else by how fast things have moved. Two years ago Ireland elected as president his nominee, Mary Robinson, a feminist lawyer: it was the rough

Dick Spring, Irish Minister for Foreign Affairs

equivalent of Helena Kennedy being elected queen of England. The scale of Mr Spring's success in this election confirms that Mrs Robinson's election was not a flash in the pan. Labour doubled its number of Dáil seats while Fianna Fáil slumped to its worst defeat since 1927 and Fine Gael to its worst since 1948. It was the most startling result for a generation.

The other victors, on a smaller scale, were the Progressive Democrats. This is significant in that the party is very much to the right in economic terms but also stresses the need for reform and new departures. Thus both the secular left and the secular right were winners, showing again that one of the key elements in the election was a vote for change.

The old Ireland has not, of course, disappeared. Fianna Fáil and Fine Gael may have had their worst results for decades, but between them they still took more than half the vote. Yet many of the familiar certainties and traditions are fast breaking down. The comfortable rural Catholic value system is still there in some areas, but so too is a new, cosmopolitan, European, outward-looking spirit.

Fianna Fáil may well decide to ditch its leader, Albert Reynolds, in the coming months or years, but the party's problems go much deeper than simply a leadership change. It is looking at a shrinking market, and has little choice but to reposition itself to take account of the new facts of life. Fine Gael faces a similar need for a shake-up. It is an open question whether either, or both, can refashion themselves and present themselves as advocates and agents of change rather than conservative forces. Whether they succeed and survive, or fail and perish, the question of change and modernisation will now be one of the keynotes of Irish politics. Ireland today presents the fascinating spectacle of a nation taking stock of itself and, more and more, coming to the conclusion that change rather than continuity should be the order of the day.

POSTSCRIPT

After weeks of negotiation the Republic had a new government, a coalition of Fianna Fáil and Labour. Albert Reynolds was re-elected Taoiseach, while Labour took six of the fifteen cabinet seats and dictated much of the new administration's programme. Dick Spring became Minister for Foreign Affairs, creating expectations of new moves in Anglo-Irish matters.

4

THE IRA

The years since 1989 have been marked
by continual violence from both
republicans and loyalists. The IRA kept up
its litany of death and destruction, not only
maintaining its campaign in Northern
Ireland but also extending its activities into
England and, for a time, continental
Europe. The foundation for its expanded
campaign was the huge arsenal donated
by Colonel Gaddafi's Libyan regime in the
mid-1980s. This included around 1,000
rifles and heavy military equipment,

including heavy machine guns, anti-aircraft guns, RPG-7 rocket launchers, grenades, mortars and two tons of deadly Semtex plastic explosive.

The Libyan connection came to light in November 1987 when a French customs patrol intercepted a trawler, the *Eksund*, off the coast of Brittany. Security force jubilation turned to dismay when it emerged that four previous shipments had got through. The *Eksund* was manned by three IRA men, Gabriel Cleary, James Doherty and James Coll, and by two sailors, Adrian Hopkins and Henry Cairns, all from the Republic of Ireland. When they came to trial in Paris, after spending some years in custody, they received sentences of between five and seven years and heavy fines.

The court heard details of lengthy statements made to French police by Adrian Hopkins, who admitted not only captaining the *Eksund* but also involvement in four previous major arms shipments to Ireland. The trial shed new light on the IRA's Libyan link, which transformed it from a struggling group into one of the world's best-equipped terrorist organisations. That link has been described as the intelligence world's greatest lapse since the Kim Philby affair.

Voyage into
business of terror

Adrian Hopkins's relationship with the IRA was, to begin with, strictly financial. As his involvement deepened he became more anxious, he told French police, and there were threats to ensure he did not pull out of his role of skippering the vessels which brought the weapons of war from Libya to Ireland. Although the French prosecutor described him as an adventurer and a romantic, Hopkins himself frankly admitted that his motivation was money. His boat-dealing business, like his other moneymaking schemes, had financial problems. According to his admissions, a great deal of IRA money was handed over to him.

He had previously had what could be described as a chequered career. After 10 years as a radio operator in the merchant navy, he returned to Ireland in 1966 to help run the family business. Two years later it failed, its offices burning down. He next launched a holiday business, specialising in renting out horse-drawn caravans, but this also was not a success. Ms Martine Anzani, president of the all-woman three-judge court which heard the case this week, noted that its offices had also burnt down. Hopkins's next venture, a travel company, grew into a substantial enterprise before collapsing spectacularly at the start of the 1980s. Once again, the judge remarked, fire struck at its offices.

In 1982 Hopkins, who is now aged 52, set up a company buying and selling boats, but by 1984–5 it too was in financial difficulties. It was at this point, he told French police in his detailed statements, that he came into contact with the IRA. The link man was his friend and associate Henry Cairns, whom he had known since their school days. Cairns, 48, had worked in casual building jobs in London in the 1960s, and as a petrol-pump attendant in the Republic. At one stage he worked as a driver for Hopkins's firm, later running a second-hand bookshop near Dublin.

Cairns, who described himself in court as an IRA sympathiser, was contacted by a member of the organisation who said they needed a means of transporting arms. He, like Hopkins, needed money: at one stage he had suggested using a boat belonging to Hopkins to smuggle whiskey and cigarettes. Hopkins said

80

he had turned the idea down because the risk outweighed the comparatively small profit involved. But when Cairns put Hopkins in touch with a man who turned out to be a senior IRA figure – Gabriel Cleary, one of the defendants in Paris – he quickly realised that large sums of money were involved.

The arms in question were to come from Libya. Colonel Gaddafi's regime had been linked with the IRA in the early 1970s, when he had given them money and sent an arms shipment which was intercepted by the Irish navy in 1973. The relationship appeared to have ended, however, in the mid-1970s. Exactly why it began again is still a matter for conjecture. It was in April 1984 that a gunman inside the Libyan embassy in London shot dead a policewoman, Yvonne Fletcher, in an incident which led to a prolonged siege of the building. Relations between Libya and Britain, never warm, were at a new low.

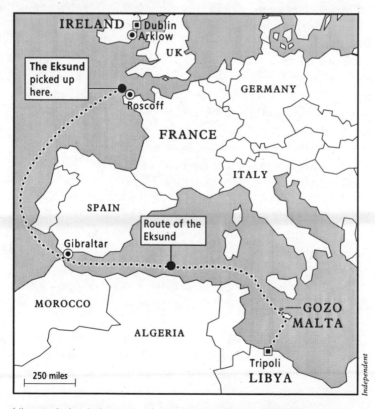

Libya to Ireland: the route of the gunrunning ship *Eksund*

By 1985 Gaddafi was promising arms for the IRA, and Cleary told Hopkins they wanted to transport several tons of weaponry. In London, Hopkins bought a 65-foot converted yacht, the *Casamara*, for around £50,000, and in August

1985 he set sail from Malta with a member of the IRA on board. Off the Maltese island of Gozo, according to his statements, he made a rendezvous with a Libyan ship, the *Samra Africa*. The Libyans on board included one man from the Libyan embassy on Malta, together with a senior figure who was to act as the IRA's main contact. This was Nasser Ashur, also known as Ali Ashoud Naser. He has been described as the number two or number three man in Libyan intelligence. A close associate of Gaddafi, the colonel had sent him to London in 1984 to negotiate the ending of the Libyan embassy siege.

Ten tons of arms, including Kalashnikov rifles, pistols and grenades, were transferred to the *Casamara*. Hopkins and others then sailed the vessel to Clogga Strand, a spot on the east coast of Ireland around 40 miles south of Dublin. The consignment was ferried ashore in high-speed rubber dinghies, and spirited away by IRA teams. Hopkins said he was paid £100,000 for his part in the enterprise, half of which he spent on buying the ship.

Another shipment was quickly arranged, for October 1985. The *Casamara* was used again, though this time Hopkins renamed her *Kula* and switched from the British flag to Panamanian colours. The rendezvous off Gozo was repeated, with another 10 tons of arms transferred and ferried again to Clogga Strand. Hopkins received £50,000. The third shipment, this time of 14 tons, followed in similar fashion in July 1986: again Hopkins was paid £50,000.

It was the fourth shipment which, in effect, transformed the IRA's capacity to wage its terrorist campaign, supplying most of the weaponry which continues to elude the searches of the security forces. Hopkins bought a larger ship, the *Sjamor*, in Norway for £45,000, renaming it the *Villa* and fitting navigational and radio equipment. The *Villa* left Malta in October 1986, this time sailing into Tripoli harbour. According to Hopkins, 30 men loaded about 75 tons of materiel, including rifles, RPG-7 rocket launchers, SAM-7 missiles and one ton of Semtex plastic explosive. This time Cairns accompanied Hopkins and the IRA crew on their voyage to Clogga Strand, where a major operation was needed to unload the armaments and disperse them to hiding places all over the Republic. It is not clear how much Hopkins was paid for this shipment.

In public, meanwhile, the Libyan regime had become increasingly open about supporting the IRA. In June 1986 – four months before the journey of the *Villa* – Colonel Gaddafi's deputy explicitly said it was planned to resume aid to the IRA. In October, just after the *Villa* reached Ireland, Gaddafi went on Irish television, proclaiming support for the IRA and declaring: "Liberation movements need arms in the fight against colonialism."

But the most extraordinary clue of all to the IRA's Libyan connection had come in January 1986, when Kalashnikovs and other guns were discovered on a Co Roscommon farm. The words "LIBYAN ARMED FORCES" were stencilled on ammunition boxes. The authorities did not regard this as confirmation, however, of the origin of the weapons: had they done so, the lethal cargo of the *Villa* might never have reached Ireland.

The *Eksund* was meant to carry the biggest consignment of all. Hopkins said he was contacted in January 1987 about a proposed shipment of 200 tons, and set about finding a boat capable of holding such a load. He saw the *Eksund* in Sweden in May, bought her in June and had her brought to Malta by an unsuspecting delivery firm in August. The ship left Malta in October of that year, making for Tripoli. On board were Hopkins, Cairns, and the three republicans, Gabriel Cleary, James Coll and James Doherty.

According to Hopkins's statements, a pilot boat took them first into the civil port and then to the military section, where they tied up between the quayside and a military patrol boat. He said the loading, which was carried out by crane and by 30 Libyan sailors, took two days and was chaotic: he was concerned that the cargo had not been stowed evenly, and might unbalance the ship. The Libyan intelligence chief, Nasser Ashur, was present, as he had been for all the previous shipments. Hopkins said that by this stage the IRA men had very close relations with the Libyan, on this trip bringing presents for his sister.

One hundred and fifty tons of armaments were loaded onto the *Eksund*, which then headed for Ireland. The trip did not, however, go as smoothly as the others had. On three occasions – off Spain, off Bordeaux and off Brittany – small planes overflew the ship, leading the crew to believe they were under surveillance. They decided to abandon the mission. The first plan was to steer to a deep spot in the Channel, known to them as the "deep hurd", and blow up the ship. Explosive charges were placed around the vessel. Later, however, they decided, instead, simply to open the valves and scuttle her. They would then head for France in one of the rubber dinghies.

By this stage, however, the ship itself was giving trouble. The *Eksund* was an elderly vessel in poor condition: Hopkins had paid £50,000 for her, and is generally thought to have been overcharged. The delivery firm which brought her from Sweden to Malta had trouble on the way with both the engine and the steering. By now the weather was stormy, and once again the steering gave problems, hindering Hopkins's efforts to reach the "deep hurd". Repairs were necessary, but were difficult because the steering fault meant the vessel was rolling and pitching, and he told the others they needed to steer towards more sheltered waters closer to France to carry out repairs.

James Coll told the court they then discussed the question of territorial limits, not wishing to enter French waters. He said Hopkins assured them that the limit was three miles. Henry Cairns said he had been told by Hopkins to stay in the wheelhouse and make sure the ship did not approach closer than five miles from the French coast, so as to leave a safety margin. Cairns dutifully monitored the radar, which had a digital read-out showing their distance from the coast. But the French limit is, in fact, 12 miles, and a French customs vessel was on its way to board the *Eksund*. When it arrived, said Cairns, the radar showed they were 5.6 miles from France. Customs officers found three of the men in diving outfits, and in the wheelhouse discovered five loaded Kalashnikovs, a machine gun and a bayonet.

Hopkins gave a detailed account in lengthy statements to French police, in which he insisted he had several times attempted to extricate himself from the operation, but had been intimidated into continuing. Cairns also spoke to police, but the three IRA men have, for three years, said next to nothing. An energetic examining magistrate, Jean-Louis Bruguière, has spent that time making enquiries all over Europe, amassing a mountain of evidence.

Although some argue that the French or the British authorities knew the *Eksund* was carrying arms, the signs are still that the customs officers who boarded her were looking for drugs. What is not in doubt, however, is that despite a series of public indications from Libya, and despite the evidence of the Roscommon arms haul, the British and Irish authorities had no knowledge of the consignment delivered by the *Villa*.

The IRA was given a new lease of life by the donation of an arsenal which left it better armed than ever before in its history. The contact with Libya is believed to have ceased but the hundreds of rifles, copious supplies of explosive and other heavy weaponry have fulfilled most of its supply needs for the rest of the century. It previously had limited resources, spending a great deal of time, effort and money attempting to smuggle in what weapons it could from the United States and the European arms market. But the Libyan connection solved almost all of the IRA's weaponry problems at a stroke, providing, as it did, an estimated 110 tons of modern weaponry. The IRA suddenly had more guns than members. Some of this has been recovered by the security forces in searches, but the bulk remains in IRA hands.

At the time of the Enniskillen bombing in November 1987, when an IRA bomb killed 11 Protestants at a Remembrance Day commemoration parade, it was possible for an optimist to believe that republican prospects were poor, with distinct signs that the strength of Sinn Féin and the IRA was fading. Sinn Féin appeared to have passed its peak, while in a single year 14 IRA activists were killed. But the Libyan link changed the face of the IRA campaign. The linchpin of the escalation in violence has been Semtex plastic explosive, which gave the IRA's bomb-makers a new cutting edge and has posed the most severe problems for the authorities. It has been used in Northern Ireland in booby traps, grenades, mortars, and roadside bombs. It also formed the basis of bombing campaigns in England and on the continent. In 1988 a British army general said privately: "The IRA's secret weapon isn't SAM missiles. The thing that has made the single biggest difference to them is the Semtex. It's impossible to overemphasise the flexibility it has given to them. Semtex is so easy, and so little of it has such a devastating effect."

An example of the way in which small amounts of the explosive could produce disproportionate results was to be seen in the appearance of the drogue bomb – a primitive-looking device consisting of just over a pound of explosives inside a tin can with a throwing handle. Despite its crude looks, the drogue bomb represents a real menace to security force armoured vehicles. The authorities were forced into an urgent search for countermeasures. In west Belfast, the area of greatest hazard, many more foot patrols were employed, while Land-Rovers stopped travelling in pairs and today travel in convoys of three. Urgent and costly research went into designing new forms of armour to withstand drogue blast, with specially reinforced Land-Rovers eventually arriving in Belfast. The drogue bomb nonetheless remains a much-feared weapon, and one which has made the streets a more hazardous place for the security forces.

The IRA also switched to using Semtex in its mortar bomb attacks on army and police bases. A half-pound of the explosive was placed in each missile, made and assembled in unofficial mortar factories in the Republic before being smuggled north. Another menace, under-car Semtex bombs, faced off-duty members of the security forces and other potential IRA targets. The IRA and INLA had for years used booby traps beneath cars, but the advent of the plastic explosive meant the IRA could considerably refine such bombs. Only two pounds of Semtex was needed, so that the entire device could be fitted into an ordinary plastic lunch box and, with the aid of an attached magnet, be fixed unobtrusively beneath a vehicle.

The treacherous little devices have claimed many lives. The greatest loss of life came in June 1988 in the Co Antrim town of Lisburn, when six soldiers who had taken part in a charity "fun run" were killed by a seven-pound bomb placed under their van. Semtex was also used in the bomb which devastated an army coach at Ballygawley, Co Tyrone, in 1988, killing eight soldiers and injuring twenty-eight others.

Since late 1987 the authorities had operated on the assumption that the IRA possessed SAM-7 ground-to-air missiles, a number of which were found on the *Eksund*. The presumed presence of the weapon forced military helicopters to take precautions such as flying lower and faster and fitting countermeasures. So far these SAM-7s have not been used, but a number of helicopters have been hit by heavy machine-gun fire. RPG-7 rocket launchers have been used on a number of occasions, posing a threat to security force bases and armoured vehicles. Kalashnikov rifles also made their way from the deep hides in the Republic into Northern Ireland, and have been increasingly used in shootings. Although scores of these have been recovered in searches, the IRA probably still has up to 900 Kalashnikovs. Troops in Belfast have also found a flame-thrower in full working order. The Warsaw Pact weapon, using a napalm-type material, is capable of projecting a jet of flame up to 80 yards.

The authorities have reacted to the escalation with a series of new policies and measures aimed at combating the increased threat, and the IRA has not succeeded in causing the level of mayhem it had hoped to create. Nonetheless, the existence of the Libyan armoury is an unfortunate fact which will cause the security forces continuing problems for many years ahead.

Armed with the Libyan weaponry, the IRA turned its attention to Britain. From 1972 on it had staged sporadic bomb attacks in England, killing more than 100 people in incidents such as the bombing of Harrods in 1983 and the Brighton bombing in 1984. But in the mid-1980s the organisation laid the foundations for a new type of campaign, this time conceived not as occasional hit-and-run attacks but as a permanent presence in Britain. British military personnel on the continent were also targeted.

As a result the IRA constituted, from 1988 on, a major threat, not just in Northern Ireland, but also in Britain and continental Europe. This campaign on three fronts received an early setback when three IRA members were shot dead by the SAS in Gibraltar in March 1988, but within months British servicemen had been killed both in England and Holland. In the European campaign the IRA killed seven servicemen, a woman, a six-month-old baby and two Australian tourists before their activities fell away in 1990. In Britain, however, each year has been marked by numerous IRA attacks. The largest casualty toll came in September 1989, when 11 army bandsmen died in an attack on a barracks in Deal, Kent.

The impact of this approach was considerable. In April 1990 the Ministry of Defence revealed that an extra £126 million was being spent on anti-terrorist security measures in Britain and West Germany. But as the authorities moved to defend military bases, the IRA switched tactics away from soldiers towards political assassination, using an under-car booby-trap bomb to kill one of Margaret Thatcher's closest friends, Ian Gow.

Ian Gow: "Some small sacrifice for Ulster"

It was in November 1985, with the signing of the Anglo-Irish agreement, that Ian Gow first came to public prominence in Northern Ireland politics. His resignation from the government in protest against the signing of the accord was in stark contrast to the general attitude at Westminster, where MPs voted overwhelmingly in favour of the agreement. Mr Gow's action was regarded as quirky and quixotic by nationalists. It was applauded by Unionists, though in the wave of anti-British feeling among Protestants, he was arguably not given the full recognition that his action deserved. He felt obliged, at a meeting in Belfast, to remind his Unionist audience that he had made "some small sacrifice for Ulster". He went on to make frequent appearances on Irish television and radio, always stressing his support for the Unionist cause and his opposition to the agreement. His projection in such appearances was old-fashioned, almost Dickensian, and occasionally pompous; it was only in private that his sense of humour and the element of self-parody became evident.

He helped found the Friends of the Union group of Conservatives and Unionists opposed to the agreement. In 1989, in an introduction to one of its pamphlets, he set out his views: the accord had brought strife and turmoil rather than stability, and the Republic should not have the right to a say in Northern Ireland affairs. The accord should be abandoned to be replaced by an approach which was both unionist and integrationist. Northern Ireland should be more tightly bound to Britain, legislated for in the same way as Britain, and the idea of legislative devolution abandoned. He believed that an ever-firmer union would eventually convince the IRA that they could not win, and lead in time to the ending of violence.

Mr Gow's interest in Northern Ireland affairs went back, of course, long before 1985, originating, in fact, during a National Service posting to Co Tyrone in the mid-1950s. His alignment was always solidly Unionist: in 1982 he told me privately that he favoured having James Molyneaux or some other Unionist appointed to a ministerial post in the Northern Ireland Office.

He was one of the leaders of a band of around 30 Conservatives, almost all tending towards the far right, who remained staunchly pro-union and pro-integrationist while almost all other Tory backbenchers were indifferent to the Northern Ireland question. Most, including Mr Gow, were admirers of Enoch Powell. The group has lost three of its most effective spokesmen with the assassination of Mr Gow and the deaths in recent years of the journalist T.E. Utley and former MP Sir John Biggs-Davison. It was this group which, in 1982, staged a Commons filibuster against the devolution bill put forward by the then Northern Ireland Secretary, James (now Lord) Prior. Marathon speeches kept MPs up all night. At that time Mr Gow was Mrs Thatcher's parliamentary private secretary and therefore part of the government; yet the fact was that he covertly encouraged and helped to organise the filibuster which disrupted the Commons and held up the government's bill.

Lord Prior was bitter about Mr Gow's role and Mrs Thatcher's attitude: she privately thought the bill was "rotten", and effectively acquiesced in the parliamentary mischief. Prior noted in his memoirs: "No one should be under any illusions about the part that Gow played in trying to undermine the Bill and all that I was seeking to do. I regard it as a disgraceful episode. Ian subsequently resigned from the government over the Anglo-Irish agreement. His position at that time was wholly honourable, but the damage in the intervening years was immense."

The car in which Ian Gow MP died

The assassination of Ian Gow may represent an attempt by the IRA to cause personal hurt to Mrs Thatcher, in an effort to goad her into overreacting to his death. The IRA would be well aware that Mr Gow was not a key figure in forming government policy and that he was, indeed, entirely at odds with Mrs Thatcher's policy of persisting with the Anglo-Irish agreement. His symbolic importance lay, rather, in the fact that he had been so closely associated with the Prime Minister, and to some extent, also, that he was identified with the Unionist cause. It has been widely reported that the death of her close confidant Airey Neave, at the hands of the INLA in 1979, affected her deeply and painfully. This theory is supported by the fact of the recent attack on the former home of Lord McAlpine, who was regarded more as a friend of the Prime Minister than as a major political figure.

In a sense Mr Gow may have been attacked as a surrogate for Mrs Thatcher, who will always be the terrorists' main target. The IRA has been unable, since the 1984 Brighton hotel bombing, to penetrate the intense security around her. His death may amount to an IRA acknowledgement that she is beyond its reach, since the protective measures which surround her will presumably now be tightened even further.

The basic republican thesis is that Britain should pull out of Northern Ireland; that this can only be achieved by IRA violence; and that this violence should be aimed at provoking reactions from both the British government and Unionists in Northern Ireland. The Gow murder fits into this pattern. The republican hope will be that the killing of the MP will drive a wedge between the British and Irish governments, affecting Anglo-Irish relations and weakening the Anglo-Irish agreement. They would most like to see the introduction of measures which they could characterise as repressive and which might produce a counter-reaction among nationalists in general.

In the wake of previous security incidents the Prime Minister has not always been able to resist the temptation to issue pointed calls on the Irish Republic to improve security co-operation. The sequence has generally been, however, for any such comments to be followed by a general smoothing of relations by ministers and civil servants anxious to send out the message that terrorist incidents will not deflect the two governments from their chosen path of co-operation.

The IRA and Sinn Féin will also hope that the assassination will damage the prospects of success for Northern Ireland Secretary Peter Brooke's efforts to bring local parties to the conference table this autumn. The IRA–Sinn Féin view is that such moves are dangerous, since any new partnership arrangement will include constitutional nationalists and will be aimed at isolating the republican movement. Their theory may be that the attack will encourage Ulster Unionist leader James Molyneaux, a friend and close associate of Mr Gow, to pull out of the proposed discussions. Both men held deep reservations about such talks.

The bitter irony is that some of the policies advocated by Ian Gow actually coincided with those of the IRA. Both strongly opposed the Anglo-Irish agreement, though for diametrically different reasons. Mr Gow regarded the accord as eroding British sovereignty and encouraging terrorism, while the IRA view it as an attempt to cement British authority in Northern Ireland. The terrorists have further been apprehensive that closer cross-border security co-operation under the agreement will make life more difficult for them. Mr Gow and the terrorists also opposed any moves towards devolution, again for opposite reasons. He suspected it as a move that would differentiate and mark out Northern Ireland from the rest of the United Kingdom, while republicans regard it as an attempt to strengthen a union which they hope to bring to an end.

The attack confirms the recent pattern of IRA activity in Britain. Two years ago, when the current sustained campaign began, the concentration was on military targets. Recently, however, the range has been broadened with bomb attacks on places such as the Conservative Carlton Club in central London. Even after more than a dozen major incidents in Britain in the last two years, the IRA is clearly still managing to take advantage of the element of surprise. This has been partly due to its strategy of varying tactics and targets, and of spacing out attacks so as to allow public vigilance to drop. But it is evidently still the case that potential targets are not paying sufficient attention to their own personal security. Many public figures take the view that embarking upon extensive precautions in itself represents a victory for terrorism. Such an attitude makes it easier for the IRA bombers to carry on their campaign.

A flurry of violent activity in late 1991 led to a rerun of the perennial argument that the reintroduction of internment without trial would be effective against the terrorists. It was generally acknowledged that it had not succeeded, and in many ways had made things worse, when used in the years 1971 to 1975. The argument was whether, two decades on, the security forces might now be able to make it work.

Internment: the big gamble for both sides

Security chiefs have reached the sombre conclusion that a defeat of the IRA is not on the horizon while current security policies are maintained. Although they proclaim their confidence that the IRA will ultimately be beaten, they say that with present policies its defeat could be 10 years or more away. According to one high-level military source: "The IRA terrorists are better equipped, better resourced, better led, bolder and more secure against our penetration than at any time before. They are absolutely a formidable enemy. The essential attributes of their leaders are better than ever before. Some of their operations are brilliant, in terrorist terms. If we don't intern, it's a long haul."

There is no immediate indication that ministers are preparing to drop their opposition to a drastic measure which, when last used in the 1970s, was considered to be disastrously counterproductive. But it is clear that the urgings of senior RUC and army officers have made internment a realistic option after a long period when it was considered out of the question.

The advocates of internment argue that it could be introduced in an entirely different way to its implementation in August 1971, when it triggered off waves of deaths, street disruptions and political and social fragmentation on a major scale. For one thing, not only republicans but also loyalists – who were not picked up in 1971 – would be locked up. According to an authoritative source: "Some of those will be among the first to be interned." Of the IRA, he added: "We know the guys who are doing this mayhem – we know them well. You can break up the command structure by picking up key individuals. The quarter-masters, for example, are the only ones who know where the arms dumps are. They might in time, perhaps, re-equip and remuster their efforts, but the command structure won't be there."

It is recognised that the Irish government and nationalist opinion within Northern Ireland is very much against internment. But, the argument goes, such considerations will be overridden if the tactic is seen to result in a quick and significant reduction in violence.

The late Reginald Maudling, one of the British ministers who authorised the introduction of internment in Northern Ireland just over 20 years ago, wrote

92

later of that decision: "No one could be certain what would be the consequences, yet the question was simply this: what other measures could be taken?" Today, with hindsight, it is clear how awful the consequences were. The experience of internment, from 1971 to 1975, was by almost universal consent an unmitigated disaster that has left an indelible mark on the history of Northern Ireland. It is hardly surprising that every administration since then has recoiled from the idea of repeating the tactic.

Yet listening to senior security sources this week, it was evident that some security chiefs have reached pretty much the same state of mind as Maudling did: a feeling that something has to be done, and that internment is one of the very few remaining options.

It came as something of a shock to hear the authoritative military assessment that internment may represent the only prospect of defeating the IRA before the end of this century. The stark fact is that this week the Northern Ireland Secretary, Peter Brooke, was told by the RUC and the army that a security apparatus of almost 30,000 troops and police, augmented by thousands of associated staff, is not enough to deal with the menace of the IRA and loyalist terrorists. One senior soldier said privately: "The fact is that the IRA are very, very good. When you're a terrorist, and a good one, you don't make many mistakes. They've had 22 years' experience. Most soldiers are here for 18 months, then away again."

On the prospects of an IRA ceasefire, he added: "I accept there are people in the movement who want to spend more time with their families, who would like to stop if they could get what they would regard as some honourable arrangement. Some important people are thinking of ceasefires – or, alternatively, maybe they are floating the idea to see if it would be picked up by the government. But a lot of them aren't interested. I mean, what the hell do you offer them? They absolutely enjoy being a terrorist. I have no doubt they find it very stimulating and challenging. There are different types. There are people, I suppose Gerry Adams and Martin McGuinness are examples, who do have a burning zeal about getting Britain out and who wish to see a united Ireland. But there are, equally, people who enjoy the power that terrorism gives them. There is a lot of extortion and racketeering, and some make money. There are others who actually get a thrill from killing and assassination. And then at the bottom end there are minions, who join from family tradition and so on. It's heady stuff for them."

The assessment is that the IRA has very substantial stockpiles of weaponry, enough recruits to maintain its campaign for the foreseeable future, and a highly experienced command structure. Its leadership has moved away from the "Armalite and ballot box" strategy and is instead placing its faith in straight militarism as the way to sap the British will.

The approach of paying less attention to political constraints means the organisation has felt free to use tactics which previously would have been regarded as unacceptable, such as bombing the military wing of a Belfast hospital and the "human bomb" technique of forcing civilians to deliver huge bombs to army border checkpoints. The human bomb device is seen as just one example of how the IRA can exploit the border with the Irish Republic. Security sources say that in some cases the terrorists have been able to move about in quite large numbers, both by day and by night, and in some clashes have actually outnumbered soldiers. According to one assessment – which differs markedly from Peter Brooke's assertion that cross-border security is highly effective – "The fact is that we don't know of any insurgency that has been defeated by government forces where the insurgents have what they perceive to be a secure frontier behind which they can go for shelter."

It is from this cheerless perspective that military and police minds have increasingly turned to the idea of internment. At the moment, they say, it is usually only minnows who get caught: "The big boys plan and launch the attack, but they don't touch." Soldiers and police have the frustration, they say, of knowing exactly who the leading terrorists are. Said one senior officer: "Our people will stop them on the road – the car will be completely clean. They are a cocky breed of people who know what they're doing. They talk to us: one of them told an army officer at a checkpoint the other day, 'We'll have a present for you for Christmas.'"

But it comes as a surprise to find that in some senior circles internment is being presented, not only as a desperate attempt to deal with a dire situation, but also as something close to a panacea. In the words of one source: "We can deliver, given a favourable, or at least not unhelpful, climate in the south. If the government can keep the Americans off our backs, and deal with the EC and the human rights people and so on, and ensure it does not become a *cause célèbre*, then yes, we can deliver. Some say to me, 'But you might only get half of them on the first day.' I say to them – that's all right, we'll get them in the following days. They'll go on the run, but that will disrupt the command structure. And if you do that, you've brought peace. Wouldn't people then say, 'This is better, this is a climate in which we'd prefer to live'?"

Such statements are, however, based on so many arguable assumptions that they are unlikely to convince internment's opponents. In 1971 it was opposed on principle; because it did not conform to international human rights standards; because many of the wrong people were picked up; and because it was accompanied by casual brutality during and after the arrests. It was also seen as an illegitimate weapon, in that part of the reason for using it was to prop up an ailing Unionist government. For more than a year no loyalists were rounded up, while republicans were kept in miserable conditions in leaky Nissen huts. On the outside the death toll rose alarmingly while riots and street disturbances became much worse. Thousands of people moved home. Alienation rose sharply in the Catholic population, thousands becoming involved in rent and rates strikes and civil disobedience. For nationalists, internment became an icon of injustice.

Most of those who lived through that appalling time will not easily accept that today the results will in effect be the opposite, and that internment would bring peace rather than another calamity. In the words of one opponent, the internment option contains "more *ifs* than Kipling". For one thing, there are doubts about just how good security force information is. Much is known about the IRA, but there are huge blind spots. For years the intelligence services were blissfully unaware of the major arms shipments that were reaching the IRA from Libya; and today, after 20 years, they are still unable to prevent the flow of weapons into the north from the Republic.

Internment is bound to disrupt Anglo-Irish relations, and is most unlikely to be simultaneously introduced by Dublin. Unless it was an immediate success, it would make the prospect of finding agreement among the Northern Ireland parties even less likely. It would certainly draw international criticism, which is why the Foreign Office is believed to oppose it. And, crucially, it is inconceivable that an organisation as formidable as the IRA is acknowledged to be would not have the most careful of contingency plans to ensure that violence will continue. For years, in fact, the terrorists have expected that the authorities would eventually resort to internment, and they have made preparations not just to survive it but ultimately to profit from it. Their theory is that since internment is acknowledged to be the last desperate measure, its failure to work would lead Britain to conclude that it had no option but to withdraw from Northern Ireland.

It is not hard to imagine how those in charge of security can be driven to look for short cuts and panaceas in violent times such as these. Yet a glance at the death statistics for 1971 and 1972 shows how much worse it might get. The death toll for 1991 is over 80; but more people died in a single month in 1972. This illustrates that internment, no matter how well planned and executed, is still the highest of high-risk strategies. It remains a gamble: it might work, but if something went wrong, it could turn the clock back 10 years.

The year 1992 brought no respite from the violence. Between 1985 and the beginning of that year the IRA killed 19 men who, it claimed, supplied the security forces or carried out building work for them. Those killed ranged from company executives to ordinary workers. This campaign cost not only these lives but also hundreds of jobs and millions of pounds, for many firms were intimidated into cutting off contact with the security forces, and the authorities were forced into taking elaborate and costly special measures.

Nonetheless, the work went on. One security source said: "It's been a monumental task but we've done it. It took some extraordinary measures but we now have half a dozen major contractors working for us. Some people get police protection – armoured car, bodyguard, personal weapon and so on. Some of the builders get paid through dummy companies. Some of the workers live in the police station five days a week and only come out at weekends."

On 18 January 1992 the IRA laid an ambush for a busload of Protestant workers who had been helping to refurbish a police station and who were being driven back to their homes in Co Antrim. The IRA decided they were part of the "British war machine" and, with a single bomb blast, killed eight of them at Teebane crossroads, Co Tyrone.

A bleak grey dawn
after the massacre

Dawn revealed the full horror of the scene. The blue van, or what was left of it, lay upside down on a roadway strewn with dirt, debris, pieces of clothing, personal possessions. It was said to be a Mercedes, but there was not enough of it left to be certain.

The morning greyness illuminated a damp, lonely countryside of green and brown, a landscape as bleak as Northern Ireland's immediate prospects. The van had been travelling along the road in the twilight, packed with working men on their way home to their families on a Friday evening. They were probably joking and looking forward to the weekend.

The countryside here is largely Catholic and republican, but it is remote, underpopulated and not noted as a particular hot spot of violence. The bombers had obviously planned the attack with cool calculation, and could have set it up in less than half an hour. Some of the gang placed the bomb in the hedge at the roadside. Others unrolled the command wire, running it along the shelter of another hedge to set up a firing point on a rise overlooking the road. In the dying light they did not bother to conceal it. When the van appeared, the man with his finger on the firing button was deadly accurate. The vehicle took the full force of the blast. Its upper part was torn asunder, but instead of being blown off the road, its momentum kept it tumbling along until it came to rest 30 yards on.

The scene at that point must have been hellish, with dead, dying and injured bodies scattered in a field, on the road, and trapped under the wreckage. Some passers-by who stopped to help were sent into shock by the sight of terrible mutilations. It took the emergency services a considerable time to work out how many had been killed.

Looking at the shredded remains of the van in the grim early light, it seemed inconceivable that anyone who was inside it could have survived. Yet seven men were left alive, to carry scars for the rest of their lives. One told a hospital chaplain he had been a front-seat passenger. He recalled an awful blast, then found himself hurtling down the road for about 30 yards. He was able to walk

97

back to the scene: he would always remember seeing his injured, dying and mutilated workmates.

Yesterday morning the human beings, and parts of human beings, had been removed, leaving the fragments of metal and personal effects. There were scraps of clothing, some of which had been used as bandages, a lunch box, and the remains of a cheap plastic purple flask with a gaping hole in its side. There was a little heap of rucksacks, some clothes, some sheets. Eight soldiers in single file picked their way through boggy ground, while others examined the track of the command wire that set off the bomb which, in one flash of devastating violence, brought ruin to so many lives.

In February 1992 an IRA member who had been active in the campaign in England met his death at the hands of the SAS. Kevin Barry O'Donnell, a student from Coalisland, Co Tyrone, was arrested in London while carrying two Kalashnikov rifles. At his trial he was, to general surprise, acquitted of possessing the weapons. But he was excluded from Britain and sent back to Tyrone.

Back home, he became part of an IRA unit which staged a heavy machine-gun attack on Coalisland RUC station, pumping bullets into the station from the back of a stolen lorry. But when the lorry drove outside the town, the SAS was waiting, and in a clinically executed ambush, four IRA members were killed.

Conflict goes on
as IRA buries its dead

In the middle of the road in the middle of a funeral in Coalisland, Co Tyrone, Sinn Féin president Gerry Adams stood and argued with a senior officer of the Royal Ulster Constabulary. The policeman told Mr Adams that he wanted an assurance that there would be no paramilitary trappings: Mr Adams responded that he did not like the officer's tone. The MP was dressed in his standard green funeral coat, whose shoulders must by now be threadbare from carrying the coffins of so many dead IRA and Sinn Féin members. The policeman was clad in dark uniform, flak jacket, protective leggings, helmet, visor, black gloves and swagger stick.

Gerry Adams, president of Sinn Féin

Behind Mr Adams were the coffins of Kevin Barry O'Donnell and Sean O'Farrell, two of four IRA men killed by the army, together with 5,000 or so people. Behind the RUC officer a phalanx of several hundred police officers in full riot gear formed a line across the road. The town has been swamped with police and troops since the shootings, the RUC's saturation policing tactics causing much local resentment.

The policeman courteously explained that his concern was to prevent any paramilitary display. Mr Adams turned and made his way through the crowd to find the parents of the dead men. Martin McGuinness of Sinn Féin stayed and needled the policeman: "You're standing there like a big child," he remarked coolly, almost casually, to him. "You're as bigoted and sectarian as ever youse were." The officer did not respond.

Mr Adams and other Sinn Féin members came back with the fathers of the dead IRA men, and the officer explained that he wanted the coffin moved forward to the front of the mourners so that police could keep a closer eye on those around it: "We want an assurance that there will be no shooting or paramilitary trappings. As soon as there are any signs of marching, stamping feet or paramilitary trappings, we will stop it," the officer said. "Are there regulations for funerals?" Mr Adams asked. The policeman said he was not going to get into any arguments. He agreed with O'Donnell's father, Jim, that the proceedings had so far been very dignified, and accepted his assurance that there would be no paramilitary trappings. The police line moved back, and the coffins made their way through the run-down little town and up to the small graveyard on the hill.

It was in the graveyard, while the police were momentarily occupied elsewhere, that the republicans surreptitiously staged their little ceremonial, a dozen or so youths, men and women in black leather jackets and white shirts carrying the coffin a few yards. It was their way of putting one over on the police, just as Kevin Barry O'Donnell had put one over on an Old Bailey jury by assuring them that he and his family would never support violence. According to his IRA obituary, he joined that organisation in 1988 and took part in numerous incidents before moving to England, where he "continued operations against British military targets throughout that country".

Earlier in the day his father, who 21 years ago named him after a republican martyr, Kevin Barry, put one over on the Catholic church. The clergy do not permit paramilitary trappings inside their buildings, but the Tricolour-draped coffins were brought to the door of the Holy Family church and kept there until the local priest agreed, with the greatest reluctance, to allow them inside. There were cheers and applause at the clerical climb-down. Later more than 100 walked out when the priest, having criticised the army for the shootings and the RUC for insensitive saturation policing, also criticised the IRA leaders who gave the dead men their orders.

Local people still cannot understand what the IRA hoped to achieve by attacking the station, which was specially strengthened last year and had ample defence against the IRA's weapons. The attack knocked chunks out of the station walls and left metal screens peppered with bullet holes, but stood little chance of causing death or injury to its occupants. One local theory has it that the whole thing was mounted for publicity purposes and was captured on film so that videos could be sent to America to be viewed by sympathisers. If so, the IRA has paid a high price for its propaganda.

East Tyrone is a beautiful place, but it harbours enmities whose origins are almost lost in the mists of time. It is a dangerous place for the security forces, but in mid-1991 the SAS hit back with an ambush in which three local IRA men were killed.

4 JUNE 1991   THE INDEPENDENT

A tribal past
lingers in modern hate

To the outsider, a trip to east Tyrone can give a feeling of intruding on a quarrel which is both ancient and modern: a place where both the immediate and the distant past can never be forgotten. Here the IRA kills Protestants, saying that they die because they are (or are mistakenly thought to be) members of the security forces. Loyalist extremists kill Catholics, in general claiming they are members of the IRA and Sinn Féin. That seems straightforward enough; but it does not take many conversations here to realise the multifold layers of history which affect everyday life. The tribal and territorial imperatives were firmly in place before the dreary steeples of Fermanagh and Tyrone, of which Churchill complained so wearily, were even built.

Some men in this area still regard Protestants as holding land which was robbed from the Catholic Irish hundreds of years ago. The killings are justified in terms of the present day, but the suspicion lingers that some, at least, are motivated by revenge for real or imagined grievances stretching back to the days of the first Elizabeth. Centuries ago Catholic woodkernes would emerge from the vast forests of the day to attack the Protestant settlers drafted in from Scotland and England during the plantations. The pattern now may not be so different: yesterday the modern-day woodkernes were caught and killed when, according to the security forces, they were on their way to attack Protestant workmen.

Catholic and Protestant do mix here in many ways, but politically the tribe is paramount. Everybody's antecedents are known, with religion as a key determinant. A person is either "one of ours" or "one of the other sort".

Coagh is a predominantly Protestant village surrounded by a largely nationalist countryside, an area which in recent years has seen the emergence of a cycle of violence following some reasonably peaceful years. The politics tends towards the extremes, with strong support for the Rev Ian Paisley's Democratic Unionist party and for Sinn Féin.

Republicans attack loyalists and the security forces, while loyalists and the security forces, in their different ways, attack republicans. The start of the present cycle is dated by locals to the killing of an Ulster Defence Regiment member three years ago. This has been followed by a large number of loyalist attacks on republicans and Catholics, together with republican attacks on loyalists. One landmark came two years ago when the IRA killed three local Protestants in a Coagh garage: one was alleged to be a loyalist extremist, but the other two were indisputably harmless elderly men. Since then loyalist attacks have continued, with the Protestant killers managing to kill many more republicans, as opposed to uninvolved Catholics, than loyalists in other parts of the country. This has led to a firm belief among local Catholics that the loyalists are being aided by the co-operation of members of the security forces.

Unlike many parts of Belfast where Catholics and Protestants are often effectively segregated from each other, the two sides live closely together here. Each is able to rhyme off the names of those whom they allege to be the other side's gunmen, and each tends to regard the other community as deliberately shielding the killers in its midst. One of those killed by the SAS was particularly well known to Protestants as a dangerous IRA activist.

If the patterns of the past are adhered to, there will be in the coming weeks, or months, or years, attempts to avenge these killings. The would-be assassins will be helped in their task by the fact that the two sides find themselves, through history and through geography, living together in such hostile proximity.

In the hills of south Armagh, where neither the security forces nor the gunmen are ever completely in charge, an element of lawlessness has over two and a half decades become part of everyday life. In rural districts such as this, little post offices serve as an important focal point of local life. They are frequented by practically everyone in the district – including, unfortunately, the gunmen.

---

17 MARCH 1992   THE INDEPENDENT

Raiders target the country post offices

"It's the same every time," said the sub-postmistress. "The most frightening thing is the masks and the balaclavas, and the eyes flitting behind them. Of course they have the guns, but you don't feel they're going to use them. Afterwards the tension builds up and you get nervy and sick." She was speaking about what has been, over the years, a recurring feature of life for many post office workers in south Armagh: the fact that every so often they will be confronted by armed and masked robbers. The raids had eased off in the last few years but, according to the post office, are now on the increase again.

On the surface the district is deceptively peaceful and often strikingly picturesque. Yet frequently the majestic sweep of a valley is marred by

103

A south Armagh post office

the fortified squatness of an army lookout post perched on a hill, a constant and obtrusive reminder that this is a trouble spot as well as a beauty spot.

Some of the men and women who staff the little post offices which dot the countryside have been robbed up to a dozen times. There are also frequent hold-ups of the vans which supply them with money. "You learn to live with these things, that's the strange thing," said another woman who, like everyone else in south Armagh, spoke on the strict condition that she should not be identified in any way. "The first time, these three men came in and I honestly thought they were joking. Then one of them held a gun to my ear, and I could feel his hand was shaking away – that really was frightening. You're nervous, but sometimes they're even more nervous. They just want to get in and out, quick. I hope I never have to face it again."

Armed robberies of post offices, banks and other premises have been such a familiar feature of the Troubles that they are now rarely reported in the media. In the past two decades more than £18 million has been stolen in no less than 17,000 such raids in Northern Ireland.

Most of the robberies of south Armagh post offices and vans are over and done with in just a few minutes. Some of the staff are extraordinarily stoic about their experiences, needing only a few days to recover from the ordeal, but others are more deeply affected. One sub-postmaster related: "It's unbelievable how you feel. Afterwards you go in and close the door and you don't want to open it again, you don't want to go out anywhere – the after-effects are desperate. That fear would be in you a long, long time." After one robbery, he went to see his doctor: "He gave me a line to go to the mental hospital but I wasn't going to go there. I just threw it in the fire."

Some staff do, however, need treatment for mental distress. According to Raymond Crea, Northern Ireland manager of Post Office Counters: "Physical injuries are mercifully rare but some people have had to be retired because of the shock. There are mental scars which can last a lifetime." One woman speaks sadly about a driver who works in the area and who was recently robbed for the first time. "That big fella was never the same after it. He used to be all great chat and jokes. Now, never a word."

According to Mr Crea, delivery staff may refuse to go back after they have been held up: "It's a diminishing band of people who are prepared to continue delivering there. After being held up at gunpoint a few times, a lot say, 'Sorry, we're not prepared to go back there.'" That option does not, however, exist for those who run the little post offices, for these are frequently set in a corner of their family grocery stores, and they live on the premises. In fact, the post offices very often run in families, the business being handed down from generation to generation.

Nobody will say whether they think the IRA is behind the robberies. A Sinn Féin supporter said enigmatically: "I wouldn't rule out totally that it was them. It's hard enough to say, now." There is certainly a code of practice in operation which suggests that the thieves have a certain communal conscience, or at least an unusual political sensitivity. In every case the post office money is taken but the cash in the shop till is left untouched. The robbers have been known to call out, "Give us the Queen's money."

A post office manager was shot dead in the area in the 1970s, though that is assumed to have been a case of mistaken identity on the part of gunmen, who thought he was a detective. The post office has always made it very clear to its employees that it does not want any dead heroes, and staff are under orders not to resist. The instruction is, in any case, hardly necessary since, as one sub-postmaster put it, "There's no man going to argue with a man with a gun."

The speed of the robberies means there is little chance of troops or police intercepting the raiders, but in any event security forces in this most hazardous of areas are not in the business of making fast responses. The dangers of the IRA staging what the RUC calls a "come-on" ambush are obvious. Staff in some post offices say that police may take days to respond after a robbery, and in some cases never visit the post office at all. RUC sources explain that every robbery is investigated but add that, given the dangers of ambush, detectives do this in their own way and at their own time.

Post office robberies elsewhere have been much reduced over the years, but in Armagh the problem persists. Following two raids on Cullyhanna post office within four months, Raymond Crea announced that the problem had reached "alarming proportions" and warned that some post offices might have to close permanently. His hope is to ensure that, for the men and women behind the counters, staring down the barrel of a gun should not be an occupational hazard.

Late 1991 saw a sustained IRA return to an old tactic, that of placing large car bombs designed to cause maximum destruction in Northern Ireland cities and towns. The centre of Belfast particularly suffered from these attacks, which caused millions of pounds' worth of damage.

15 JANUARY 1992   THE INDEPENDENT

IRA attacks take shine off Belfast's Golden Mile

The IRA man believed to be the key figure in the organisation's current campaign to blast the heart out of Belfast is a regular visitor to the RUC's main interrogation centre at Castlereagh in the east of the city. Like other top IRA figures, he is frequently picked up by the police and army and taken in for questioning sessions. In the past he has complained of being physically ill-treated while in custody in Castlereagh. Although the law says he can be held for up to seven days, his stays are usually shorter than that since, in line with standard paramilitary practice, he generally says absolutely nothing and therefore gives detectives nothing to go on. Unusually, however, he did say something on his arrival at Castlereagh before Christmas. Formally asked his occupation, he answered dryly: "I create car parks."

The results of his efforts can currently be seen right across the face of Belfast. Six large bombs have gone off in the city centre since the end of November, causing substantial damage over wide areas. Shops and offices have been wrecked, businesses put out of action, thousands of windows shattered, hundreds of vehicles destroyed: one observer called it vandalism on a colossal scale. More than a month after some of the explosions, repair work is still going on all over the city. There are still vast stretches of hardboard where windows should be, with a few defiant BUSINESS AS USUAL slogans on the hardboard. Thousands of people have been affected, from office people to workers in large and small shops. As well as the big bombs, there have been a great many incendiary bombings – attacks which are less spectacular but which can also be tremendously disruptive, for the fires sometimes damage a building beyond repair.

In addition to the physical damage, public morale appears to be at its lowest for years, with many complaints to be heard that the IRA is either winning, or at least holds the initiative. People ask how the security forces, with all their experience and their thousands of men, cannot stop the bombers getting through. The knock to morale is all the greater because of the undoubted improvements to Belfast city centre over the past decade. All over the city new shops, arcades and office developments have appeared, together with a bustling Golden Mile of crowded bars and restaurants. Most of the citizens of Belfast have taken a quiet pride in the rejuvenation of a city which was devastated by IRA bombs in the 1970s. They also noted that the IRA, while clearly resentful of such progress, generally refrained from launching a concerted attack on the new buildings. It looked as though political constraints were saving the city and that Sinn Féin, fearful of alienating its supporters who worked, and shopped, downtown, was arguing for a more selective campaign of violence. Sinn Féin's influence has dwindled, however, and today straight militarism takes precedence over political niceties. Thus the magnificent Grand Opera House, the symbol of the urban renaissance, has been blown up along with the much-bombed Europa Hotel, an action which a local columnist called "an indescribably depressing piece of *déjà vu*".

For the general population, perhaps the most depressing feature has been the suggestion of a return to the really bad old days of the early 1970s. Last November brought a wholesale slaughter of civilians, with 1970s-style attacks on pubs full of people. Now the car bomb and the van bomb have returned.

The present security force reaction is to swamp the city with permanent checkpoints on every road into the centre, for they know IRA members will not approach a checkpoint while carrying a bomb. This has brought a respite from the explosions, but a price is being paid in the form of major road congestion, which can add more than an hour to short car journeys. Belfast papers are now carrying advice on how best to pass the time in traffic jams.

The government's attempts to foster an image of normality have taken a severe dent, and the city will take time to recover from its battering. Yet it absorbed even greater punishment than this in the past, and emerged from it with a communal determination not to allow the IRA's creator of car parks to succeed in his aims.

IRA bombs affect everyone: big businesses, small enterprises, churches, houses, restaurants. One large device left beside an RUC station caused enormous damage to homes, offices, shops and other premises near Belfast city centre.

One of hundreds of buildings damaged was the handsome Victorian headquarters of Relate, the marriage guidance organisation. Sitting in his shattered office a few days after the blast, John Chambers, Relate's chief officer, outlined the effect of the bombing on his organisation.

Defiance and despair in bomb's aftermath

John Chambers of Relate, the marriage guidance organisation, in his bomb-damaged office

"I arrived at a quarter past seven in the morning and it was absolute chaos. The place was devastated: windows and doors blown in, ceilings down, cracks in the walls, papers everywhere. A storage heater had been blown off the wall and was scorching the carpet – if I hadn't found it the place could have gone up in flames.

"I have to say that my first reaction was utter despair. We had just spent £30,000 on a major renovation scheme on the building. In a charity like this it was a scramble to get that money together, and it was very difficult to work on through all the building. Suddenly, my God, we were just back to that all over again, only far worse.

109

"Then I thought, right, we'd better get something practical done. We had a good builder who had done our renovation work for us, so I phoned him about twenty to eight and by nine o'clock the builders were here with their hardboard to board up windows and so forth. The builder advised me to appoint an assessor to examine the damage, and the assessor was here by a quarter past nine.

"The first thing was to get a structural engineer in to make sure the building wasn't actually going to collapse, because it must be over 100 years old. At the top of the building there were cracks right underneath the roof. Later in the morning I had the builder and the assessor and the architect all in together, deciding on how we would plan things. The police were round too, of course, and other people were calling in to sympathise.

"Then we had a guy from the Northern Ireland Office having a look round, jotting things down, essentially saying there's extensive bomb damage, go ahead and get all the essential first-aid stuff done, make sure the building is windproof and damp-proof and secure from burglary. By that stage we were all talking about what's going to happen about the windows and so on. Some of the frames have gone, and are we going to replace them with the same wood or put in PVC or whatever?

"The bank manager came round as well and advised me to open a separate account. He said he would advance us overdraft facilities – obviously builders will have to be paid.

"The staff here went through a very high level of distress. They weren't in tears, but they were just very upset because all of them had put a great deal of time and effort into this place. But it was amazing how that spirit of distress very quickly gave way to a feeling that we should get the place tidied up. And everybody slaved and we were back in operation by Wednesday.

"Some of the rooms were vacuumed about five times because they were cleared up and then something else happened and they were covered in dust again. But there certainly was that immediate knee-jerk reaction that we were not going to give in to these buggers.

"After a few days, though, a touch of depression was setting in again. You come in every day and it's still chaos. You've still got to do all the work you had to do anyway, plus now all the coping with the bomb. There's the awful dawning that this mess is actually going to go on for quite a while. There is no doubt that the toll it takes on the staff is a very serious one, and they're all absolutely exhausted.

"Our budget is about £300,000, and we get grants of £170,000 and have to find the rest. Fund-raising is difficult because we don't come across as an emotive charity, yet what we do is one of the most emotive jobs there is. We get people in here whose hearts are breaking, not to mention the children. We

110

give people a weekly appointment, on the same day, at the same time, for an hour. Quite apart from what the counselling actually does for them, it is something to hang on to, for people whose lives are in a state of chaos, to know that they're going to see a helpful, understanding person every Tuesday from 10 to 11. Some of the counsellors told me that the clients were so relieved to see them that it was almost as if they didn't notice the state the building was in.

"Some of the walls have glass embedded in them. And as you go on, you discover things that have been damaged or lost that you hadn't realised, and I'm sure that will go on for weeks.

"The engineer, the architect and one of the assessor's staff have been here a lot. I've also spent quite a lot of time with the builder. He reckons he could have it all done in three months, but part of the work can't be done until we get clearance from the NIO. Hopefully, by the end of the week we'll have most of the glass back in again.

"I haven't really an idea about the cost, but I would be very surprised if it's less than £50,000. I'm told the assessor will come up with his figure and then negotiate with the NIO, who may not give us 100 per cent. Apparently they could say, 'That room hadn't been painted for years, so you're benefiting from having it redone, so why should the NIO cover your costs when it would have been repainted anyway?' When we'll get any NIO money, I do not know.

"When you feel you're providing a very useful service, on a cross-community basis, on a shoestring budget, helping people of all sorts who are distressed, when something like this happens you really do start to wonder – what on earth is it all about? The thing just doesn't make any sense at all."

Six months later John Chambers
described what the public never hears
about: the protracted aftermath of such an
explosion.

Bombing takes high financial and emotional toll

"When we spoke in March I said I thought the damage would be round about £50,000. It turned out that that was a gross underestimate, because the main building work is costing us £82,500 plus VAT. The compensation offer from the Northern Ireland Office is £72,000 plus VAT. In addition, the bill for damaged contents is round about £7,000 plus VAT. We still haven't settled the contents claim, but that's likely to be less than the full cost of the contents. So we are facing a considerable shortfall. It's compensation, but it's partial compensation. The notion that you can do all this work and that it isn't going to cost you anything really is a myth.

"What really frustrates me is that, because we had increased our output in terms of counselling last year, we finished up with a working deficit of £17,000. If I had that £72,000 to spend, we could have wiped out the deficit and doubled our output of work: but this is money.

"To begin with, we had a negotiation as to how much of this work was actually caused by the bomb, and how much may have been due to weaknesses in the building in the first place. We suffered some structural damage, and in fact we had engineers in to put ties in the walls because the walls have actually moved out as a result of the bomb. Now it may well have been that that was a process that was happening anyway, and was exaggerated by the bomb.

"The other NIO argument is that when it's all fixed up we will have betterment in the building, which they are not prepared to pay for. Basically, they say that all we're entitled to do is to replace our building as it was at the time of the bomb. But of course you can't do that, because the whole building has to be redecorated. And the point is that if you're painting a building after it's been bombed, there is much more preparation work than if you're simply repainting. You have to replaster, you have a lot of holes here, there and everywhere which have to be repaired.

"Looking back, what I think of is just how long-drawn-out the whole thing is. Right at the start there is that knee-jerk reaction, when everybody pulls all the stops out, but then within a few days you begin to get tired because it's going on and on. Well, I would have to say that the tiredness gets worse as the months go on and everybody in this organisation, including myself, was absolutely gasping for the holidays. There is an ongoing level of stress that builds up over that period of time, that you're not necessarily aware of until you wake up one day and you're absolutely knackered. You feel as if you've been working very hard and not really getting anywhere.

"We have a very good builder, but even so, the work was extremely dusty and dirty and noisy, and at times it was cold. Our counsellors were often seeing clients in very unsatisfactory circumstances. The noise, for example: you're talking to people who are already finding it difficult to say some of the things that they have to say, and that they need to say. If there's a lot of banging going on outside the room it makes it that much more difficult.

"This is, in any case, always a very stressful organisation. The amount of stress that comes through our door and over our telephone on any day of the week is enormous. We have group meetings to help us all cope with that, and what we've attempted to do in all our gatherings is to give space for people to talk about how they're feeling. I suppose the danger in an organisation like this is that people, because they're used to coping with stress, think they can cope with the extra pressure. There is a danger that you actually don't recognise the serious effect it's having. There was a lot of anger and a lot of frustration. There were people who lost their rooms, who really felt a deep sense of loss. It was almost a kind of bereavement.

"But on a more positive note, the work should all be complete by the end of this month, and after the summer people have come back with a new sense of hope and energy. We have had our symbols of success, like getting our book shop reopened. Little signs like that are critically important, because people need to see that progress is being made, that this agony is not going to be sustained for ever.

"For me, the final sign that it's over, the last thing I shall do, is to remove the broken clock from my wall. It's stuck at ten past two, which was the time that bomb went off in the early hours of 24 March."

The ordeal of Relate and John Chambers
was almost over, but the bombings
continued. Just before Christmas 1992
a Londonderry town which had escaped
the worst of the Troubles suffered
serious damage.

13 DECEMBER 1992   THE INDEPENDENT ON SUNDAY

Brave faces and bargains amid the ruins

Moore's department store was a bit of an institution in Coleraine, a big old shop that retained its traditional character. It was the type of place that still stocked things like reels and needles, the sort of thing the large multiples may not bother with any more. The store opened in 1925 with John, the son of the founder, taking it over in the 1940s. He has run it as a real family concern: seven family members work there, each running their own section of the shop. Over the years Moore's expanded to 20,000 square feet, employing a staff of 40. This year the building had a half-million-pound refurbishment.

The IRA van bomb went off a month ago on Friday 13 November, blasting buildings in the town centre. It was left at the other end of the Moore's block, and at first it seemed that the old store had had a miraculous escape. As often happens in bombings, the blast had gone in some directions but not in others, and Moore's windows were undamaged. One of the family, Neville, opened the security shutters to let firemen inside: "At that stage you could have walked in the front door," he recalled. "All the displays were intact and untouched. But then the fire started to come through from the back and you could see the flames and the smoke. Then the fire suddenly came down the stairs with a tremendous whoosh, and it really got a grip."

John Moore heard the explosion at his home some miles away, but thought it was thunder. Fifteen minutes later somebody rang to say there had been a bomb in the town, and he set off to drive into the centre. The night sky was lit up. "We saw the smoke and the flames as we got nearer and nearer, and I thought, that must be close to us." When he arrived his store was an inferno.

The next morning a woman member of staff fainted when she saw the scene. Moore's store was a shell, only its outer walls still standing. Inside was an enormous heap of blackened, wet, smouldering rubble. Her place of employment, and more than 60 years of tradition, had gone.

The rest of the block has now been demolished, leaving a sea of mud in what used to be the busiest shopping block in Coleraine. The town is struggling to come to terms with the damage and make the most of what is left of the Christmas shopping season. There were a fair few shoppers around, some of them attracted by the bomb-damage sales which many premises advertise on their hardboarded windows. A newspaper advertisement for one of the sales announces cheerily: "What's gone up now comes down." A sprightly matron from outside the town, who had just bought a bag for her daughter in a bomb sale, said: "It's sad when you see the big empty space there. It would have made you weep the first day, it was very moving. The shops are quite busy but they haven't great stock, they've nothing left really to sell just yet. It was such a prosperous town, friendly and relaxed."

The reason why Coleraine was so relaxed was that, like a surprisingly large number of other places in Northern Ireland, it has been almost totally bypassed by the Troubles. Some people died in terrorist incidents in the largely Protestant town in the early days, but it is 17 years since anyone was killed. A local newspaper noted sadly: "For so long we have had the luxury of telling prospective visitors that we are exempt from the horrors that have afflicted the rest of the province." Now the papers talk of Black Friday.

The centre of Coleraine now looks like Coventry after the blitz. The town hall, which was right next to the blast, was almost wrecked by the bomb. Its windows and doors are boarded up, its sandstone exterior pitted with holes gouged out by shrapnel. The roof of the building lifted in the air and came down again, smashing some of the heavy rafters. It will take years to restore. The council, in a gallant but unconvincing attempt to create a Christmas atmosphere, has put festive decorations over some of the hardboard and broadcasts seasonal music from loudspeakers. The carols were periodically drowned out by the hammering of workmen and the revving of the heavy engine of a crane working on the local Bank of Ireland. The listed building was shattered by the blast and is now desperately unsafe. The walls are shored up with thick timber beams as workmen try to save the structure of the building. Another bank, the Northern, escaped more lightly, though its all-glass front has now become an all-hardboard front.

The words BUSINESS AS USUAL are everywhere to be seen, though some shops have had to move. Warren Frew's fruit and grocery shop was badly damaged.

He now, enterprisingly, conducts his business in two Portakabins erected in a car park round the corner. Mr Frew, 26, said: "Our business is about halved, because we were in a prime spot and now we're off the main road. But we're hoping our regular customers will find us again. It's all been pretty stressful. I imagine it will be six months to a year before we can move back, though some people are saying two years."

John McClements runs an interesting little book shop strategically placed in a small street between the town centre and a large car park. Damage to his doors and windows has been repaired but he now faces a much longer-term problem. Because of an unsafe building, a wooden barricade has been put up across the street, transforming what used to be a handy little short cut into a dead-end street cut off from the whole town centre. He has been left stranded, the passing trade gone. "On Friday I had one customer, who bought one book, for £1.50. That was it. That's the worst day I've had in the 16 years I've been here. Even if people know I'm still here, they've a long way to trek round here in bad weather through the dug-up streets. I've written to everyone, but no one can tell me how long the barricade is going to stay up."

The Moore family is already trading again, having quickly taken over other premises for use as a toy shop for Christmas. But they know it will take two years to rebuild on their old site: when they do, they promise that it will be a building of traditional character. In the meantime, they have had to pay off half their staff, 20 people who have received, courtesy of the IRA, the bitter Christmas present of unemployment.

More misery followed a huge IRA bomb blast in south Belfast. It wrecked its target, the forensic science laboratories, but it also caused damage to no fewer than 1,002 homes in the vicinity, principally in the Belvoir Park housing estate.

Blast victim faces
a bleak Christmas

It has clearly all been too much for Margaret Chapman. She sits, grey-haired and wheezing asthmatically, in a damp mobile home, talking of builders and assessors and loss adjusters and estimates and compensation. She is baffled by it all, fretting over bills and trying not to think of Christmas.

Her own house, a neat little modern terrace, is just round the corner. The IRA bomb that damaged it, and 1,000 other houses and flats, exploded exactly three months ago, on 23 September, but repair work has yet to start on her property. The roof is still off, the windows are still boarded up, and soggy furniture sits where it was tossed on the night of the blast. Many others in the district have made much more rapid progress, but Mrs Chapman is obviously out of her depth. She will spend Christmas in a little compound of mobile homes which has been erected on some open space in Belvoir Park housing estate. A dozen families have been housed in this neat little shanty settlement, a parody of a seaside caravan site.

The bomb which devastated forensic science laboratories also damaged 1,002 homes, 100 of them severely. The Northern Ireland Housing Executive, following an effort which has been little short of heroic, recently announced that all its 574 tenants are now back in their homes. The other 400-odd families, who owned their homes, have been affected in various ways. Some did not have to leave; some left and have now returned; some, like Mrs Chapman, cannot yet go back. In the beginning she hoped to be back home by Christmas, but now her target is Easter.

Belvoir Park is in a quiet area, sitting several miles outside Belfast on gentle hills which afford a panoramic view of the city. It was a model estate, which the Housing Executive always held up as an example of what an estate could be. Many families who moved there in the 1960s were thankful they left Belfast before the Troubles started, and have stayed on. It thus has a large number of elderly and retired people who enjoyed its sedate environment.

Today Castledillon Road, which bore the brunt of the blast, is a site of desolation. Workmen are everywhere, dumping shattered material into skips filled with rubble, plaster and broken timber. Unrepaired roofs are draped with incongruously gaudy yellow and orange tarpaulins, which lend a dash of cheerless colour to the dismal scene. The Church of the Transfiguration, which was badly hit, is still covered in hardboard. The nearby Presbyterian church bears the warning DANGEROUS BUILDING – KEEP OUT, and is shrouded in scaffolding as work continues on the bell tower and the roof. Between the churches are 11 families in their mobile homes, including Margaret Chapman and her two daughters. The mobiles shake in high winds and are hard to heat. This Christmas she will be trying to keep warm, but is fearful that using the electric heater too much could bring in a bill that she cannot afford to pay.

With the IRA's campaign in Britain and Northern Ireland attracting more and more attention, the *Independent on Sunday* went back to basics and asked a series of simple questions about the organisation.

A plain person's guide to the IRA

OUR DAY WILL COME

IRA mural, west Belfast

HERBIE KNOTT

1 How did the Provisional IRA get its name?

Until 1969 there was only one IRA, but late that year a split developed. Most of the old leadership stayed on in the smaller faction, which styled itself the Official IRA. The larger section became the Provisionals, the name being a reference to the provisional government declared by those who rose against Britain in Dublin in 1916.

The Provisionals said the old leadership had become too left-wing and lacked militancy. The Official IRA still lingers on, though it has largely given up terrorist violence and concentrates instead on running clubs and rackets.

Over the years two other splinter groups emerged, the Irish People's Liberation Organisation and the Irish National Liberation Army. The first degenerated into drug-dealing and has just disbanded after the IRA shot some of its leading members. The second is small and disorganised.

2 How did the IRA start?

The IRA claims lineage running back through the 19th-century Fenians, past the rebels of 1798 and going back into the green mists of Irish history to encompass just about anyone who ever took up arms against the British. In this century it claims direct descent from the 1916 rebels who laid the basis for the south's independence. Its men refused to recognise the limited form of home rule originally granted by Britain, fighting in the bitter civil war of the 1920s against those who favoured settling for a compromise treaty with the British. The 1916 Proclamation of Independence is the nearest thing the IRA has to holy writ.

Over the decades most of those who had opposed the treaty swallowed their pride and, like Eamon de Valera, slipped into political life. The IRA moved out of the mainstream and became the refuge of the diehards. At times membership was down to a couple of dozen, but the outbreak of the Troubles in 1969 brought a huge expansion.

3 Do they believe in God?

Most do, some do not. Most IRA members go to mass – its membership is almost all Catholic – while others, especially from the cities, have not seen the inside of a church for years. Mass attendance in some of the strongest IRA areas is relatively low. The IRA flatly rejects the pronouncements of the Irish Catholic bishops, who regularly denounce terrorism in general and the IRA in particular. But IRA members, even the deeply religious ones, have a long tradition of ignoring church advice on political matters.

In previous decades the church went so far as to excommunicate IRA members, to no great effect. Some of those penalised in this way in the 1920s went on to become pillars of society, and indeed of the church.

4 What does the IRA want?

In two words, Brits out. It believes that Ireland's endemic violence and most of its economic and other problems are the direct result of the British presence. It wants Britain to admit defeat and declare its intent to withdraw from Northern Ireland. It then wants talks on the best way to effect a withdrawal; and later it wants Irishmen of all persuasions to sit down and decide together on how to run Ireland in the aftermath of a British pull-out. But most immediately, it wants the British to engage in talks with its political wing, Sinn Féin, to start the ball rolling.

After withdrawal, the republican theory goes, the border will melt away and nationalists and Unionists will live in peace in a Brit-free Ireland. The IRA says it would not attempt to seize power, and that Ireland's precise form of future government would be decided democratically. Not everyone believes that: a British minister once warned that the IRA's goal was "a new Cuba off our western coast". Although the IRA went through a flirtation with Marxism in the 1970s, its language today is less and less left-wing. It is also softening its anti-EC line to take account of the fact that most Irish nationalists are enthusiastically pro-European.

5 Does the IRA have an intellectual élite?

The IRA's leadership shades into that of its political wing, Sinn Féin. Although few of those at the top have any third-level education, the republican movement contains some sharp thinkers and able debaters such as Gerry Adams, Danny Morrison and Mitchel McLaughlin. Almost all of them are working-class. Many received their political education behind bars, where republican prisoners continually debate and discuss their cause. The Maze prison near Belfast has the best educational record of any UK jail, largely because of the IRA prisoners who take A-levels and Open University degrees in political studies.

Republican publications are literate and of a high standard. IRA people can often display a surprising flexibility of mind, but one option always seems to remain a no-go area: that of calling off their campaign.

6 How many members does the IRA have?

The security forces estimate around 500, though this is a hard core of activists who can depend on a much wider circle of second-rank supporters and sympathisers. Over the last 20 years, 5,000 or more have passed through the ranks before being imprisoned, shot, or retired for various reasons. At the moment there are approximately 650 IRA members in jail in Northern Ireland, more than 100 of them serving life sentences for murder. When those held in the Republic, Britain and the continent are added, that figure rises to about 750.

IRA numbers are deliberately kept down on the principle that every 20th member is likely to be an informer working for the police or army. Recruits are generally in their teens or twenties. When they apply they are given a "cold bath" – a stern lecture pointing out that they may well end up imprisoned or shot by the SAS.

Sinn Féin has thousands of members. A small proportion of these are also in the IRA but for the most part they are drawn widely from among the working-class Catholic population. Both the IRA and Sinn Féin have a fair sprinkling of women.

7 How many members does the IRA have in Britain?

Nobody knows. The most recent security force estimate is up to 25, but this seems to be based, not on hard intelligence, but on the number which police calculate must be needed to sustain the British campaign at its present level. However, the recent increase in the volume of bombings suggests that more than 25 people may be active.

8 Has the IRA's British operation been penetrated by the police, army or MI5?

All the signs are that it has not. The RUC in Northern Ireland, and the Gardaí in the Irish Republic, pass on lists of people who are missing from their homes in Ireland and who may therefore be active in Britain. But clearly, police in Britain do not know how the IRA members slip into England: if they did, they would either pick them up or launch close surveillance operations on them. They do not know how the Semtex explosives and guns are brought over. They also do not know where the IRA members live in or around London.

In Northern Ireland the security forces use informers to penetrate the IRA structure, but this is not possible in England: the IRA pick their English teams very carefully, and are not going to send over people capable of being "turned" by the Metropolitan Police Special Branch or MI5. This means the RUC's most valuable anti-terrorist weapon is simply not available to the security forces in Britain.

9 Is the present IRA campaign in Britain different from those in the past?

Yes. IRA bombs have been going off sporadically in England since the early 1970s: there were the Birmingham and Guildford pub bombings, explosions which killed soldiers in Hyde Park and Regent's Park, and the bombs at Harrods and the Grand Hotel in Brighton. But most of those were hit-and-run attacks. The difference now is that the IRA is intent on waging permanent war in England. With hindsight, it can be seen that it took a strategic decision in the mid-1980s on how to use the large quantities of Semtex plastic explosive and other material supplied by Libya. The IRA decided it had enough equipment not only to step up its campaign in Northern Ireland but also to wage a major campaign in Britain.

A Semtex find in Cheshire in 1987 held up its plans, and it was not until mid-1988 that the bombing of army premises at Mill Hill heralded the start of the present campaign. Since then the IRA has had its successes and setbacks, but it has kept up the pressure with a stream of attacks over the past four years.

10 Why this increased emphasis on bombing Britain?

The cliché that one bomb in London is worth twenty in Belfast is quite correct. In Northern Ireland last year there were 230 explosions, only a handful of which rated any detailed mention in the British media. Almost any bombing in England, by contrast, will attract coverage. Since the IRA is trying to affect British public, and hence political, opinion, it makes tactical sense for it to strike in Britain as much as possible. In four years it has exported to Britain many of the features of Northern Ireland terrorism, including bombings of various kinds, shootings, mortar attacks, incendiaries and so on.

The theory is that the public will come to realise that bombs will be a permanent fixture of life in Britain so long as the troops remain in Northern Ireland. The public will then, the IRA hopes, put pressure on British politicians to bring the soldiers home.

One problem for the IRA is that four years of a sustained bombing campaign has not noticeably increased troops-out sentiment in Britain. When told that it has not worked, they reply that it has not worked – yet.

11 How is the IRA organised?

The traditional terms such as brigades, battalions, chief of staff and so on are still used, but the IRA has learnt over the years to be as flexible as possible. For one thing, this hampers the security forces, who tend to think in terms of identifying patterns.

In the Republic of Ireland there are teams who supervise the hiding of weaponry, while others specialise in moving it across the border. In the north quartermasters distribute weapons to the "active service units". Intelligence units choose and check out targets for attack. An "engineering department" develops new types of improvised weaponry, including new kinds of bombs, refined booby trap devices and new mortars and grenades. Although technically these are home-made weapons, army experts have a healthy regard for their effectiveness. There is also a "security department" whose job it is to ferret out security force informers and agents planted in the IRA ranks. Further sections deal with tasks such as finding sources of weaponry abroad and working out how to get supplies into Ireland. A "finance section", a sort of IRA treasury, deals with raising money and allocating it to other departments.

A seven-person "army council" oversees the whole operation. In addition to running these various sections, it has also proved successful in establishing special units whose existence is unknown to the security forces. Thus the unit which ferried in the Libyan supplies in 1985–7 was a mystery to the security services until it was accidentally uncovered by French customs. Similarly, the authorities appear not to have appreciated, until comparatively recently, just how extensive the current British campaign would be.

12 Is it true that the IRA acts as a community police force in some parts of Northern Ireland?

In some areas, particularly those where the security forces find it most difficult to operate, the IRA acts against those deemed guilty of "anti-social behaviour". This can refer to those suspected of joyriding, drug-dealing, burglary, sex offences or other crimes. "Community policing" in this context is a euphemism for shooting youths in the knees, or, in extreme cases, the elbows and ankles as well. Enforced exile is another alternative, with people sometimes ordered out of the country on pain of death.

Over the years the republican community has come to regard such methods as an alternative form of justice. In many cases, in fact, non-republicans have asked the IRA to intervene against elements felt to be beyond the reach of the police and army.

13 What is the true level of IRA support, north and south?

A difficult question to answer, but one measurement is the vote for Sinn Féin, which gives an idea of the numbers prepared to support or tolerate IRA violence. Sinn Féin received 78,000 votes in this year's Westminster election, which amounted to exactly 10 per cent of the total vote and 30 per cent of the nationalist vote. This is significantly down from its 1983 high point of 102,000 votes, which was more than 40 per cent of the nationalist vote. This gradual decline is bad news for Sinn Féin but even worse is their vote in the south, which has dwindled almost to vanishing point – 1.2 per cent.

It also has to be understood that those who support the IRA have the power to impose certain rules upon it. Many of those people, for example, approve of killings of soldiers or policemen but frown on civilian casualties. The IRA knows it has to pay attention to such judgements.

14 Are the IRA racketeers?

It depends what you mean by racketeers. The IRA is a multi-million-pound business: all the figures are guesstimates, but it is reasonable to suppose it raises and spends perhaps £5 million a year. If its leaders had sticky fingers and were keeping money for themselves, those 78,000 voters would disappear overnight. It is true that they extract money from businesses and enterprises like clubs and taxis, but it is done for the cause rather than for personal gain. The reluctant givers tend to be large concerns rather than small local businesses, because the local community would not stand for it. Such community constraints help to explain why the IRA has never been tempted to go for the easy money available in, for example, drug-pushing.

15 Will the government ever talk to the IRA?

One can never say never. [Indeed one can't.] Governments have held talks with them in the past, and the IRA claims to be confident they will some day be back at the conference table. Many feel the only reasons a government would talk to it would be to accept its surrender, should it ever decide to call off its campaign, or to surrender to it. The IRA has made it clear that it is only interested in discussing how the British would withdraw, and will not settle for some compromise arrangement.

Britain has little selfish interest in remaining in Northern Ireland: it no longer has any military or strategic importance, represents a constant drain on the UK economy, and brings nothing but trouble and bad publicity. There is, however, the moral argument that a government should not capitulate to terrorism. In addition, those who fear that a pull-out would destabilise Ireland and lead to much worse bloodshed include not only northern Unionists but also many northern nationalists and southern Irish politicians.

There is certainly a British instinct to put an end to its involvement, but these other factors exert powerful pressure to stay. The IRA has done great damage in Northern Ireland and in Britain, but it has united the British and Irish governments in a determination that terrorism should not succeed. It has successfully sustained a two-decades-long campaign of terrorism. Its durability is not in question; but after 20 years all the signs are that it is no closer to achieving its aim of forcing British withdrawal.

5

THE LOYALISTS

Although loyalist paramilitary groups have always received much less publicity and public attention than the IRA, they have been one of the biggest takers of life in Northern Ireland, accounting for around one-quarter of all Troubles deaths. In the early 1990s violent loyalists actually overtook the IRA in terms of the number of people they killed. Such groups have similarities with republican organisations, but also many points of difference.

Loyalist killers
have criminal element

In 1966, two years before the Troubles really began, an embryo loyalist group killed three people in the backstreets of Belfast. Twenty-seven years on, such groups have, by a rough calculation, been responsible for around 900 of the more than 3,000 deaths. This is roughly half the republican death toll. Yet even after making such a substantial contribution to the slaughter, loyalist paramilitary organisations remain one of the most underresearched elements of the conflict. [The best study of the subject is *The Red Hand* (Steve Bruce, Oxford University Press, 1992).]

The fact that republicans are good at propaganda and loyalists are not is one of many differences between the violent loyalist and republican groups. Many of those dissimilarities, close observers agree, stem from the fact that the IRA and the loyalists are made up of people of very different character. One of the keys to understanding this lies in the fact that, according to security sources, most republicans have not been in trouble with the law before joining the IRA. A majority of imprisoned loyalists, by contrast, have previous criminal − as opposed to terrorist − records for offences such as burglary and assault. Nationalist sources argue, and security sources readily agree, that most of those locked up on the republican side would not be in prison had it not been for the Troubles. Most loyalist groups, however, contain a strong criminal element. Many of the republican−loyalist differences flow from this. The IRA genuinely thinks of itself as an army, with units responding to commands from a central structure which lays down strict policies. The loyalists are more based on strong local personalities who rule their own areas and come together in a much looser, more confederal structure.

Both sides raise money through racketeering, extortion and other illegal means. The crucial difference is that loyalists have much more of a reputation for having sticky fingers − keeping part of their haul for self-gain. In its own strongholds the IRA has, despite much official propaganda to the contrary, preserved a reputation for using the money for "the cause" rather than personal enrichment.

127

Loyalist mural, Shankill Road

IRA members are clearly more secure in their own minds about what they see as their political status. In 1981, for example, 10 republican prisoners went on hunger strike to the death rather than accept that they should be treated on the same basis as nonterrorist inmates. Loyalists have never made such a sacrifice, and many more of them have shown remorse for their violent actions and renounced their former activities. For example, a significant number, while in prison, declare that they have been "saved" and become born-again Christians.

Republicans have become highly skilled over the years at presenting their case and attempting to justify their violence: one IRA member has described their campaign as "armed propaganda". The loyalists, however, have made a poor fist of presenting their views, being highly suspicious of journalists and the media. While most republican publications and propaganda tend to be of a reasonably professional quality, productions from the loyalist side are often characterised by amateurism. Loyalist groups give far fewer interviews and press conferences than the republicans.

An American journalist who has paid frequent visits to Belfast summed up the differences he found: "A lot of the republican leaders are smart, they're foxy, they're highly politicised and they can always give you a very good argument. The loyalists really don't like the media – they're defensive and they're not as bright. They lie more often and they just strike me as basically sectarian. What really gets me is all the tattoos they have – that really gives me the creeps."

128

The characteristics of the loyalist groups are reflected in their victims. Of the 900 killed by them, around 170 have been Protestants, while of the remainder well under 100 have had significant republican links. This means that their main contribution to the death toll is the killing of more than 600 uninvolved Catholics. The attitude that "any Catholic will do" has been illustrated often over the years. One man told police he had shot a man dead "because he was a Fenian bastard". Another said he had killed a woman "because she was a Taig-lover". Another said: "The only reason I did this was I was told the man was a Taig and it was Taigs who killed my father."

The IRA, meanwhile, has had many civilian victims, but for the most part those it has targeted have been members of the security forces or were in some way connected with officialdom. The loyalists have often demonstrated that they regard the Catholic community as a whole as their enemy. In the 1970s this led to no-warning bomb attacks on Catholic bars, while more recently it has resulted in indiscriminate machine-gun attacks on Catholic betting shops. In recent years there have been attempts at more selective targeting, with 18 people with Sinn Féin connections killed in the last five years. But this clearly represents only a small proportion of the total loyalist death toll, and attacks on random Catholics, and those targeted for no apparent reason, have continued. Republican leaders often spell out in chilling detail exactly why IRA victims had to die, cold-bloodedly relating the rules that govern who should live and who should die. The loyalists give an impression of being more hot-blooded and fired by straight sectarian hatred. Often they do not even bother to claim responsibility for the attacks with which they terrorise the Catholic community. They clearly feel the deed speaks for itself and needs no explanation: for them, the murder is the message.

Violent loyalists killed a total of 91 people in the five years from 1986 to 1990, but 1991 saw a significant rise in the death rate. That year, 42 people died at the hands of loyalist groups, principally the UVF and UDA.

One particularly active UVF unit, centred around the Co Armagh town of Portadown,

established itself as an especially vicious
and unrestrained killing group. Reputedly
led by a loyalist nicknamed "King Rat",
the group killed many people, including a
number of women. In one attack they shot
dead an elderly Catholic couple whose son
was in prison for IRA offences.

---

9 SEPTEMBER 1992   THE INDEPENDENT

Protestant assassin
who revels in
world of fear

As soon as it was broadcast that an elderly Catholic couple had been killed
in their Co Tyrone cottage, the word went round: King Rat did it; King
Rat has struck again; nobody is safe; who's next?

It remains to be seen what involvement the Portadown Ulster Volunteer Force
leader who is known as King Rat actually had in the murders of Charlie and
Teresa Fox. He may have pulled the trigger; he may have helped to plan the
attack; or he may have had no part in the affair. In the tense, anxious atmosphere
of that part of Northern Ireland, it hardly matters. King Rat is now firmly fixed
in the grim folklore of Tyrone and Armagh as the relentless, merciless embodi-
ment of the loyalist death squads. He is destined to go down in history as one
of the foremost, and certainly one of the most feared, Protestant assassins.

His identity is one of Northern Ireland's many open secrets: his name, as they
say, is known to the dogs in the streets. The town of Portadown, where he
lives, is a small, bitter place where both sets of extremists know each other well.
Sometimes the loyalists paint the names of their intended victims on the walls
of the shabby housing estates. King Rat has accepted his celebrity, or notoriety.
He has given several interviews to newspapers and even television, in which

he spoke frankly about the right of Protestants to take the law into their own hands. He comes across as not particularly bright, and impervious to argument.

The general area has seen more than a score of loyalist killings since 1988. Clearly, a large number of men have been involved in these, but almost all have become linked in the public mind with King Rat. One of the features of the attacks has been a readiness to shoot women: apart from Mrs Fox, two teenage Catholic girls were gunned down in a mobile shop, and a bus carrying Catholic women and children was machine-gunned. Some of the attacks have been indiscriminate, though others have killed people with republican connections. This fact has led to allegations that King Rat and his men have received aid and assistance from the security forces.

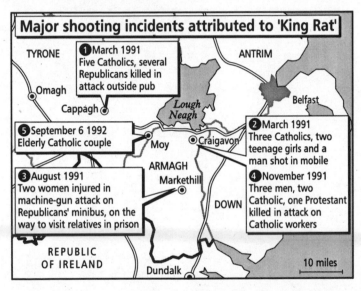

Major shooting incidents attributed to 'King Rat'

TYRONE

① March 1991
Five Catholics, several Republicans killed in attack outside pub

Omagh

Cappagh

ANTRIM

Lough Neagh

Belfast

⑤ September 6 1992
Elderly Catholic couple

Moy

Craigavon

② March 1991
Three Catholics, two teenage girls and a man shot in mobile

ARMAGH

Markethill

③ August 1991
Two women injured in machine-gun attack on Republicans' minibus, on the way to visit relatives in prison

DOWN

④ November 1991
Three men, two Catholic, one Protestant killed in attack on Catholic workers

REPUBLIC OF IRELAND

Dundalk

10 miles

A previous bout of killings produced an earlier icon of violence, a man known locally as the Jackal. The local tabloid press regularly features both King Rat and this older man, who is said to be still active, frequently printing stories which build up their images. Acts of IRA violence are often followed by stories that either King Rat or the Jackal is furious and bent on vengeance.

Republicans in Armagh and Tyrone speak frequently about King Rat and his associates, and they and everyone else know where they live. A number of other loyalist paramilitary figures who have become public personalities have met their deaths at the hands of republicans over the years. King Rat, in a Dublin newspaper interview, acknowledged that he is a marked man: "People are writing stories about me, Catholics, nationalists, left-wingers. I know what they are trying to do. Personally, I'm a dead man. It would be morally wrong to back

131

off. I have to give my life now. I am married, I have kids, but morally I have to lay down my life now. If I was shot dead in the morning, I would laugh in my grave."

The relatives of the victims of King Rat and the other loyalist killers find it hard to understand why he is at large and giving interviews rather than behind bars. He and his associates are, in fact, regularly questioned by the RUC but, almost always, released for lack of evidence that would stand up in court. The same happens with suspected republican terrorists.

Figures like King Rat often remain active for a long time, but most, in the end, either wind up in jail or in an early grave. When their profile becomes so high, as King Rat's has, intense pressure goes on both the police and the IRA to deal with them. The question may be which one will get to him first.

Early 1992 was a black time for Belfast. On 4 February a policeman walked into Sinn Féin offices on the Falls Road, shot dead three men, and later took his own life. The next day there was another blood bath when UDA gunmen opened fire indiscriminately inside a crowded betting shop on the Ormeau Road in south Belfast. Five Catholic men died and another nine were injured, one of them critically. A priest who gave the victims the last rites said it was "too much horror, blood, death, too much for any one day", while a Catholic bishop spoke of an atmosphere of "gloom, death and near-despair" in the city: "The murderers, the arsonists, the bombers are plaguing us, they are plunging us more and more into what seems to be a fathomless pit of agonising darkness."

Tragedy of Ulster's relentless cycle of violence

Distressed women after a loyalist betting-shop attack which killed five Catholic men

BRIAN HARRIS

133

Little knots of women stood on the Ormeau Road, one of Belfast's main thoroughfares, and compared notes on the grim facts of life and death: who had been killed, who had been injured, who had escaped.

Most of the men were silent, wearing that mask of impassivity affected by Belfast onlookers, though one small man, agitated and distressed, wrenched off his glasses, swore, and offered to fight the RUC man who would not let him through the cordon of white tape.

The women displayed their feelings more, taking a local GP by the arm and begging him to come and comfort a woman who had been taken to a nearby house. A relative of hers was said to be dead. The doctor, who has over the years gone through the lexicon of condemnation of those who keep killing his patients, glared angrily towards the bookmaker's, which in a moment of frenzy had come to resemble a butcher's shop.

The relentlessly mounting death toll has had an extremely demoralising effect on the public in Belfast and elsewhere. The week's bloody events, on top of last year's increased death rate, the slaughter of eight workers by the IRA in Tyrone last month, and the huge bombs that have pulverised Belfast, have created an atmosphere of great tension and apprehension.

Both republican and loyalist terrorists display a terrifying appetite for violence. The fact that each new incident brings the near-certainty of retaliation never prevents either side from continuing their campaigns.

Seasoned observers, asked how they gauge the general mood, speak of a sense of hopelessness; of misery piled on misery; of the incessant roadblocks turning Belfast into a war city; of the expectation of both more republican and more loyalist blood-letting; of a community in shock. Scores of roadblocks all over the city have partially paralysed the traffic flow, but they have not broken the cycle of violence. Many people have a sense that things are out of control.

There is also a feeling of *déjà vu*, and the dread of a return to the really bad days of the 1970s when almost 500 people were killed in a single year. One of the real horrors lies in the way paramilitary groups can successfully reproduce themselves: members may come and go, but recruits can always be found who are ready to bomb and shoot people. Individuals may learn and develop and turn away from terrorism, but the organisations themselves never lose their commitment to violence.

On the night of 2 May 1974, a group of us stood on practically the same spot after the bombing of a pub on the same block as the bookie's. Loyalists had thrown a bomb into the Rose and Crown bar, killing six men and injuring a score of others. Witnesses said they had heard laughter from the getaway car as the loyalist gang made their escape. A hospital casualty doctor later told me how she had burst into tears when the doors of an ambulance were opened to reveal a jumble of unrecognisable flesh.

134

Two of the bombers were later caught and given sentences of life imprisonment: both, it turned out, were aged 16 at the time of the bombing. One of them has been released on licence after almost a decade and a half behind bars and is now a very different man, as he told the Belfast *Irish News* in an interview two years ago. He said: "I was recruited into the junior wing of the Ulster Volunteer Force when I was 14. It was a logical step: I had got involved in a number of sectarian riots and fights, beating up a few Catholics.

"When I heard the number killed in the bar I couldn't believe I was responsible for something so drastic. The going rate [for a pub bombing] was usually one or two dead and that somehow gave the situation a sense of normality. A fellow loyalist knew one of the men who died and he said he was a brilliant guy, just a normal Joe Bloggs who enjoyed a drink and a chat. My mother worked with one of the victim's brothers and she said the family were ordinary decent people and in no way sectarian.

"But any doubts were drowned by hatred. We dehumanised the other side and branded them animals. We didn't think in terms of them being people. If we couldn't get the IRA, we would have to slaughter members of the Catholic community, who, after all, seemed to support them."

In jail he gained an honours degree in psychology. He met republicans and found, to his surprise – "There's a lot of decent blokes in the IRA just like there's a lot of decent blokes in loyalist paramilitary groups." He concluded: "When I planted that bomb I wasn't old enough to legally drink or vote. I was a Grange Hill terrorist. I am now 32 years old. Thirteen years of my life have been spent in jail. I will carry the memory of what happened that night in 1974 until the day I die. After all these years of paramilitaries and prisons, a sad reality I've faced is that people must often be hurt or killed before the value of human life is realised."

Those who blasted the bookie's shop may well be caught and in time learn their lesson and come to regret their actions. But it is too late for those who have been killed, and for the bereaved; the pity of Belfast is that so many lessons have to be learnt the hard way.

[The released life prisoner later wrote to thank me for not printing his name. He now works in a community scheme aimed at steering young people away from the paramilitary path that led him to killing and to prison.]

In August 1992 the government reacted to the steadily rising tide of loyalist violence by reversing its 20-year-old policy and banning the largest Protestant paramilitary group. The ban put the Ulster Defence Association on the same basis as the IRA, making membership an offence punishable by up to 10 years' imprisonment. The move brought to an end the anomaly under which the UDA remained a legal organisation while directing an assassination campaign which resulted in the killings of hundreds of Catholics. There was some mystery as to why the government did not respond at some earlier stage to nationalist calls, which stretched back a full two decades, for proscription of the organisation. The move was welcomed by the Irish government and northern nationalists.

The 1990s saw the emergence of a new UDA leadership which the RUC characterised as harder, more aggressive and more ruthless. These Young Turks presided over the killing of 17 people in 1991 and 14 people in the first seven months of 1992. Their apolitical approach removed the argument that keeping the UDA legal might at some stage encourage it to move away from violence.

In the early days the UDA, which began as an amalgam of vigilante groups, had more than 25,000 members and was often said

to be too big to ban. It went into steep
decline from 1977 on, however, and was
tainted by associations with racketeering
and drug-dealing.

Young Turks are blamed for rise in loyalist violence

A briefing document prepared in 1988 for foreign journalists by the Northern Ireland Office contained an extraordinary statement about the Ulster Defence Association. It said: "There is no evidence that it is engaged in organising terrorist attacks." That assertion would be regarded as an astonishing whopper by almost everyone who has closely observed the Troubles and knows anything of the activities of the UDA. It is an indisputable fact that it and the other main loyalist paramilitary group, the Ulster Volunteer Force, have been responsible for the killings of hundreds of people, most of them civilians. The best estimate is that the UDA has killed close to 400 people.

Evidence of UDA involvement in violence is abundant. More than 100 UDA members have been sentenced to life imprisonment for murders committed in an assassination campaign that began on a large scale in 1972 and which still continues. Hundreds more have been jailed for lesser offences. Judges hearing cases involving UDA men have repeatedly denounced it as a terrorist organisation. Those coming before the courts are not junior or fringe members, but senior individuals in its structure. At least four former members of its ruling "inner council" are behind bars.

Earlier this year the trial of Brian Nelson, an agent inserted into the ranks of the UDA by military intelligence, heard evidence that he had been personally recruited by members of the inner council to improve their information on republicans earmarked for assassination.

In private, neither army nor RUC sources – nor the UDA itself – would maintain for a moment that the group was not heavily involved in violence. But the government, as can be seen in the 1988 document, has always preferred to play

137

down its terrorist character. This helps to explain why the UDA remained legal for so long. The government has chosen, especially when addressing foreign audiences, to project the IRA as by far the principal threat to life and order in Northern Ireland, either ignoring the loyalists or presenting them as an essentially reactive sideshow.

In Northern Ireland terms, the police have had much more success in dealing with the UDA and UVF, who are particularly prone to infiltration by informers and agents, than they have had with the IRA. The conviction rate for loyalists is several times that of republicans.

The UDA began life in the early 1970s as an umbrella group of localised vigilante organisations made up of Protestants concerned by growing IRA activity and by nationalist political advances. At its peak it had around 26,000 members, many of whom paraded in paramilitary uniform in the streets of Belfast. Its members ran drinking clubs and took part in some community activity, but by the summer of 1972 it became clear that some of its members, including its leaders, were heavily involved in violence. Today about 20 UDA members are serving life sentences for murders committed in that year.

The numbers involved fell away drastically as the years passed, the organisation contracting geographically into hardline Protestant ghettos in and around Belfast. Its killing rate fell, but the killings never entirely stopped and in recent years they have increased significantly. In both 1989 and 1990 the UDA and UVF together killed 19 people in each year. But in 1991 this rose significantly, the UDA alone killing 17. So far this year it has already killed 14 people, 5 of them in an indiscriminate attack on a Belfast bookie's shop.

It retains a certain amount of community support, but this has tended to fall over the years as the organisation has been linked with drugs and racketeering. Its prestige took a further blow this summer when a well-known UDA member was charged with sexually abusing an underage girl inside UDA headquarters. [He was later convicted.]

The past five years have seen an almost complete removal of the organisation's top leadership: some were jailed, others expelled, and two were killed. The Young Turks who have replaced them are held responsible for the increase in violence. The old guard occasionally dabbled in the political sphere, which meant there was at least a notional possibility that they would one day turn away from violence and into politics and community affairs. But now the rising tide of violence and the emergence of this new apolitical leadership may be the strongest of the factors in persuading the authorities to opt for a ban. The government may well have concluded that since their replacements have shown themselves to be completely uninterested in politics, it is not worth while to keep them legal and thus make it easier to have talks with them at some future stage.

138

6

AFTERMATH OF VIOLENCE

After more than two decades of the Troubles, coping with the casualties of atrocities has almost become routine for Belfast's emergency services. These are interviews with people at the sharp end: an ambulance man who has taken charge at the scenes of atrocities, and five consultants who daily deal with the injured at Belfast's Royal Victoria Hospital. Their stories are told in their own words.

The scars of violence

HARRY WHAN, divisional ambulance officer for the city of Belfast

The first shooting at a bookie's shop in February [where 5 men were killed and nine injured when loyalists sprayed a Catholic betting shop with gunfire] was for us just one incident among very many. The call came into ambulance control and right away it was classed as a multiple shooting, so they mobilised a number of ambulances and myself to the scene. The police stopped the traffic and allowed me to go down a one-way street the wrong way, so I arrived within about three minutes of the initial call.

As incident officer, my first job was to identify myself as the person who was going to take charge of the incident. When something like this happens, there has got to be control at the scene and proper communication and that was my responsibility.

I went in and had a quick look inside the building. The scene was horrific, with bodies everywhere. In that confined space there was a smell from the gunfire and all the bleeding and whatever that you couldn't describe. I identified one of the crews and asked how many, roughly, and he said roughly 15 casualties. I asked the control centre for seven vehicles and asked them to put the hospital on full stand-by for approximately 10 serious casualties and some minor injuries. I then started to co-ordinate the movement of vehicles. I asked one person to do triage and not to treat, triage being identifying who were the priorities among the casualties. The length of time from the moment the call went in until the last live patient left the scene was 21 minutes.

The first person to arrive at casualty ultimately died. The second person went to intensive care. The third person required theatre and then admission, and thereafter the people who arrived were treated at casualty. In other words, the system worked.

I must admit, the first thing I did afterwards was, I rang home. Now it maybe sounds silly, but I just wanted something normal, wanted to get back to reality. But a lot of the crews couldn't do that, because this incident was just one of many. Little Mrs Brown was still tripping and falling and hurting herself on the other side of the city, and needed an ambulance. So control had to keep co-ordinating the shooting but everything else as well, and as soon as I reckoned I didn't need a vehicle, it was made available and gone. Overall, Troubles-related incidents are quite a low percentage of our work.

My heart goes out to those ambulance staff who had to mop their vehicles out and go straight to the next emergency call, because they didn't get the opportunity to get back to normality. Imagine it: you've just dealt with that blood bath, the adrenalin is pumping, and you're suddenly told to hurry up and get your vehicle cleared, there's another emergency call for you.

It has an effect on you as an individual. I get flashbacks to it, I get visions of what was going on. Even now talking about it, I get flashbacks to the original scene as I walked through the door: the smell, the feeling of being there. For other ambulance men it was worse: they were knee-deep in it, dealing with the dead and dying.

Recently we've started to offer stress counselling, where people have a chance to go and discuss what they've dealt with and air their feelings, their fears, their worries. One of the big fears is that maybe you could have saved the life of someone who ultimately died. The stress counselling isn't just Troubles-related. You might require some form of debriefing and counselling after something like an explosion, where there are a lot of very severe injuries and trauma, limbs amputated by the blast and so on. But sometimes the thing that can bring the ambulance man to his knees is something like the child in its own home, that dies in his arms.

CASUALTY: LAWRENCE ROCKE, consultant in accident and emergency medicine

There are always cases that you remember a long time, particular ones that stick in your mind, like the Abercorn bomb [an IRA device exploded in a crowded Belfast café in 1972, killing and injuring women and children]. It was a Saturday afternoon.

Down around the resuscitation room there were five patients, all girls, all late teens or early twenties, and every one of them had lost at least one limb, some of them more than that. They were stabilised and went to theatre, and I went down there to help out. That was 20 years ago; but it's something that I will never forget.

I started here as a houseman in August 1971, the exact month the killings really started in earnest, so the Troubles have been going on for all my working life and some of my student life. The vast majority of the work is entirely unrelated to the Troubles, though they probably do have a disproportionate effect.

I remember a couple of bombs when you got a lot of patients in and you had to use this principle of triage to sort people into categories – people who were critical and needed immediate treatment, people who could wait for a while and people who, though they were technically still alive, had injuries that were clearly not survivable.

Nowadays most people coming in here have been shot, and if there's any evidence that they're alive, then you do what you can. Sometimes it works and sometimes it doesn't.

There have been some terrible days and terrible nights in here, when we've been operating and amputating right until dawn. Then again, people can be incredibly lucky. I remember a taxi driver who was shot by a man who stepped out in front of the taxi and went bang, bang, bang through the window. He was shot between the eyes, twice. The first bullet went slightly downwards, just skirted underneath his brain, and was sitting at the back of his neck. The second bullet had gone in, hit the bone and stopped – it didn't even damage his eye. When he came in he was talking to us, and he has survived very well.

Another guy came in who had been shot in the back of the head; they said he was an informer. The bullet hit his skull, and either he had a very thick skull or maybe it was an old bullet, but it just made a dent in his skull and lodged there. He's OK.

It's incredible how lucky they can be, but by the same token people can be unlucky. People can be shot in places where you might, nine times out of ten, expect them to survive. But they don't, maybe because the bullet happens to hit a major blood vessel or you get catastrophic bleeding that can't be controlled or whatever.

There's a difference in dealing with the relatives of Troubles casualties. As well as the grief, the inevitable grief, there's often an element of anger and frustration. It's nearly always somebody who is young, who has been fit and healthy with a normal life expectancy, and that makes it more difficult. Very often the family arrive here to find that the relative is already dead, and it's dreadful for them. And there's more of an emotional element for the doctors and nurses concerned because it just seems so absolutely needless and pointless. At the time you're just reacting and doing your job. It's only afterwards, when you're driving home, that you think how totally futile it all is.

I don't know how these people can do it, and keep on doing it. There are times when I really cannot comprehend how one individual can do something like that to another person, no matter who they are or who they perceive them to be. I just don't understand it.

HEAD INJURIES: DERMOT BYRNES, consultant in neurosurgery

One man I remember had been hit in the head, and he was life-and-death for a few days. A lot of his frontal lobe was damaged, but it was far enough forward to spare his motor areas, so his limbs and speech and memory were all right. He's a bit sluggish, but apart from that he doesn't seem to have any deficits
142

at all. But then there's another man, who was just thumped a bit and ordered out of the district. He didn't suffer much physically but the poor guy has never recovered from the fact that he had to move, under violent conditions, from the house where he'd lived for most of his life. Physically he's fine, but he has a lot of psychological scars and I doubt if he'll ever get over it.

Nowadays the Troubles don't impact on our department the way they did in the early seventies. One reason is that, tragically, a lot of assassination attempts are now successful, instantly, because they're often directed at the head.

In the seventies it was virtually every night. We used to stand at the door of the department and cock an ear, and if there was a lot of shooting the registrar on call would just stay in the hospital. The Royal is in the middle of the Falls [Road], so if you went home you might not be able to get back in because of the location.

We learnt a lot as the Troubles went on. Many of these gunshot victims originally looked not too bad, but within half an hour they would deteriorate rapidly. We had to become very slick in terms of resuscitation. It became clear that it wasn't possible to examine the patient at your leisure and work out what was needed. Traditional medicine required diagnosis and then treatment, but that began to reverse. You had to do the treatment before diagnosis, because there wasn't time to wait to work out all the extent of the injuries. We made step-by-step advances, not dramatic breakthroughs. There was no Monday morning when we changed the face of modern neurosurgery; but each week that passed we learnt that bit more. We also learnt the ones that you were wasting your time on, too, that has to be said.

In American cities injuries caused by the handgun, the low-velocity weapon, are common as mud. But in Belfast we have high-velocity rifles being used, and that's very different: they can have 25 times as much energy as revolvers and can be much more devastating. So here, for the first time, we had battle-field weapons being used on the streets outside a university hospital, which was unique.

It angers me as a member of the community, the fact that I am trying to undo something that has been deliberately done by somebody else. I think if the terrorists knew what a delicate, wonderful piece of equipment the body is, I would hope they'd never do it again. The destruction that they wreak on a delicate and incredible machine, and the fact that it can't be fixed, that saddens me.

CHEST WOUNDS: JIM MCGUIGAN, consultant thoracic surgeon

There was one chap who was knocking on the door of a house when a bomb went off and the door collided with him. You can see on his chest the number

27 and you can see a door knocker and you can see a letter box, all tattooed on his chest. This looked awful, but actually we were able to send him home in a few days. With explosions it tends to be that either you're blown to bits, if you're right beside the bomb, or it can be minor.

Some people have the assumption that a high-velocity bullet going through the chest would just blow the lung to pieces, but our experience has been totally the reverse of this. We've seen lots of bullets go straight through the lung and do very little injury: of 53 gunshot wounds to the chest, a lot of them high-velocity, we had only one death. In the case of one chap, the bullet went very close to the big artery to the lung but didn't disrupt it, and went straight past all the critical structures. He actually wasn't that badly injured. I remember great big planks of wood going through guys' chests, with very little injury. Sometimes what looks like an absolutely horrific injury is survivable: they're not always as bad as you think.

Here in Belfast we're known as a bunch of hawks, because we would tend to operate on about 80 per cent of the gunshot wounds to the chest. In England they don't tend to do that, so we're seen as aggressive. We think we can prevent a lot of the long-term problems of chronic shortness of breath and repeated infections and all the rest by getting in and getting the whole thing cleaned up quickly. We also think that by doing that we can all relax a bit because we know exactly what's going on inside. In the US a lot of these handgun wounds to the chest are treated conservatively, they don't open the chest at all. We can clean out properly any clotted blood and infected material that's in there and repair any holes in the lung, which we think decreases the chance of infection.

These cases are distressing, extremely distressing. I hate it. A lot of us are being stressed by these situations. You spend your days explaining to people with lung cancer that they can't have an operation, then you spend your nights seeing kids of 18 and 19 shot through the chest. I find talking to the relatives very stressful, very difficult. The relatives are wonderful, they're super, you'd be amazed. I don't know how it happens but sometimes they end up comforting us rather than the other way around.

In the seventies there were far more horrendous injuries coming to us: I suppose a certain amount of amateurism in the terrorist organisations was responsible for that. Now you know how cold-blooded these killers are today — they'll knock somebody over with a shotgun and then go and shoot them in the head as well. How they can do that, I just don't know. I don't understand how anyone can do that to fellow human beings.

INTENSIVE CARE: DENNIS COPPELL, consultant in intensive care

People think that shooting is all that happens in Northern Ireland, but in fact in each year more people have died on the road than from violence. Apart from one year, the Troubles has never been more than 10 per cent of our work.

I've been at it for 22 years now, and Troubles cases don't particularly affect me any more. They did at the beginning, when I lived through the Abercorn bombing and other terrible explosions. It did have a psychological impact and sometimes I couldn't sleep at night. I think it was mainly seeing young people whose lives were in danger through no fault of their own and who, if they did survive, were going to be severely disabled. I still see some of these patients, meeting them socially or getting messages from them, and I remember them very clearly – who they are and what was wrong with them. I remember them better than the car crashes, because there are a lot more of the car accidents, whereas the shootings and the bombings are a smaller group, much more dramatic, with a higher profile. Very many more people die or have their lives devastated in car crashes.

In gunshot cases, if they're shot in the head, that is usually bad news and at least 50 per cent will die, more if it's high-velocity. Chest injuries, especially low-velocity ones, have a much better chance of survival. But if you get shot in the abdomen, in the gut, and it goes through the bowel, the mortality is still very high despite surgery, despite antibiotics, despite intensive care.

Bombing injuries can be quite deceptive. Some patients have obvious injuries, like loss of limbs or wounds that are bleeding, and you know what you've got to deal with. But I've seen patients that have died when they only seemed to have flash burns, because they had internal injuries in the chest or the abdomen because of the pressure that is generated by the explosions. One of the main lessons we have learnt is that someone who has been in a bomb explosion may need to be admitted to hospital and observed for these other injuries.

When a bomb has gone off we've sometimes had 100 patients arriving in Accident and Emergency. Ninety per cent of them are only shaken and confused and they don't know where they are, and in a couple of hours they can go home. You've got to be able to sort them out and find the ones who need to stay.

KNEE-CAPPINGS: JOHN HOOD, consultant vascular surgeon and clinical director of surgery

The so-called knee-capping is a very barbaric form of punishment, with a sort of severity scale to it. The most common is being shot in both knees, then there's being shot in both knees and both ankles. And then most severe is both knees, both ankles and both elbows. We haven't had very many of these, probably no more than two or three. One of these chaps, I remember, ended up in a very bad way, with a stiff arm and a hand that is now next to useless.

145

Knee-capping is the most common type of Troubles injury that I see. It has been going nearly since the start of the Troubles – the first one I remember was in 1974. In my department we see about 15 per cent of the punishment shootings, who are the most serious cases. Since 1979 we have had around 400 of them, but there have been only three amputations that I'm aware of in this hospital. That's less than 1 per cent.

Over the years there have been significant advances in the treatment of these injuries. In the Vietnam War the amputation rate for people with damage to blood vessels behind the knee was around 20 per cent, while in the Korean War it was well over 50 per cent, so you can see the improvement.

We deal with the whole range of vascular injuries as a result of the Troubles. The commonest by far is the punishment shooting with a handgun, then the next most common are shotgun wounds at pretty close range. They provide very different problems because there's an awful lot of soft tissue loss, and you can have multiple injuries because of the pellets. The victims are nearly always young men in their late teens or twenties. They're usually very frightened and in some degree of pain and shock. Nowadays a lot of them are home after a week to 10 days, but it's certainly not something that the victim forgets. Yet we've had a number who have been knee-capped on two occasions and a few who have had it three times.

I remember the night the Troubles really started. I was a final-year medical student and all these people were arriving with gunshot wounds, something we had never seen before. Three of us volunteered to go to a first-aid station and we ended up in a church hall down the Falls. We were really green. There was burning all around and you could actually see the tracer bullets flying up and down the street. We got back to the hospital at five in the morning, as dawn was breaking, lying flat on the bottom of the ambulance. A lot of the Falls was smouldering: that made a big impression on me, it was so incredible. Nobody thought then that after all these years we'd still be patching up the victims of the violence.

Loyalist and republican groups may differ in many respects, but both kill people and destroy families. The grief of widows is just the same – just as touching, just as heart-rending – no matter who kills their husbands.

Some areas have been so scarred during two decades of violence that it is difficult to imagine their wounds ever healing. Individual families, and in some cases whole communities, have been savagely damaged by the violence. Every part of Northern Ireland has been touched, but some in particular have suffered a concentrated and apparently endless stream of deaths. There are places where the hooded gunman returns regularly and relentlessly to claim victim after victim, leaving shattered families in his wake.

Different areas are affected in different ways. Along the border many Protestant communities have lost people as the IRA picks off isolated members of the security forces. Some little country churchyards hold more than half a dozen graves of members of the Ulster Defence Regiment and Royal Ulster Constabulary. Tightly knit communities are devastated by loss on such a scale. The IRA insists that those men were killed not because of their religion but because they wore the uniforms of British forces. But most Protestants in these areas are unshakeable in their belief that the IRA acts from a sectarian rather than a political motive. Community relations are further damaged by the belief that the killers strike from across the border on the basis of information supplied by local Catholics.

Many miles away in the Catholic ghettos of north Belfast, it is Protestant gunmen who have wreaked most havoc, generally among the civilian population. Here there is almost total segregation of the working class, but although a number of huge peace lines slice through the streets to keep the two sides apart, the area's patchwork quilt of Protestant, Catholic and mixed enclaves affords the gunmen easy access to their prey. Hundreds have been killed, sometimes in the most barbaric ways.

The murders leave behind families which are cut to the heart. The two widows interviewed here felt the authorities did not care enough about the plight of the vulnerable. They had very different perspectives, being separated by distance, religion and politics. But in the end their situations are the same. The gunman has bestowed on them and their families an equality of misery, grief and irrevocable loss.

Divided by religion but united in their grief

Kathleen Finlay is a small, dark woman who is welcoming to those who call at her spotlessly clean tidy bungalow near the hamlet of Victoria Bridge, not far from the border in west Tyrone. She has two children: Brian, who is ten, and Andrew, just turned three. Until last month she also had a husband, Ronnie, a 47-year-old farm labourer who had retired from the Ulster Defence Regiment three years earlier. The IRA said little about his killing, but the word in republican circles is that they had not realised he had left the UDR. His death was "all a mistake". Such reports do not change Mrs Finlay's view that he was shot, not because of any security force connection, but solely because of his religion.

Mrs Finlay is nervous and fidgety. The visitor knows she has been through a lot; yet nothing quite prepares for her account of the horror which last month befell her family.

"We left for work as usual, as a family. I always dropped Ronnie off at the farm, with the children in the back. He got out of the car and he spoke in to us again, and said to Brian about work – we always give him work to do every day for his 11-plus. He said to Brian, 'You have your work finished for this evening', and then he said goodbye. He'd just straightened himself, just closed the car door, when there was a noise. I couldn't relate to it as being a gunshot. I could see that Ronnie was trying to balance himself, you know, keep himself upright on his feet.

"And I thought, something has happened to you, and I looked all round but I couldn't see anything. I got out of the car and was making my way round to him. He had fallen at this stage. I thought he had taken a heart attack or something, because I could see nothing around. But just as I was about to go to him there was this burst of automatic fire, and I knew immediately that we were under attack and what they were at.

"And all I can remember then is being back in the car and trying to force

149

DAVID ROSE

Kathleen Finlay, whose Protestant husband died at the hands of the IRA

my children down onto the floor of the car, to protect them. Andrew, my youngest, he clung to me and in that moment I thought, I've got to get them to the farmhouse for protection.

"As I ran to the house with Andrew in my arms, this gunman confronted me and told me to get back. I don't remember ever coming back to the car, but I remember then standing beside it and shielding Andrew between the car and myself. The gunman stood at my right-hand side with his gun trained on me.

"And then they just pumped Ronnie with automatic fire, with the children there, and they made their getaway. And I just walked about three-quarters of a mile for help. My legs were all punctured with shrapnel, streaming with blood.

"Brian was hysterical, Andrew was OK. I tried to carry him and pull him after me, and tried to be as cool and calm as I could, for Brian's sake. He was asking about getting a doctor and getting help for his dad. I just tried to reassure him as best I could at that stage, but I knew the worst had happened.

"I raised the alarm and phoned several people, and came back to the farm-yard again. The ambulance was there when I got back. After that I just left and came home. There was nothing I could do."

A copy of the Good News Bible sits in Mrs Finlay's living room. Ronnie was rector's churchwarden at the local parish church, helping with the hymn books, the alms dishes and the bell. Mrs Finlay has taken over that post from her husband. She says he was a hard-working, honest and decent family man. As we talk a relative, Carol, brings coffee and biscuits. Carol was married to Ronnie's brother, Winston, who was a police reservist. He too was shot by the IRA, gunned down before her eyes four years ago.

Kathleen Finlay, slight, vulnerable, deeply hurt, feels let down by the British government. Her family and that of her late husband both have a tradition of serving in the security forces. "When Winston was killed, Ronnie and I were both very angry. But we felt we could not vent our anger, we had to respect law and order. He learnt to accept it and get on with his life. Ronnie was the 14th Protestant from this community to be murdered in the past eight years. No one has been apprehended or brought to book. You do be angry, really angry, at the fact that no one ever seems to be caught for all these cold, callous and premeditated murders in our area. You have such a sense of frustration that you can't see anything being done.

"I believe that the government should have a sense of duty to the law-abiding citizens of this part of the United Kingdom. All our married life we have lived under threat, just because we support the legitimate government. I want people in Britain to see the plight of the ordinary decent citizen here who has striven, just like people on the mainland, to play an honourable and decent role in society and in their community. We have served loyally through the generations, but people in Britain look at us as if we weren't part of the United Kingdom."

Ronnie Finlay served in the Ulster Defence Regiment for 18 years, but on the day he was gunned down he was a civilian, having left the force in 1988. The family's view is that he was shot not because of any security force connec-tion but because of his religion. According to Mrs Finlay: "To Andrew and Brian and me Ronnie was everything that was good and true in life. I think they saw that, and they wanted to smash a good Protestant family."

Three-year-old Andrew is coping well, she says, but Brian has been much changed by his experience. "He's ten and a half, he's at a very impressionable age. He's a different boy; he's scared. He's practically my shadow at the minute, he's just finding it hard to cope.

"That morning and what happened dominates your thoughts. You do your best, especially for them. You have to be strong, you have to keep going. I believe they want to smash me as well, emotionally, but we can't let them do that. We must strive for what is good and true in life, really, and we want to be supported by our government and those in authority to help us achieve that aim."

The north Belfast street Maura McDaid lives in is completely Catholic. One end of it, which gives on to a Protestant area, is walled in to keep the two sides apart. The district has seen many shootings and disturbances. Her children, 12-year-old Tracy and 10-year-old Patricia, play outside in a street which at the moment is peaceful.

Mrs McDaid is small and dark. Sometimes she manages a smile but at other times tears well in her eyes as she speaks. She keeps a tissue handy. We sit in her cosy front room because she cannot bear the living room where the life of her husband Terence, a 30-year-old bricklayer, came to a violent end one night in May 1988.

"We were in the house with Terry's mother and father, who always came round on a Tuesday night. Tracy and Patricia had their juice and their biscuits and we had our tea. I said to them, 'Say night-night to Daddy and Nanny and Granda and get to bed because you've to get up for school in the morning.'

"I put them into their bunks. I normally say their prayers with them but that night I didn't. I said, 'Say a quick Hail Mary and go to sleep quickly, I'm away down to Nanny and Granda.'

"Soon after I went downstairs and sat down, there was this horrendous thundering noise, it was a terrible noise. It didn't sound like a door opening. Terry and I just sat and stared at one another. At that, the living-room door flew back to the wall. Two men were standing at the door, they were completely clothed, there was no flesh to be seen. They ran in and just started firing. They just kept shooting round the room. It was totally deafening. I screamed at them to get out, get out. I shouted, 'There's nobody here, there's nobody here, go away, go away, stop it, stop it, stop it.'

"I turned and grabbed the hose of the vacuum cleaner and I hit one of them on his left arm. His hands went down, but then he brought the gun back up and put it to my head. I can still remember looking down that hole. He fired two shots: how he missed I'll never know. I threw my hands over my head and I went down onto the settee.

Maura McDaid, whose Catholic husband was killed by loyalists

"All this time there was firing going on in the room. I jumped off the settee and got up in between the two gunmen, but Terry screamed to me that they had got him and I turned round. As I turned, they shot him twice in the chest. At that, they ran out of the room.

"The children were screaming at the top of the stairs, they were hysterical. I rang for an ambulance. I could see one bullet wound at the back of Terry's neck, just a very small round hole. He wasn't bleeding badly, but he had already started to lose consciousness. I just told him not to panic, that he'd be OK, that I'd called an ambulance, that he'd be all right.

"Terry was shot seven times. The house, from the front door to the back, was just completely black with forensic dust and the smell of gunpowder. It was really, really horrible, and there were bullet holes everywhere.

"The next morning, I was up at half six and tried to clean the house before the children would see it, tried to get the black all off and get rid of the gunpowder smell. My sister and I got buckets of water and kept washing. But it just wasn't our house any more.

"When they brought Terry home the children had never seen anybody dead before, and Tracy constantly wanted him out of the coffin. You see, that night, just after the shooting, she had heard somebody saying Terry was still breathing. She said, 'But Mummy, I heard them saying my daddy was still breathing. Would you put him on the chair and see would he breathe?'"

Mrs McDaid says, and security sources confirm, that her husband was not involved with any paramilitary organisation and was an innocent victim. For more than a year, Mrs McDaid believed her husband had been shot simply because he was a Catholic. But then information emerged to put the killing in a different light. It came out, through court proceedings and subsequent journalistic enquiries, that classified security documents had reached loyalist terrorists. The real target may have been one of Terence's brothers, who was a republican and who resembled him closely. But it seems the wrong address was given on a security document: the killing of Terence McDaid, like that of Ronnie Finlay, was all a mistake.

In 1989 a corporal in the Royal Scots and a woman member of the UDR admitted passing the documents to extreme loyalists, and were given 18-month suspended sentences. The UDR woman resigned, though the Scottish corporal was allowed to remain in the army as a training instructor in England. Mrs McDaid was shocked: "I cannot find the words to describe what that does to me – that a soldier in a British uniform helped lead to the death of an innocent man and was given a suspended sentence for it. How he can be training other soldiers is beyond me. If that's justice, I give up. If that's British justice, there's no such thing as it."

Meanwhile, a man has been charged with her husband's murder. A court has already been told that the man, a west Belfast Protestant, was an army agent for more than 10 years. Mrs McDaid is anxious to find out more. [More information about the background to the killing of Terence McDaid emerged later. See p. 164; "Army defends 'brave' agent", pp. 165–8; and "Thin dividing line in secret world of army agents", pp. 168–71.]

She finds it hard to help her children come to terms with the loss of their father while coping with her own grief. "Something I discovered recently is that there's actually no support group or help-line for children who lose their father like this, apart from getting them psychiatric treatment. There should be something for them. I'm so badly scarred and hurt by it that I can't deal with them and they can't deal with me, in the sense that they don't want to hurt me by saying anything. Patricia can be very withdrawn. She was Daddy's girl, always sat beside him – nobody was as tall as her daddy, there was nobody in this world like her daddy. Sometimes she just comes home and sits in this room and stares into space. Some days now she seems like a normal, happy wee girl, but those days are few and far between. They used to sit beside their daddy, one on each arm of his chair. I just thank God they weren't there when he was shot."

7

COLLUSION
CONTROVERSIES

In the early 1990s information emerged to
shed much new light on the murky world
of intelligence and infiltration of loyalist
paramilitary groups. The story emerged
slowly in stages, and the whole tale has
almost certainly not yet been told.

It had been known for many years that
information reached violent Protestant
groups from within the security forces.
This was demonstrated in a number of
court cases, and, indeed, loyalist sources
had made little secret of their access to
police and military material. A major
political controversy developed when the
Ulster Defence Association showed
security force material to a BBC reporter in
support of its claim that one of its victims
was in the IRA.

Security leak puts credibility of RUC and army at risk

Loyalist sources have often claimed to journalists that despite appearances, many of the Catholics killed by the UDA and UVF appear on police and military lists of suspects. On a number of occasions in the 1970s security force documents were shown to reporters in Belfast. Nonetheless, the available evidence fails to support the assertion that most – or even a substantial proportion – of those killed by loyalists have had strong republican connections. Since 1969 loyalists have been responsible for roughly 700 deaths, amounting to one quarter of all those killed. Around 90 per cent of all loyalist victims were civilians.

An analysis of the most recent loyalist killings shows that the evidence for increased selectivity is inconclusive. Thirty-seven people have been killed by loyalists since the beginning of 1988, and only three of these were acknowledged members of the IRA. Another was lawyer Pat Finucane, while a fifth was a Sinn Féin councillor, John Joe Davey. Two others were not IRA members, but were shot while attending an IRA funeral; another was the brother of a Sinn Féin councillor; another was the father of two sons who are republicans. Three were the victims of internal loyalist disputes, and four killings were clearly mistakes. Seven victims were simply shot at random. Of the remaining fourteen, loyalist sources claim eleven had IRA connections and three had associations with the INLA. None of these was given a republican funeral and none was claimed by these organisations as a member.

It remains possible, however, that some were active republicans, since the IRA does not always claim those killed as members. One example of this was the loyalist killing of William Carson in north Belfast in 1979: he was not acknowledged as an IRA member and for years was presumed by many to have been the victim of a straightforward sectarian assassination. Today, however, he appears on the IRA's "roll of honour" as one of its dead members. Nonetheless, many of the 14 alleged to be active republicans appear on the face of it to make unlikely IRA or INLA activists, and the limited information given in inquests often throws little light on the facts of any alleged republican involvement.

Security force montages of republican suspects, obtained by loyalists and sent to the *Independent*

It is also clearly the case that loyalist extremists, whatever the information available to them, often regard Catholics in general, rather than republicans in particular, as the enemy. Thus they continue to carry out acts which are completely indiscriminate, such as the machine-gunning of a bar in which three men died last year.

In other instances the fact that someone is believed to be related to an active republican has been enough to seal their fate. Others killed have served jail sentences in the 1970s but appear to have been inactive at the time of their deaths. And in other cases the security force information may be inaccurate in itself or may be out of date when acted upon. Last year, for example, a Catholic man shot in his north Belfast home was killed in error for another man who had lived in the house but had moved out more than a year earlier.

The collusion controversy brought much political debate on the record of the Ulster Defence Regiment.

31 AUGUST 1989   THE INDEPENDENT

Previous conduct leaves regiment under suspicion

The chequered record of the UDR has meant that its members have traditionally been prime suspects for leakages of information to loyalist terrorist groups. Sixteen are serving life sentences for murder while another seven have been convicted of manslaughter. Most of the offences were of a sectarian nature. In addition, it is estimated that more than 100 in all have been jailed for serious offences, including passing on information to loyalist organisations.

The 6,400-strong regiment once had a sizeable number of Catholics in its ranks but the percentage has now dwindled to around 3 per cent, leaving it with an overwhelmingly Protestant membership. For more than a decade it has

159

been a controversial force, with nationalists complaining that its members have acted in a sectarian manner both on and off duty.

The regiment's defenders say that the vast majority of UDR men and women join the force to play their part in the battle against terrorism, pointing out that 180 of its members have been killed while serving, with another 49 former members killed after retiring.

Its critics complain of harassment of Catholics at vehicle checkpoints and allege UDR involvement in recent loyalist violence. The UDR itself has acknowledged that loyalist infiltration has been a problem, and has made periodic efforts to tighten its vetting procedures.

But allegations against the regiment and court appearances by its members are a regular feature in Northern Ireland newspapers, serving as continual reminders that in some quarters the regiment is viewed in a decidedly sinister light. Scores of its members have been convicted of rioting, robbery, possession of firearms and many other offences. UDR men have figured in some of the most notorious incidents of loyalist violence. One of the Shankill Butchers, a UVF gang that killed up to a dozen Catholics with knives in the late 1970s, was a member of the regiment at the time. Two UDR NCOs, a sergeant and a lance corporal, received record sentences for their part in the Miami Showband massacre, when three members of a Dublin-based pop group were killed in a bomb and gun attack in 1975. They were sentenced to life imprisonment, the judge recommending that they serve at least 35 years each.

Some military sources argue that any cross section of the community will have its bad apples, pointing out that only a tiny proportion of the more than 30,000 men and women who have passed through the UDR's ranks have been in trouble with the law. One soldier said privately: "Look, a lot of other regiments in the army, if you totted up their activities in Germany and Hong Kong, would have a much worse record than the UDR, especially some of the Scottish regiments."

The critics respond that security forces in such a sensitive situation as Northern Ireland must aim for the highest of standards, and contend that the UDR, instead of being part of the solution, has become part of the problem.

The collusion issue demonstrated the extent of Britain's reliance, for security purposes, on the Protestants of Northern Ireland.

The Dirty Harry syndrome

M embers of police forces all over the world are prone to the Dirty Harry syndrome – the notion that they are justified in breaking the law in order to uphold it. It is an occupational hazard that policemen will become frustrated with seeing those they know – or think they know – to be criminals or terrorists walking free.

Critics of English police forces claim that this belief can give rise to the framing of suspects, with unscrupulous officers planting evidence or inventing, distorting or forcibly extracting confessions. The belief is widespread in Ireland that English police have been guilty of such tactics in some celebrated cases involving Irish people.

The long-haul security strategy in Northern Ireland can intensify the frustration. With internment ruled out, the only way to put terrorists behind bars is by producing evidence that will stand up in court. The courts themselves have been changed almost beyond recognition, yet they remain an imperfect mechanism for dealing with terrorism. The additional complicating factor here is political. Until 1972 Britain administered Northern Ireland via Unionism, with a Protestant government at Stormont keeping order by means of the exclusively Protestant B Specials and a predominantly Protestant RUC. Ever since Stormont collapsed, the government has been hopeful of bringing it back – though this time, crucially, with a partnership government involving both communities. The principal reason why it has not managed to accomplish this is the continuing resistance of Protestants, in particular working-class Protestants, to the idea of sharing power with Catholics. Successive Northern Ireland Secretaries of State and their aides have privately fulminated against the unreasonableness of the Protestant working class. But the irony is that the authorities are, in the security field, heavily dependent on that section of opinion which they regard as politically obstructive.

There are around 30,000 members of the security forces in Northern Ireland, of which 11,000 are regular army. The other 19,000 are members of the RUC and UDR, forces which are more than 90 per cent Protestant. This means that 64 per cent of the security forces are locally recruited, almost all of them from the Unionist community. This percentage has risen over the years as the

161

authorities have sought to "Ulsterise" the conflict: back in 1973 locals made up only 47 per cent of security force numbers. The trend is also evident in the casualty figures. In 1972, 70 per cent of security personnel fatalities were regular troops. Today more than 70 per cent of those killed are RUC and UDR men. In other words, a large part of the war against the IRA is carried on by Protestants in uniform.

Most of these have little but contempt for loyalist paramilitary organisations, whose actions have been tainted with gangsterism and a savagery which has often surpassed that of the IRA. But at the same time most of those 19,000 are drawn from the same manpower pool – the Protestant working class – which supplies the paramilitary groups with their recruits. An unknown percentage of that 19,000 has clearly been prepared to collude with the assassins. The problem is obviously one of scale – any group of 19,000 is bound to contain some renegades – but it also has its roots in the Ulster Protestant's singular view of the nature of law and order.

Northern Ireland itself came into being as a direct result of a threatened revolt by Protestants in 1912. When home rule for Ireland seemed to be on the cards, the Unionists of the north-east organised an Ulster Volunteer Force, tens of thousands strong and armed with 25,000 rifles smuggled in from Germany. Although their leaders stressed their readiness to act outside the law to oppose a united Ireland, conflict with Britain was averted when the First World War broke out. Much of the UVF joined the army *en bloc*, becoming the 36th (Ulster) Division, thousands of them dying at the Somme. After the war many of them joined the RUC and B Specials.

This confusion of legality and illegality has been built into the Protestant psyche, and the concept that a higher cause can excuse actions outside the law remains in the Unionist folk memory. It can be seen in the minds of those who collude: their belief is that the fight against the IRA – and Irish nationalism in general – can properly be carried on both within and outside the law.

The current controversy has galvanised the authorities into taking urgent measures, and a tightening of procedures, some sackings, and perhaps prosecutions may follow. But the basic fact will remain unchanged: so long as the authorities look to the Ulster Protestant to provide most of the security manpower, the security forces themselves will inevitably display some of the distinctive characteristics of the Protestant community.

The prolonged collusion controversy led the RUC to call in an English police officer to investigate the issue. The job went to John Stevens, who was then Deputy Chief Constable of Cambridgeshire and later became Chief Constable of Northumbria.

After experiences such as the Stalker affair, hopes were not high that the inquiry would get to the bottom of the matter. The Stevens report, published in May 1990, concluded that many documents had been leaked to loyalists, but that only a small number of security force personnel was involved. The abuse was said to be neither widespread nor institutionalised. The most important consequence of the Stevens inquiry, however, was something not mentioned in the report: the unearthing of a small, insignificant man who was at the centre of an extraordinary web of infiltration, spying, and manipulation.

That man was Brian Nelson, a key figure in UDA intelligence-gathering. It turned out that for years he had also functioned as a British army agent. Detectives working for John Stevens had him arrested and charged with possessing documents likely to be of use to terrorists. The move sent UDA leaders into a near-panic, for Nelson was the organisation's chief intelligence collator in Belfast. His job was to co-ordinate a large mass of material, much of it leaked from security force members, on

163

suspected republicans and IRA members. He was right at the heart of the organisation, and early on word leaked out that he was co-operating with the Stevens team.

The arrest also caused major waves within the security apparatus, for Nelson had been a valued Military Intelligence agent whose services were rendered useless when he was picked up. It was evident that he had been involved in extensive illegalities, but a major high-level debate ensued on whether or not he should be brought to court.

The *Independent*, believing the issues involved to be of major public importance, carried extensive reports on the case even before it came to court. It was not until June 1991 that Nelson, then aged 43, was charged with thirty-four offences, including two of murder. His trial eventually opened in January 1992. He originally denied all charges, but when he reached court a last-minute legal trade-off saw the crown drop two murder charges in return for guilty pleas on lesser charges. (One of the murder charges related to Terence McDaid, whose widow was interviewed on pp. 152–5.)

The trial brought an unusual development – the appearance in the witness box, in open court, of a senior

Military Intelligence officer. Called as a
defence witness, the officer, who was not
named, was introduced as a former head
of Military Intelligence in Northern Ireland.
He said Nelson had put country before
family and continually risked his own life
for the lives of others.

The colonel, a bald-headed man with a
Scottish accent, gave the first detailed
military perspective on the controversial
affair.

---

30 JANUARY 1992   THE INDEPENDENT

Army defends
"brave" agent

The colonel, who commanded Military Intelligence in Northern Ireland from 1986 to 1989, said that in January 1987 they had reviewed their current agent coverage and identified a gap in surveillance of loyalist paramilitaries. They had decided to re-recruit Brian Nelson, who had been an agent in the past and was then living in Germany. Nelson had been flown to Heathrow and there agreed to return to Belfast to infiltrate the UDA, at a salary of £200 per week. The witness explained: "He was not paid by results. That is a singularly ineffective way of running agents." He agreed with Nelson's counsel, Desmond Boal QC, that this was less than he had been earning in a good job in Germany.

The colonel said the difficulty was that they wanted inside knowledge, but did not want Nelson to get involved in the UDA murder gangs. They therefore decided to infiltrate him into the organisation's intelligence structure.

Military Intelligence had run him as an agent, passing on information in all cases to senior RUC Special Branch officers at regional and headquarters levels, he added. Asked about guidelines on the behaviour of agents, the colonel said there were no laid-down guidelines to the situation in Northern Ireland. There were Home Office guidelines, but these, in his opinion, were more appropriate to dealing with the criminal fraternity in the East End of London. Agents were not supposed to break the law, but in Northern Ireland this could not be observed, since agents had to join terrorist groups. Military Intelligence had to get Nelson into a position where he had the confidence and trust of his associates, and where he would be privy to life-saving information on potential UDA targets.

Once in the organisation, the UDA had given Nelson a large amount of material, which included hundreds of documents from all sections of the security forces, together with the UDA's own documents. He had taken this to Military Intelligence, who photocopied it and gave it back to him. He had later passed on copies of other documents as the UDA acquired them. At one stage Nelson had transferred his documents from his home to another house which was thought to be safer. Military Intelligence had facilitated the transfer by making sure he had a secure passage.

As senior intelligence officer, he had to obey the orders of his UDA superiors: when they asked for someone's photograph or address, obviously he would give it to them, though later he would tell the army. He met his handler on a regular basis, usually around once a week. Between 1985 and 1990 Military Intelligence had produced, on Brian Nelson's information, something like 730 reports of threats to the lives of 217 separate individuals. Only three of these had been killed by loyalist paramilitaries.

The colonel said Nelson had been a prolific provider of intelligence, supplying a great deal of information of life-saving potential. A number of people owed their lives to him, including some well-known personalities, one of whom was Sinn Féin president Gerry Adams. Nelson had been in a particularly hazardous situation, possibly facing brutal interrogation and equally brutal death. Ninety-five per cent of the time he was on his own, seeing handlers only a few hours a week. "He was, to quote a cliché, out in the cold," the colonel said. He was a courageous man in a very difficult position: "It's not surprising, certainly not surprising to me, that he didn't get it right all the time." He was bound to make mistakes and undoubtedly he had, but they were all very understandable. "There is absolutely no doubt in my mind that he was not loyal to the UDA. He was loyal to the army. His prime motivation was to save life, to help bring down paramilitary organisations. He was a soldier by tradition, we shouldn't forget that, and he wanted to continue to be a soldier."

His reports were regarded as accurate and of high value. The information was circulated to senior army, RUC, security and political figures. Asked by the judge why Nelson had provided names to UDA gunmen when asked to do so, the witness responded: "He had to show willing." He had to be very careful how he played it, and was not in a position to refuse to give a name. Nelson's motivation was much more honourable and reliable than many. His incentive was to make up for his past demeanours (he had been jailed in the 1970s for kidnapping a Catholic), to save life and to bring down terrorist organisations, but probably the biggest motivation of all was team spirit, loyalty to the army. "He actually put country before family, because of the risks he took," the colonel said.

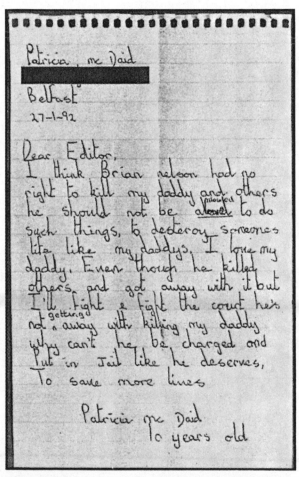

Patricia McDaid wrote a letter to the *Independent* telling of her sadness and anger at the death of her father.

The witness said it embarrassed him personally that the system had been unable to recognise the real difficulties of running agents within terrorist organisations. He felt a personal moral responsibility for Brian Nelson, but the real moral responsibility lay with the system.

167

Under cross-examination, the colonel said there had perhaps been errors of judgement, but there were mitigating circumstances. An agent was bound to be involved in criminality. When several instances of Nelson's allegedly willing participation in planning murders were put to him, the colonel said he had not enough detailed knowledge to comment.

Passing sentence, Lord Justice Kelly commented that the law made it clear that if an undercover agent committed a crime he could not expect to be immune from criminal prosecution and punishment. "In our system of criminal justice there is no refuge or halfway house in criminal culpability in these circumstances," the judge said.

Nelson had been tasked by Military Intelligence to penetrate the UDA but not to get involved with their assassination gangs. On the other hand the UDA had instructed him, in Nelson's own words, "to build an efficient intelligence network to enable it to properly target known republicans for possible execution". On five occasions Nelson had chosen to cross to the wrong side of the dividing line between criminal participation and lawful intelligence-gathering. His activities in these five instances amounted in law to nothing less than conspiracies to murder. He sentenced Nelson to ten years' imprisonment.

The court proceedings had lifted a small part of the curtain which normally hides intelligence activities from the public gaze.

---

4 FEBRUARY 1992   THE INDEPENDENT

Thin dividing line in secret world of army agents

The bespectacled unnamed Military Intelligence colonel, in the witness box at Belfast Crown Court, had it put to him that Brian Nelson, his spy inside the UDA, had been a willing participant in at least one murder conspiracy. The colonel said he could not comment on that, but added that Nelson had given information and taken other actions which had saved lives. He held out his hand palm downwards and declared in his Scottish burr: "Lives were saved, so how do you balance it off against this particular incident?" And the colonel tilted his hand back and forward to indicate that these were difficult and delicate matters, involving conflicting considerations and fine judgement.

The colonel did an effective job of defending both his former spy and his own organisation. He did so principally by pointing out with some force, and with complete accuracy, that at the heart of the informer system lies a legal nonsense. Although there have been extraordinary technical advances in surveillance technology, the key weapon in the battle against both republican and loyalist terrorists remains, as it has for centuries, the well-placed informer. To be effective an informer must be a functioning member of a terrorist group, participating in its activities. This means that he himself must be involved in illegalities: indeed, in some groups, such as the IRA, simple membership is itself a crime. In all such organisations the planning and commission of killings and other serious offences is the stuff of daily routine.

Yet there are, as the colonel said, no legal or official guidelines as to which illegalities are acceptable for an informer and which are not. His point was that involvement in some illegality is unpalatable but unavoidable. There is, he indicated, no legal justification for this: the only justification is a moral one, for if the purity of the law was preserved, then there would, quite simply, be no agents and, it follows, more killings.

The fact that a legal deal was done in the Nelson case has meant that the media and the public have gained only glimpses of what happened. The full story has not emerged, and suspicions will always remain about what dark secrets have been kept under wraps. Yet even the very limited picture that has emerged has been enough to raise the most far-reaching questions about how the intelligence services, and army intelligence in particular, conduct their clandestine business.

To begin with, Nelson as an individual pleaded guilty to 20 separate offences. The prosecution said he had passed on a great deal to his handlers but had failed to relay some important information, giving reports which were not as comprehensive as they could and should have been. They said, furthermore, that on occasion he had been a willing participant in the targeting of potential assassination victims.

In 1987 the colonel and his associates had outlined some rules of thumb to Nelson when they persuaded him to infiltrate the UDA. He was told that he should not get involved in the actual assassination gangs, but that he could be involved in gathering and organising information for them, so long as he then told the army what they were up to.

In giving his mitigation evidence the colonel advanced reasons as to why

Nelson should have overstepped the mark. He actually had to function as a UDA man to win the organisation's confidence, and he faced death if uncovered. These are factors which show how an informer will, in the nature of things, be tempted to act beyond his brief. They also show how important it is for those who control him to be aware of such pressures, and to make sure he resists them.

The Nelson case showed starkly that nothing of the kind happened. Even from the limited evidence available, and even if the colonel is taken at his word, the charges to which Nelson pleaded guilty show he repeatedly broke the rules, and did so with apparent impunity. He functioned as an agent for more than two and a half years, yet many of the offences he admitted happened within his first twelve months in place. His subsequent statements to his handlers made it obvious they knew exactly what he had done shortly after he had done it, yet no action was taken to prevent a recurrence. In other words, he was plainly breaching Military Intelligence's own *ad hoc* guidelines, but he was not made to stop. Furthermore, the only reason any of this has been aired at all is because of the Stevens inquiry, when detectives from Britain were brought in to do another job and made an unexpected and most unwelcome foray into Military Intelligence territory.

There must, over the course of the Troubles, have been hundreds, if not thousands, of informers in both republican and loyalist groups. Many of them, like Nelson, must have overstepped the mark. Yet no one has ever heard of any of them being prosecuted for doing so; and no one can believe that Brian Nelson would ever have wound up in court had it not been for the *deus ex machina* of the Stevens inquiry. The colonel knew at the time, from the reports of the handlers, that Nelson was committing offences. But he did not charge him, and in court he gave the impression, by his demeanour and in his fulsome tributes to Nelson, of strongly believing that no charges should ever have been brought.

Clearly, tough decisions have to be made on a daily basis in Northern Ireland. One of the revelations of the Nelson case is that some of these are being taken, on no legal basis, by an agency, Military Intelligence, which seems accountable to no one. The full facts of the Nelson case have not yet emerged, but enough was seen to show that enormous power lies in the hands of an agency which invented its own rules and then failed to keep them. A world was revealed where decisions on matters of life and death rest not on legal, or even political, factors, but on the tilting of an unnamed colonel's hand.

In his report on collusion, John Stevens said he received "full co-operation" from the army. As he wrote those words he must have had his tongue firmly in his cheek. It emerged that far from helping Mr Stevens in his quest to track down security force documents, Military Intelligence had actually hidden the UDA's central documents dump from him – in army headquarters at Lisburn, Co Antrim. They did not tell him that a full 18 months before his inquiry was ever established, they had surreptitiously photocopied the UDA's main store of documents, then returned them to the organisation.

The paper trail began in the spring of 1987, when Brian Nelson became a UDA intelligence officer. The UDA handed over to him its large store of documents, many of which had been leaked to it by members of the security forces. He promptly took these to the army, who photocopied them and told him to give them back to the UDA. His handlers similarly made copies of any fresh material as and when it reached the UDA. There is no indication, however, of the army ever making use of this valuable evidence to find out which security personnel were doing the leaking.

When the Stevens inquiry was set up in September 1989 Nelson gave all his material to the army for safekeeping – safekeeping, that is, from Mr Stevens. The English police team only learnt of the documents from Nelson after four months, at which point they went to army headquarters and were given a suit-case and a large cardboard box full of material. Copies of all this material are, however, still in the hands of loyalist paramilitaries, for Nelson made five photocopies of it and gave them to different people in the UDA. All of his material is, therefore, still out there in the hands of the assassination gangs.

8

HUMAN RIGHTS

Since early in the Troubles some of the most controversial aspects of security force policy and behaviour have concerned incidents in which people have been shot dead by troops or police. In all, the security forces have been responsible for around 350 deaths, many of which have caused bitter disputes and ill-feeling. The authorities have resisted calls from nationalists, Catholic clerics and human rights activists who argue that changes in procedures and the law could increase confidence in the security forces and prevent deaths.

One case concerned Fergal Caraher, a member of Sinn Féin in south Armagh. He was shot dead by Royal Marines in December 1990 in an incident at what appeared to be a routine road check. Two versions of events emerged – that of the marines and that of local people. Two marines were charged with the murder of Caraher; exactly three years later they were acquitted.

Army challenged over shooting

It would be naïve to believe that a full public inquiry into the death of Fergal Caraher would win the security forces new friends in the south Armagh hamlet of Cullyhanna, where he lived and died. This is a highly politicised little village, decorated with a large number of IRA slogans and posters. Fergal Caraher himself was a member of Sinn Féin. Just across the road from its main housing estate stands a well-tended granite monument commemorating three dead IRA volunteers. It lauds "one of Ireland's noblest sons, Captain Michael McVerry, OC First Battalion South Armagh Brigade, killed in action by British forces of occupation".

There is no RUC or army base. "Policing" is carried out by squads of troops helicoptered in from time to time to stage searches and checkpoints: the little roads that wind their way through the picturesque hummocks could too easily be mined and are unsafe for the security forces to travel. Last year a soldier was shot dead a mile away. There are next to no Protestant families in the vicinity: this is a quintessentially Irish village which does not accept its official status as part of the United Kingdom. The hearts and minds of the people of Cullyhanna are not to be won over.

Yet there is also a strong body of opinion elsewhere which insists that even in the most difficult environment the authorities have both a moral and a political duty to ensure that the actions of the security forces comply with the principles of justice. Foremost among these, in this instance, has been Cardinal Cahal Daly, leader of the Catholic church in Ireland, who, in relation to the Caraher shooting, declared: "Many responsible people are completely unconvinced by the accounts so far given by the British army." This comment is based on the fact that a substantial amount of eyewitness evidence contradicts the official version of what happened. This was set out in an RUC statement which said: "Police are investigating an incident when it is reported that a car failed to stop at an army checkpoint near the village of Cullyhanna and knocked down two soldiers, one of whom was carried some distance by the vehicle. Other soldiers opened fire, and the vehicle continued to drive on."

In the car were the Caraher brothers, Fergal, 20, and Mícheál, 23. Fergal was dead on arrival at hospital and Mícheál, who was driving, was seriously

173

injured. A rifle bullet passed through his body, missing a vital organ by less than an inch.

Local people, who include the brothers' relatives and friends, at the weekend gave a version of events which contradicted the official account. They and others have made statements to the Caraher family's solicitor.

All the relevant events took place on a short stretch of the Tullynavall Road on the outskirts of the village. The sequence began when Mícheál Caraher and a friend, Liam Murphy, stopped their car to help a motorist whose vehicle had broken down. According to Murphy, a 35-year-old unemployed lorry driver, they helped restart the vehicle. Just then, Fergal Caraher pulled up in his car, to talk to himself and Mícheál. A patrol of four soldiers came around a corner and, in routine fashion, asked the three men for their names and addresses, enquiring where they had come from and where they were going. This exchange of information, Murphy says, took five to ten minutes and involved no unpleasantness. The three men then decided to drive across the border to Dundalk for a drink, taking only one of their two cars.

Ahead of them in the road, soldiers were conducting a vehicle check-point, mainly inspecting cars coming in the opposite direction, from Dundalk. Murphy says that first Fergal's car, and then his own, were waved through without being searched. Fergal, according to Murphy and others, then pulled into the large car park of the Lite 'n' Easy bar, just past the checkpoint, sweeping round in a U-turn to face the road, and waiting to rendezvous with Mícheál and Murphy. Murphy stopped his car just past Fergal's vehicle, let Mícheál out, then drove a short distance down the road to a shop to deliver his car to his wife.

Several newspapers have quoted military sources who said that in the car park Fergal encountered a third section of soldiers, suggesting he drove at two of them at speed. Three people told the *Independent* that they saw Fergal in the car park, standing beside his car, talking to one or more soldiers. These witnesses were Murphy; the owner of the bar, Pat Martin; and another Caraher brother, 24-year-old Francis, whose house overlooks the scene.

Pat Martin says he locked up the bar and was driving out of the car park as Fergal drove in. He says theirs were the only two cars in the car park, and that there were no soldiers there. He says he pulled out and joined the queue of cars waiting to get through the checkpoint, but watched what happened next in his wing mirror, from a distance of about 25 yards. According to Martin, Fergal got out of his car and stood beside it. A soldier detached himself from the checkpoint and walked over to him, passing Martin's car in the process. He was joined by another soldier, and then a third. Martin says he saw Mícheál get out of Murphy's car and walk over to join his brother. According to the publican, Mícheál got into the driving seat and Fergal into the passenger seat. He

174

says there was "no shouting or baying" as the soldiers watched the car moving off, but as it began to drive away the shots were fired.

No one says they saw soldiers being hit by Fergal's car. Mícheál remains seriously ill in hospital and has not yet given his version of events.

The position of the authorities is that no further comment is possible on the incident because the circumstances are under investigation by the RUC. In the meantime, the versions of the Cullyhanna villagers are being given widespread publicity. Eyewitness evidence, as lawyers point out, can be notoriously inaccurate or partisan, though in this instance a certain consistency is evident. In this, as in any such case, it is possible that witnesses could be concealing, or might simply be unaware of, facts which might throw an entirely different light on the incident.

The fact is, however, that in this, as in other cases, a blanket of official secrecy has now descended, with past experience suggesting that a full and balanced story is unlikely ever to emerge. The nature of the system of investigation which will now operate in the Caraher case means, the critics say, that justice will not be seen to be done.

On-duty members of the security forces have been responsible for more than 300 deaths: in 1990, for example, troops killed 10 of the 76 people who died. The deaths fall into a number of different categories. There have been shootings at checkpoints, of nonparamilitary criminals during robberies, of civilians caught in crossfire, and of members of paramilitary groups. A great many of the shootings – for example, where armed members of republican or loyalist groups have met their deaths – have caused little or no outcry. But scores of incidents, of which the Caraher case is the latest, have excited considerable controversy. Among the best-known of these is the sequence of shootings of six unarmed republicans in 1982, which were later investigated by John Stalker, former Deputy Chief Constable of Greater Manchester: the controversy surrounding this episode lasted almost a decade, and important aspects of it remain unclear.

But there have been many other episodes. Seventeen people, for example, have been killed by rubber or plastic bullets; 10 joyriders have been shot dead in the past 11 years, usually after failing to stop at checkpoints. Going further back – for memories are long in Ireland – 14 people were shot dead in 1972 by paratroopers on Bloody Sunday, which is still commemorated each year in Londonderry.

Arising from the scores of controversial incidents, there have been 21 prosecutions of members of the security forces for killings using firearms, committed while on duty: 19 of these were found not guilty. One was convicted of manslaughter and given a suspended sentence. The 21st, Private Ian Thain, was found guilty of murder and given a mandatory life sentence. An appeal was turned down but it later emerged that, without publicity, he had been released from prison after serving less than three years and reinstated in the army. Critics say this record provides statistical evidence for the argument that the primary concern of successive British governments has been not to ensure justice but to protect those members of the security forces who pull the trigger. The IRA says the record demonstrates that there is one law for the army and the RUC and another for everyone else.

There are a number of legal and other factors which, in sum, constitute a formidable series of hurdles which help to ensure that soldiers and policemen are not convicted of offences in connection with fatal shootings. A cardinal principle is that members of the security forces are subject to the same laws as other individuals. The 1967 Criminal Law (Northern Ireland) Act states that "such force as is reasonable" may be used to prevent crime or apprehend offenders or suspected offenders.

In the mid-1970s the then Labour government sought guidance from the Law Lords on the use of lethal force when the issue arose with the acquittal of a soldier on a charge of murdering a Co Tyrone farm hand, Patrick McElhone. When a soldier approached McElhone to question him, he ran away. The soldier shot him in the back. McElhone, a court accepted, was clearly unarmed and had no involvement in terrorism. The soldier argued that he believed he was shooting at an escaping terrorist. The Law Lords declined to make a specific ruling on the lethal force issue, saying, instead, that it was up to a court to decide, in each case, whether the force used was reasonable. They concluded, however, that the shooting of McElhone was a reasonable act.

Critics argue that the Law Lords' attitude left the security forces too much licence in questions of lethal force. Successive administrations have rejected recommendations from the government-appointed Standing Advisory Commission on Human Rights for a review of the law to define more precisely when the use of lethal force is reasonable.

Investigations into all fatal incidents are carried out by the Royal Ulster Constabulary: the criticism most often heard here is that the police are entrusted with investigating their own men, or their military colleagues. The suspicion is also that investigations in such cases might be less than wholehearted. John Stalker said he found the RUC reports into the six killings he investigated quite inadequate. He wrote: "We had expected a particularly high level of inquiry in view of the nature of the deaths, but this was shamefully absent. The files were little more than a collection of statements, apparently prepared for a coroner's enquiry. They bore no resemblance to my idea of a murder prosecution file. Even on the most cursory of readings I could see clearly why the prosecutions had failed."

In each case a report is sent to the Northern Ireland Director of Public Prosecutions, who decides whether or not to bring a charge. The Law Lords made it clear, in the McElhone case, that a charge of manslaughter is not appropriate in such cases: in effect the only possible charge, where a soldier or policeman is judged to have used force unreasonably, is that of murder, which carries a mandatory life sentence. Murder is the most serious charge in the law, and one of the most difficult to prove. Lord Colville QC, who has carried out a number of reviews of emergency legislation for the government, pointed out the dilemma: "The policeman or soldier, his family and friends, say that it is monstrous that a minor misjudgment in a man's reaction to a split-second emergency should lead to a sentence of life imprisonment. But the victim's family and friends will be outraged by an acquittal."

The DPP takes many factors into consideration before reaching his decisions. He is in regular touch with the Attorney General for consultation on such sensitive matters. He has regard, for example, to the question of the public interest and to the likelihood of a prosecution resulting in a conviction. It may be that the DPP privately considers that an offence has been committed, but concludes that the evidence available would be insufficient to secure a conviction. All such deliberations take place, however, behind tightly closed doors. When the DPP orders that a charge should not be brought, the iron rule is that he gives no indication of his reasons, and makes no comment on his decision.

When cases come to court, judges — there are no juries in Troubles-related trials in Northern Ireland — have often appeared inclined to acquit. The late Lord Justice Gibson, assassinated by the IRA in 1987, caused a political uproar when, in acquitting policemen of murder, he praised "their courage and determination in bringing the deceased men to justice, in this case to the final court of justice". On another occasion he declared: "If you watch wild west films, the posse go ready to shoot their men if need be. If they don't bring them back peaceably, they shoot them. And in the ultimate result, if there isn't any other way open to a man, it's reasonable to do it in the circumstances. Shooting may be justified as a means of arrest."

Inquests generally provide little new information into controversial incidents. The policemen or soldiers who carry out the shootings do not appear at the hearing, the inquest is forbidden to apportion any blame, legal aid is not available to families, and there are other restrictions on the proceedings.

Disputed shootings are often followed by calls for a full public inquiry. Such demands are regularly turned down by the government, which points out that the standard investigative and legal procedures will be set in train.

The system is characterised by substantial delays and by secrecy. There are criticisms to be made of each link in the chain — the law itself, its interpretation, the DPP's decisions, the judges, the inquest proceedings. For the critics, the bottom line is that the system which each year puts hundreds of suspected terrorists behind bars has resulted in the jailing of only one soldier; and he was subsequently surreptitiously released. Thus it is that, certainly on the nationalist side, the belief is that the dice are loaded in favour of members of the security forces; and that, even when in error, the system gives them preferential treatment.

POSTSCRIPT

In June 1993 a member of the Parachute Regiment was jailed for life for opening fire in a 1990 incident in which two joyriders were killed in west Belfast. He was only the second on-duty member of the security forces to be convicted of murder.

In December 1993 two Royal Marines were cleared of murdering Fergal Caraher and attempting to murder Mícheál Caraher. As the Northern Ireland Lord Chief Justice Sir Brian Hutton delivered his judgment, members of the Caraher family led several dozen relatives and friends in a silent walkout from the court. By contrast, relatives and friends of the two accused soldiers cheered the verdicts. Sir Brian said there had been a complete conflict between prosecution and defence witnesses, and he had concluded that he could not rely completely on either. He said there was, however, objective and undisputed scientific evidence which gave some support to the soldiers' evidence.

Memories are long in Northern Ireland. As January 1992 brought the 20th anniversary of Bloody Sunday, when paratroops shot dead 14 Catholics during a civil rights march in Londonderry, old debates on the issue were reopened. The Catholic Bishop of Derry, Edward Daly, who retired in 1993, spoke of his memories of that day and its long-lasting effects.

Legacy of Bloody Sunday

E dward Daly, who is destined to go down in Irish history as the priest who waved the white handkerchief on Bloody Sunday, was appointed Bishop of Derry two years later. Most people in Londonderry call him Eddie. He has, for a bishop in a church with many attendance problems, the most extraordinary "street cred", not just because of his behaviour on that day but because he is the most informal and approachable of prelates, and a man in close touch with his flock.

His diocese contains many republicans, with some of whom he is on first-name terms, yet his attitude towards Sinn Féin and the IRA could not be clearer. He has delivered some of the Catholic church's most direct, comprehensive and unequivocal condemnations of republican violence. He once declared: "I believe that the work of the IRA is the work of the devil. They are following the gospel of Satan." His pronouncements carry particular weight, according to one local journalist, because he conveys personal involvement: "You can see the emotion and people do trust it. People trust that emotion. Cardinal Daly denounces the Provos in a doctrinal way: Eddie does it for the grief that they're causing."

The experience of Bloody Sunday, Bishop Daly said this week, had a major effect on his own life. "I think, perhaps, before that I might have been somewhat equivocal about the use of violence, the use of guns and weapons. It changed my attitude completely in that regard. After that I became utterly and completely anti-violence of any kind and anti-gun. I cannot come to terms at all with the use of guns or weapons. I've almost become paranoiac in my fear of them.

"But I know it had the opposite effect on quite a lot of other people, particularly the younger people in Derry. A lot of those who may have been more pacifist before 30 January 1972 became quite militant as a result of it. It was certainly a major influence on the growth of the IRA in Derry and, I think, on a broader scale as well. People who were there on that day and who saw what happened were absolutely enraged by it and just wanted to seek some kind of revenge for it. In later years many young people I visited in prison told me quite explicitly that they would never have become involved in the IRA but for what they witnessed, and heard of happening, on Bloody Sunday."

How can he be as certain as he is that those who were killed were unarmed

179

when shot? "I'm 99 per cent certain of that: one could not be 100 per cent without actually seeing them falling. But I saw one being shot, I was in the vicinity when others were, I was on the scene very shortly after some were shot. I certainly did not see anything that would suggest that they were carrying weapons or were engaged in any kind of activity that would have justified them being shot. And the demeanour of the soldiers did not suggest that they believed anybody was firing at them. A lot of them weren't even bothering to take cover, they were standing right out in the open, or were down on one knee.

"It all still baffles me. I said at the time it was mass murder and I believed it was. I would love to know why highly trained, highly skilled, highly disciplined soldiers would do that. With one exception, all those shot were teenaged or in their early twenties, and I think they were all specifically targeted. There wasn't all that much automatic fire. There were a lot of shots but they were single rounds."

On Bishop Daly, as on others in the city, there are two layers of scar tissue left by the event: the first left by the actual shootings, the second by the conclusion of the former Lord Chief Justice, Lord Widgery, that the shootings had "bordered on the reckless". The Widgery report has entered Irish nationalist lore as a classic example of an English cover-up.

The bishop says of the report: "I was aghast by it, by the fact that the British Lord Chief Justice would not acknowledge the innocence of the victims and made a rather feeble attempt at exonerating those who actually pulled the trigger. But even though Widgery did engage in a whitewash, the evidence of the Paras was taken apart by our lawyers, and I think it was shown up as the fabrication that it was. Some years ago a senior minister in the Northern Ireland Office, and I cannot recollect who it was now, said to me that of course it was generally acknowledged the people were all innocent. But that was very much off the record and very much in a private discussion. I think it is important that the record be set straight – that it be acknowledged by Britain that these people, all of them, were completely innocent and completely without blame.

"I'd actually prefer not to talk about Bloody Sunday at all. But when you have been a witness to something like that you are forced, out of duty to those who were murdered on that day, to insist upon their innocence until everyone acknowledges the fact that these were completely innocent people and were unarmed.

"After the Birmingham Six were exonerated I felt that a healing had taken place in my own mind about it. I forgive those responsible for Bloody Sunday – as a Christian, I have to. But at the same time I do feel that some acknowledgement, an admission of the innocence of these 14 people who were murdered, would help put to rest this awful incident."

For more than two decades one of the most persistent critics of the security forces has been a Catholic clergyman who is also noted for his condemnation of the IRA. Father Denis Faul, a priest who is headmaster of a Co Tyrone school, has for years preached that the authorities are using the wrong methods in their battle against violent republicans.

8 AUGUST 1991   THE INDEPENDENT

Priest puts faith in justice to overcome Troubles

"Justice is the big thing, justice is the solution. Most of the problems in the 1980s were created by the British government. We could have wiped out the Provos long ago if the government had put proper discipline onto the RUC, the British army and the UDR. All we've ever asked for is for the security forces to behave themselves, to behave within the law – don't torture, don't shoot to kill, don't unjustly harass people. You can see it time and time again: the Provos rely upon atrocities by the security forces to bail them out. The Provos love harshness and cruelty and misery. It suits them down to the ground."

After the Rev Ian Paisley, Father Denis Faul is probably the best-known cleric in Northern Ireland. The two men are dissimilar in most respects, but on some points they come surprisingly close. Both agree, for example, that the Provisional IRA must be defeated. Mr Paisley, who sees the IRA as a lethal threat to the Protestant people and their political aims, insists it will only be beaten through the ever-heavier use of military force. Father Faul's perspective is that it is a menace in the first instance to Catholic youths, whose lives are ruined when they are tempted into IRA membership. He holds that military severity is counterproductive. His theme is that his own flock holds the key: "The only way to beat the IRA is to be kind and just to the Catholic people and take them

181

away from the Provos. Only the Catholic people will tell them to stop, will throw the guns out on the streets."

IRA leaders may denounce him as "Thatcher's priest", but he commands widespread respect throughout the Catholic community, and many republicans listen carefully to what he has to say. One reason for this is his extraordinary personal independence: he has often been willing to espouse the most unpopular causes and has more than once, years later, been proved correct in his stands. Right from the start, for example, he said the Birmingham Six, Maguire Seven and Guildford Four were innocent. He and Father Raymond Murray of Armagh, his close collaborator over the years, produced an 80-page booklet, *The Birmingham Framework*, as long ago as 1977. This was just one of an extraordinary stream of substantial pamphlets which the two priests have produced over two decades, dealing with human rights abuses by the military and police in Northern Ireland. Their subjects have included security force harassment of civilians, the ill-treatment of suspects in custody, loyalist assassinations of Catholics, the use of plastic bullets, the "shoot-to-kill" incidents, supergrasses and many more.

One reason why their efforts were not given more credence is that for years they were regarded as "Provo priests" by many people, including nationalists. Both served as prison chaplains, and their barrage of booklets and statements critical of the authorities seemed to serve the propaganda purposes of the IRA. "We were regarded as crypto-Provos," Father Faul admitted. "The image of being Provo priests was thoroughly unjustified, because if you look back at the newspapers during the 1970s, you find we were always condemning the Provo atrocities. But people didn't notice that then."

The big change to his public image came during the republican hunger strikes of 1980 and 1981. Ever since the priest acted to bring the protest to an end, he has been *persona non grata* with the hardline IRA prisoners, who have made it clear that he is no longer welcome to say mass in the Maze. The leaders of the IRA and Sinn Féin now hate him, but his record on human rights makes him a difficult target. He is still often critical of security policy and practices, but it is more widely accepted that his primary concern is with issues of justice.

Now he says: "Our biggest task is to persuade the Catholic people that there is an alternative to violence. Violence only sets up more violence. The big obstacle to everything is the Provos. They're the obstacle to a united Ireland, to the unity of the Irish people, to justice and fair play and reconciliation. Yet at the same time my attitude to the Provos is that they're prodigals. We must always hold out lifelines to them. They've come out of the slums, they've sprung from bigotry and sectarianism, from ill-treatment by the British army and RUC, from internment, from being burnt out of their homes. They've produced terrible atrocities, but at the same time they're like wayward children. We must always

182

have a very Christian outlook on them: they are Christians gone astray. We must reconcile them, bring them back into a better way of working for Ireland."

One of the most horrifying incidents in the Troubles took place in March 1988 in west Belfast, when a car drove into the funeral of an IRA member who had been killed by loyalist Michael Stone in Milltown cemetery three days earlier. Its two occupants were armed and the mourners, believing it was another loyalist attack, surrounded the vehicle and dragged out the two men. They were, in fact, plain-clothes soldiers, members of the Royal Signals Regiment who had, it seems, simply stumbled into the funeral. Their mistake was fatal: they were brutally attacked and shot dead.

The incident led to an unprecedented four-year series of prosecutions. But the process, and some of the verdicts, created mounting unease among civil liberties groups.

---

6 MAY 1992   THE INDEPENDENT

Soldiers' deaths that haunt west Belfast

The events of 19 March 1988 were among the most shocking in Northern Ireland's recent tortured history. Television cameras captured the scene as two soldiers accidentally drove into the middle of an IRA funeral. Dozens of the mourners took part in a frenzied attack on their car. Derek Wood and David Howes, two signals corporals, were hauled out, savagely beaten and stripped, and later driven away to their deaths. Television film showed the attack on the car while newspaper photographs showed a shocked priest crouching over their lifeless bodies. It later emerged that army helicopter film had recorded, in almost pornographic detail, the actual moment of their deaths.

Today most people who recall the soldiers being killed simply remember it with a shudder as a particularly gruesome episode from the past. In west Belfast, however, an extraordinary set of legal sequels means that the event is still a live issue more than four years later.

Thirty-four men, aged from 19 to 63, have been prosecuted in seven major trials, while seven more have been charged and are awaiting trial. The actual gunmen who pulled the triggers have not been charged, but the RUC is believed to be looking for still others in connection with the incident. The exercise has been one of the most intensive police operations ever mounted in the United Kingdom, with a large team of detectives and very substantial resources devoted to the inquiry. The outcomes have varied considerably: five men have been jailed for life, with others imprisoned for terms of up to nine years. But more than half the defendants have been acquitted or received noncustodial sentences.

In the view of the authorities the substantial effort put into the case is the inevitable corollary of a unique event of which, thanks to modern technology, unique evidence exists. From another perspective, however, the large-scale series of trials has involved features which have given rise to community resentment and civil-libertarian disquiet. A Casement Accused Relatives' Committee has been set up to campaign against what it characterises as vindictive official persecution of the west Belfast community. Two highly detailed reports due this month criticise many aspects of the trials, highlighting the fact that special procedures and new features have been appended to the Diplock no-jury system, which is itself already controversial.

The Belfast-based Committee on the Administration of Justice focuses attention on allegations of community harassment and concern over the special procedures, and says several of the sentences seem dramatically out of proportion. The Haldane Society of socialist lawyers describes some of the convictions as "an affront to common sense" and says they would not have been possible in a court in England or Wales. Among the major criticisms levelled at the series of trials are an alleged diversity of approach by different judges, inconsistencies in sentencing, and a failure by some of the judiciary to take sufficient account of the extraordinary context of the events.

To outside observers the whole episode represented an almost animalistic and completely unjustifiable onslaught. The Casement campaigners argue, however, that the incident followed an unprecedented sequence of events which helps to

184

explain some of what happened. Earlier that month three IRA members from west Belfast had been killed in Gibraltar by the SAS in a shooting incident which many in the area, including opponents of the IRA, regarded as murder. Their bodies were brought back to a district which resented both the killings and the very heavy security force presence which accompanied the coffins. Then, during the funerals of the Gibraltar Three, a loyalist gunman, Michael Stone, appeared, firing indiscriminately and throwing hand grenades at mourners. Three men were killed and dozens injured.

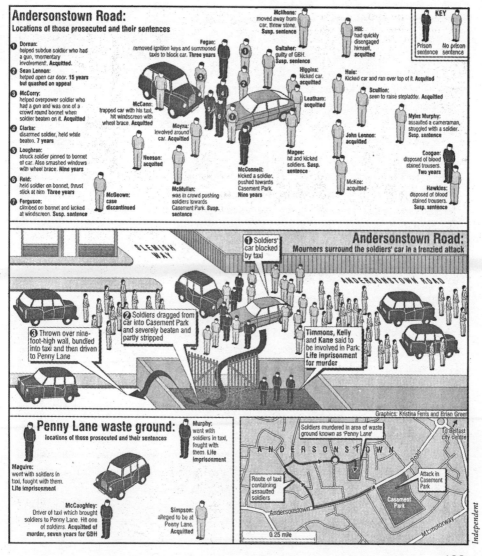

Andersonstown Road:
Locations of those prosecuted and their sentences

KEY — Prison sentence / No prison sentence

Dorman: helped subdue soldier who had a gun, 'momentary involvement'. Acquitted.

Sean Lennon: helped open car door. 15 years but quashed on appeal

McCorry: helped overpower soldier who had a gun and was one of a crowd round when soldier beaten on it. Acquitted

Clarke: disarmed soldier, held while beaten. 7 years

Loughran: struck soldier pinned to bonnet of car. Also smashed windows with wheel brace. Nine years

Reid: held soldier on bonnet, thrust stick at him. Three years

Ferguson: climbed on bonnet and kicked at windscreen. Susp. sentence

McCann: trapped car with his taxi, hit windscreen with wheel brace. Acquitted

McGeown: case discontinued

Neeson: acquitted

Moyna: involved around car. Acquitted

McMullan: was in crowd pushing soldiers towards Casement Park. Susp. sentence

Fegan: removed ignition keys and summoned taxis to block car. Three years

McConnell: kicked a soldier, pushed towards Casement Park. Nine years

McIlhone: moved away from car, threw stone. Susp. sentence

Gallaher: guilty of GBH. Susp. sentence

Higgins: kicked car. acquitted

Leatham: acquitted

Magee: hit and kicked soldiers. Susp. sentence

Hill: had quickly disengaged himself, acquitted

Hale: Kicked car and ran over top of it. Acquitted

Scullion: seen to raise stepladder. Acquitted

John Lennon: acquitted

McKee: acquitted

Myles Murphy: assaulted a cameraman, struggled with a soldier. Susp. sentence

Coogan: disposed of blood stained trousers. Two years

Hawkins: disposed of blood stained trousers. Susp. sentence

Andersonstown Road:
Mourners surround the soldiers' car in a frenzied attack

① Soldiers' car blocked by taxi

② Soldiers dragged from car into Casement Park and severely beaten and partly stripped

③ Thrown over nine-foot-high wall, bundled into taxi and then driven to Penny Lane

Timmons, Kelly and Kane said to be involved in Park. Life imprisonment for murder

Graphics: Kristina Ferris and Brian Green

Penny Lane waste ground:
locations of those prosecuted and their sentences

Maguire: went with soldiers in taxi, fought with them. Life imprisonment

Murphy: went with soldiers in taxi, fought with them. Life imprisonment

McCaughley: Driver of taxi which brought soldiers to Penny Lane. Hit one of soldiers. Acquitted of murder, seven years for GBH

Simpson: alleged to be at Penny Lane. Acquitted

Soldiers murdered in area of waste ground known as 'Penny Lane'

To Belfast city centre

Attack in Casement Park

Route of taxi containing assaulted soldiers

0.25 mile

Independent

185

The funeral which the soldiers blundered into was that of Kevin Brady, an IRA member who was one of those killed by Stone. It was taking place in a highly charged atmosphere, marshalled by republican stewards who were on the lookout for a similar attack. When the soldiers' car appeared, the immediate assumption was that they were loyalists intent on repeating Stone's attack. There is clearly no conceivable justification for the eventual killing of the soldiers, but most observers, including most of the judges, accepted that those who originally surrounded the car acted from a desire to defend those attending the funeral against what they thought were loyalist assassins.

The tragic events of 19 March fell into distinct phases. In the first, mourners surrounded the soldiers' car and, after a frenzied attack, dragged them from it and beat them. They were then shoved and pushed into a nearby sports ground, Casement Park, where they were again severely beaten and partly stripped by some members of a smaller crowd. After five and a half minutes in the park they were, sickeningly, thrown over a nine-foot-high wall, bundled into a black taxi and driven away. They were taken to waste ground known as Penny Lane, where after a struggle they were repeatedly shot.

An analysis of the court cases shows that 25 of the 34 men dealt with were alleged only to be involved in the initial attack on the car. Of the 25, only 5 were jailed, while 6 others were given noncustodial sentences and 13 were acquitted. Most of the judges clearly took into account the possibility of mitigating circumstances and the concept of self-defence. Some judges, however, clearly had difficulty with such points. One handed down a 15-year sentence to a defendant who had helped open the car door, saying he must have known he was involved in a malicious attack. The conviction was quashed on appeal, however, a more senior judge stressing what he described as the atmosphere of "tumult, alarm and confusion".

The case which is likely to attract most attention among legal critics concerns three men who were said to be among those inside Casement Park while the soldiers were being severely assaulted and stripped. One defendant, Michael Timmons, admitted being in the park while two others, Patrick Kane and Sean Kelly, denied this. The case was heard before Mr Justice Carswell, who has a reputation as one of Northern Ireland's sternest judges. In his 72-page judgment he mentioned the complex background to the case in the most cursory fashion, dealing with it in just two lines.

The facts, as determined by the judge, were as follows. Timmons had helped push one of the corporals into Casement Park, had apparently helped to close the gate behind him, and moved around within the group of people inside the park. He kicked one of the soldiers on the foot and took off his running shoes. At one stage during the episode, which lasted five and a half minutes, he lit a cigarette. The judge rejected Timmons's claim that he went into the park through "nosiness" and that he had become panicky and nervous but was unable to get out of the park. He ruled Timmons had at first lied to RUC detectives in Castlereagh interrogation centre when questioned about the incident.

In the case of Patrick Kane, the judge found he had been in Casement Park and had kicked a soldier once. He had also been involved in opening and closing the park gate. He had later switched jackets to mislead police, and had lied both to police and to the court. Mr Justice Carswell rejected the explanation that he had kicked the soldier "just to be a big fella like the rest". Kane spent in all less than four minutes in the park, according to the judge. In court Kane denied being there.

The judge found that Sean Kelly had joined in the attack on the car, helped push a soldier into Casement Park, then helped close the gate. He also appeared to take part in carrying a corporal over to the wall. Kelly, who was 19 at the time of the incident, denied being in the park.

The involvement of all three defendants ended when the soldiers were thrown over the wall and driven away to Penny Lane, where they were shot dead. The law states, however, that under the doctrine of "common purpose", defendants not directly involved in an actual killing may be guilty if they are judged to give implied approval to a range of crimes. Mr Justice Carswell ruled that during the five and a half minutes in the park (or in Kane's case, less than four minutes) the three defendants contemplated that murder was one of the range of crimes which might be carried out by the persons who took charge of imprisoning the soldiers. With this reasoning, he found all three guilty of murder and sentenced them to life imprisonment.

The doctrine of common purpose is well established in law but, in the view of the critics, it was in this instance stretched to its limits and, indeed, too far. They argue that in the fear, chaos and confusion of the moment it might well be that none of the defendants were thinking at all rationally.

When the case went to appeal, the Northern Ireland Court of Appeal clearly had difficulty with some aspects of the Carswell judgment. The three-judge court found a number of errors in the judgment, but nonetheless confirmed the verdicts and the sentences. In confirming the verdicts, it changed the basis of the convictions, though it upheld Mr Justice Carswell's reliance on the principle of common purpose.

The main problems arose in that section of the judgment dealing with Sean Kelly. Mr Justice Carswell had said a figure which appeared to be Kelly was visible in the film taken from an army surveillance helicopter. The film "tends to show" he was in the park, the judge said, though he said he had reservations about making an identification because of the quality of the film. He went on, however, to say that there were other facts which "might point" to his having been in the park. First, when the soldiers' car arrived he was "plainly an active participant on the onslaught upon them". Then, in court, he had declined to give evidence on his own behalf, a refusal from which the judge said he was entitled to draw an adverse inference. (Judges may do this under new rules introduced several years ago which human rights groups criticise as an erosion of the right to silence.) Finally, he could clearly be seen on film near the taxi as it drove away with the soldiers inside. Next, the fact that he had denied these facts while under interrogation by detectives in Castlereagh showed he had lied to police. The judge said that these facts, when taken together, satisfied him that Kelly was an active participant in Casement Park.

The 34-page appeal court judgment found that Mr Justice Carswell had been completely mistaken on several important points. The judges said that film evidence showed that Kelly had been near the car, but there was nothing to suggest that he had participated in the assault on it. They further said that Mr Justice Carswell had been incorrect in saying that Kelly had been seen near the taxi, since on reviewing the evidence they could not find him or anyone who resembled him. The judges went on to disagree with Mr Justice Carswell about identifying Kelly inside the park from the helicopter film. Whereas he indicated he could not be sure from the film that Kelly was there, the three judges said they had studied the film and were satisfied beyond reasonable doubt that they could see him.

Legal sources say an appeal court does not normally interfere with a judge's findings of facts. But because they were sure they could see Kelly in the park, the judges went on, it was not necessary to take an adverse inference from his refusal to go into the witness box. The convictions were therefore upheld.

To date the Casement trials have not attracted much attention either in Northern Ireland or outside it. West Belfast campaigners have little confidence in any aspect of the legal system, while legal observers express concern about a number of the features of the trials, in particular the cases of Timmons, Kane and Kelly.

POSTSCRIPT

Concern about the convictions subsequently became more widespread, with legal sources and the British Labour party expressing unease. The campaign gathered further momentum after March 1993, when BBC journalist John Ware raised fresh doubts in a *Rough Justice* programme. The Northern Ireland Secretary, Sir Patrick Mayhew, said in May 1993 that he was examining the case. At the time of writing he has not indicated the outcome of his deliberations.

While many aspects of security force policy attracted criticism from nationalists and from civil liberties groups, one conspicuous exception to this was the approach of the authorities to people sentenced to life imprisonment, usually for murder.

In Britain successive Home Secretaries made it clear that life sentences would generally mean that a prisoner could expect to serve at least 20 years. But in Northern Ireland a more liberal system has been tried, and seems to work.

14 OCTOBER 1993   THE INDEPENDENT

Questions raised over terrorist's home visits

Just over 14 years ago a Belfast judge told a group of loyalist terrorists that the murders they had committed were so cruel and so revolting as to be beyond the comprehension of a normal person. He told the gang of 11 that their actions "will remain for ever a lasting monument to blind sectarian bigotry". He was correct: a decade and a half later the actions of these men, the Shankill Butchers, are still remembered with a particular shudder.

Members of the gang killed 17 people, half a dozen of them in the most gruesome fashion, using knives, meat cleavers and hatchets. In one typical instance they bundled a drunken Catholic road sweeper into a taxi, fractured his skull with a heavy wheel brace, then drove him to a quiet spot where they bashed his head with a baton and cut his throat back to the spine with a butcher's knife. Even hard-bitten Belfast found their blood-letting shocking.

189

One of the gang's leaders, Robert "Basher" Bates, an unshaven 30-year-old with long unkempt hair, got 14 life sentences. Recommending that he should never be released from prison unless he contracted a terminal illness, the judge told him: "I mean life imprisonment to mean life imprisonment."

With the gang receiving a total of 42 life sentences, along with 1,892 years in concurrent jail terms, society believed itself rid of the Shankill Butchers. It came as something of a shock, therefore, when it recently emerged that Basher Bates has for some years been allowed home for parole during the summer and at Christmas. The news led to a tabloid furore and a chorus of disapproval. A brother of one of those killed said: "The Shankill Butchers deserve the same as their victims and they should just rot in hell. They couldn't be human." Presumably the judge was surprised to learn that Bates has been back on the streets half a dozen times. Many other voices said Bates should never be released; some said he deserved not compassionate parole but capital punishment.

The one-time 'Butcher' has undergone a religious conversion in prison. According to Ian Major, a Baptist missionary who works with prisoners: "Bobby has changed, he's been changed internally. He has come to Christ. I suppose a secularist would say he's had some sort of psychological turnaround, but he has a new outlook on life." There will always be scepticism about jailhouse conversions and whether or not they are genuine, or feigned to secure earlier release. But one of the surest touchstones is the collective opinion of the group of 25 or so born-again Christians in Maghaberry prison. One source said: "They live together 24 hours a day – they can spot a fake a mile off, and they're satisfied Bobby is absolutely genuine."

Bates is now a hard-working prisoner and head of the unit in Maghaberry which translates school and college textbooks into Braille. He has severed his paramilitary links and is a model prisoner. One source said: "When he first came in he had the long hair, he was wild, he was a mess. He's now a shell of a man, very quiet and inoffensive in a bland kind of way. The hair has gone, he's prematurely bald. He has found the Lord and he's no threat to anyone. Really, the only question is how much time he has to do before he's seen to have paid for the awful crimes that he committed." A welfare source added: "The notion that he's gone Christian is for real. He's a broken, spent force. He has repented and he is remorseful. The question is how long you keep someone like him inside in order to satisfy society. There is no risk factor involved."

Bates's paroles have come under prison rules that allow most life prisoners summer and Christmas home leave after they have served 11 years. Contrary to some reports, he is not on a pre-release programme, and it is understood he will probably not be considered for final release before the turn of the century. His case highlights, however, the fact that more than 250 prisoners given life imprisonment for terrorist murders have already been released into the community.

The 250 are roughly half republicans and half loyalists, with 300 lifers still inside. The release scheme, which is markedly more liberal than policies operating either in Britain or the Irish Republic, means many lifers have been set free after serving 11 or 12 years. A number of criteria for release are considered, including the nature of the original offence and the prisoner's behaviour in jail. The crucial calculation, however, is whether he is likely to reoffend.

The authorities, and most local politicians, are quietly happy with the scheme, though the bulk of public opinion is probably in favour of sterner treatment. The question is whether those like Bates should be locked up and the key thrown away, or whether society should treat him with a compassion he never showed to his victims.

Such a unique penal experiment would be unimaginable under a Home Secretary such as Michael Howard. Under the terms of release they can be arrested and recalled to prison without notice and without judicial proceedings. This threat of instant recall acts as a powerful deterrent, and the authorities say they are satisfied that none of those freed has become reinvolved in terrorist activity.

There have recently been complaints that a change in the approach of the authorities means ministers are insisting on longer terms for those sentenced for killing soldiers. In practice this would mean republicans serving longer terms than loyalists.

Welfare workers say most of the released lifers have difficulties in readjusting to the outside world, but say a majority of them become involved in community work of some kind. Many of them are now active in youth work, for example, working with joyriders. Said one worker: "They're not like fixed-term prisoners, a lot of whom just go back to violence. Some of them develop businesses, some get involved in useful community work, some − both Protestants and Catholics − get into Christian work. All the evidence is that released lifers are spending their time atoning."

There have been many complaints about the conduct of British troops in Northern Ireland. But sometimes, as this glimpse of their living conditions revealed, the troops themselves have good reason to complain.

Six months with cockroaches for company

The tattooed Jocks drinking tea in the canteen were totally unfazed by the presence of a gaggle of officers. "This is a cockroach-infested hole," one private said bluntly. "It's bloody awful. It's not so bad when you're out there on the streets doing your job, but when you're back in here it's terrible." The army would say improvements have been made to this elderly building, but another soldier chipped in: "I was here two and a half years ago and it hasn't changed one bit. There's cockroaches everywhere. We lifted a floorboard and there were dozens of them, running everywhere. You wake up and they're all over the floor, in your bed sometimes." Other soldiers nodded in agreement, one adding: "It's got worse. There's about two million cockroaches. It would be bearable if it wasn't for them."

A room on the top floor had a badly stained carpet and greasy yellow walls. Grimy windows high on the walls let in some light and air. Paint peeled off the ceiling. Around the walls were eight narrow metal cots, five of them occupied by sleeping soldiers. Some of them stirred groggily as we walked in. When an officer said, "Go back to sleep", they promptly did. Strewn on the floor were boots and packs, mess cans, radios, flak jackets. A single plastic chair stood beside each bed, holding a clock, or a radio, or an ashtray. There was a smell of sweat and grease. "It's a lot worse in the summer," an officer said. "Basically, there's no ventilation and the smell gets really bad, a real problem."

Other rooms holding four or six soldiers were cramped, with beds and lockers jammed into a small space. Most of the men have their rifles by their beds, or stacked in a corner. Asked if he at least felt safe here, one Jock replied: "No way. This place is falling down round us."

In many rooms a radio or television was switched on, even when men were sleeping. "Old army trick," explained an officer. "If they keep it noisy all the time then they don't wake up when people clump in and out of the room." The soldiers said they worked 16 to 18 hours a day, either outside on foot or vehicle patrol or inside on other duties. An officer described the routine as basically one of work, eat and sleep.

192

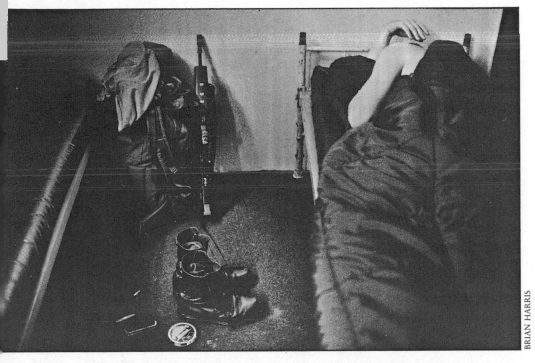

A soldier snatches some sleep in North Howard Street barracks, off the Falls Road

The NAAFI – which is "dry", meaning no alcohol – is smallish but serviceable. The canteen food looked reasonable, though some of the men described it as not great. The shower area was refurbished earlier this year and there is now a sauna and some sun beds. But overall there is a sense of claustrophobia and overcrowding, of an old building pressed into service for an unsuitable purpose.

The base is North Howard Street mill, a four-storey Victorian building erected by a Scots businessman some 148 years ago, between the Falls and the Shankill roads. It was never intended to last for a century and a half, and was certainly not designed to serve as headquarters of the 1st battalion, the Queen's Own Highlanders, housing 19 officers, 35 senior NCOs and 190 men. It gives the impression of being an emergency billet, where soldiers have been hurriedly stacked until somewhere more suitable can be found. Yet North Howard Street mill has been an army base for two decades and there is no sign of it closing.

A mile or so up the road from the mill is Fort Whiterock, which houses more Highlanders. The purpose-built base sits perched on the edge of the mountain, high above west Belfast. This means it is more spacious, but also more open to attack, and complex constructions of anti-mortar mesh are everywhere to be seen. Conditions here are rather better than in the mill, with more modern buildings, more space and more air. There is a mini-gym with weights facilities which are obviously well used, for many soldiers are into bodybuilding. The canteen is brighter and more pleasant.

One soldier, on his first tour of duty, said: "I thought it would be worse." Another, a cook who was tenderising sizeable sirloin steaks for lunch, said: "It's OK, it's not bad. I've saved loads of money here, because there's nothing to spend it on." But the men are still sleeping six to a room, and it is obvious that this is not a popular posting. The big garage has no heating or ventilation and is "like the bloody Baltic" in winter.

One Jock, whose wall was plastered with revealing Polaroids of his girlfriend, said: "The toilets are abysmal – we have to clean them when we come back off patrol. The washroom is all right, but there's only four washing machines and four driers for two companies. That's 280 men. Any time you go to use them there's a big queue, so I wind up doing it at four in the morning." His work pattern, as a member of the QRF (quick reaction force), was 24 hours on followed by 12 off. In the canteen another soldier said he had had 5 hours off in the last 48, though this was exceptional. Extra hours mean no extra money: there is no overtime in the army.

From the outside the heavily fortified bases look reasonably secure, but inside there are constant reminders that an attack could come at any time. Outside there are signs warning soldiers not to loiter unnecessarily in the open air. The canteen is crisscrossed with brick walls to limit casualties from bomb blasts.

The soldiers face risks both inside the base and when they are outside on patrol, either on foot or in vehicles. The reactions they receive from the locals, in this hardline republican area, puzzle them. One said: "I've never got used to the way one street will be friendly enough, then round the corner they shout abuse at you." A soldier who patrols two adjoining Catholic areas said: "New Barnsley is totally different from the Murph [Ballymurphy]. You say good morning to people in the Murph and it's such a tight place they won't say good morning back, or if they do they keep their voices down. New Barnsley is better. When a guy got injured there a woman came out with a blanket for him and gave him a cup of tea. That's new, even the RUC were amazed at that." Asked how they regarded the danger, one said: "Every time you walk out the gate you think, 'Christ, it could happen to me.'"

Asked whether they prefer foot or vehicle patrols, a soldier replied: "The guys prefer foots because time passes quicker and there's a better feeling, though there's a bit of bad feeling with the RUC. The RUC don't keep you in the picture, they don't always inform you what's happening."

A sergeant major later says that that soldier may have had a bad experience with some RUC constable, but that in general co-operation is absolutely first class. That soldier's opinion would not be typical, the sergeant major said: "If you take one message away from Fort Whiterock, it should be that we get on the best with the police, the very best."

Northern Ireland has more than 100 army bases of various sizes and functions, many of them bearing little resemblance to North Howard Street and Fort Whiterock. Many of the 11,000 regular army troops live in comfortable accommodation in reasonably safe bases. A few miles outside east Belfast, for example, stands Palace Barracks. Here soldiers live, many of them with their families, in pleasant housing estates and modern blocks. Newly converted accommodation is light and airy. NCOs have rooms that would not be out of place in a two-star hotel, while soldiers share four-man rooms with lots of space, lockers and cupboards.

The perimeter is closely guarded, but inside the atmosphere is relaxed and peaceful. The sprawling complex has its own swimming pool, playing fields, churches and community centre. This is home for several thousand people, soldiers and their families, who live here for at least two years. They leave the base to shop and eat in local towns. Children attend local schools, and in some areas families live, not in the base, but out in the local community. One officer who has completed eight tours of duty said: "This is our second home. I really mean that – my two kids were born here, my wife is in local toddlers' groups and so on."

But the Highlanders in North Howard Street mill and Fort Whiterock, and other hardline areas such as south Armagh, are in the front line of the undeclared war, and very different rules apply. Off-duty soldiers are generally not allowed off the base, and even when not on duty they are on permanent stand-by. Tours of duty last only six months, for the soldiers are pushed close to the limit by the constant danger, long hours and rough-and-ready conditions.

If North Howard Street mill were a hotel it would presumably be immediately shut down by public health inspectors. But it is in a strategic position, close to the centre of the IRA's Falls Road heartland, and it does not make military sense to close it down. In 20 years, dozens of units have passed through its squalid doors, and many more seem destined to serve their six-month sentences in this dark, satanic mill.

9
THE STUFF OF POLITICS

Peter Brooke succeeded Tom King as
Northern Ireland Secretary of State in July
1989, and shortly afterwards became
immersed in a lengthy period of "talks
about talks", in which he attempted to
coax the local parties and the Irish
government to the conference table.
Dozens of bilateral meetings followed, until
in January 1990 he indicated that he
believed a basis for wider talks existed.
Few originally shared his optimism, but by
mid-1990 the atmosphere had brightened
somewhat. His politely relentless style
appeared to be paying off, and the
prospect of real talks came closer.

Poised on the threshold of negotiations

On the most optimistic reading, Northern Ireland may be standing on the threshold of real political headway. Peter Brooke has surprised almost everyone by winning a measure of general agreement, on the basis of which serious political negotiations can take place. With a little imagination – and on the assumption that good will exists on all sides – it is possible to map out a scenario in which considerable progress will take place by the end of the year. The deal worked out among the British and Irish governments and the constitutional parties envisages a summer spent making arrangements, followed by an intense period of negotiations in the autumn. Mr Brooke has already made a breakthrough of sorts, simply by keeping the disparate elements in play. The years of talks about talks appear to be drawing to a close: the likelihood now is that real talks are set to begin.

The rapidity with which things have changed has surprised almost everyone. In November 1989 the Taoiseach, Charles Haughey, declared in the Dáil: "The preconditions for devolution do not exist, and there is no enthusiasm for it in any main political grouping in Northern Ireland at the present time." There was widespread public and private agreement with his view. As recently as April, Dr John Alderdice, leader of the nonsectarian and determinedly optimistic Alliance party, told his annual conference that unless there was a significant change of heart he saw no likelihood of inter-party agreement in the foreseeable future.

Yet there has been a significant change of heart – or at least a significant change of approach – since Dr Alderdice spoke. That change has taken place in the two Unionist leaders, James Molyneaux and Ian Paisley, in a manner so sharp and so sudden that most politicians were taken aback.

The two Unionist parties have not been fully involved in the political processes since the signing of the Anglo-Irish agreement in November 1985. The rival parties, Mr Molyneaux's Ulster Unionists and Mr Paisley's Democratic Unionists, sank their differences and formed a pact to oppose the accord. Unionist MPs resigned their seats and fought by-elections, boycotted parliament,

197

and staged rallies and protests against the principle of the south's involvement in northern affairs. Some advocated rebellion, or the threat of it, against Britain, attempting to form paramilitary groups to defy London's authority.

The protests petered out, having failed to budge the agreement. The pact, though battered, remains intact. The early anger was replaced in the Unionist community by a sullen resentment. Local politics atrophied. Many second-rank activists, both moderates and extremists, drifted out of politics. Mr Molyneaux and Mr Paisley eventually dropped their boycott of ministers and held a series of meetings with Mr Brooke's predecessor, Tom King. But they were unproductive, the Unionists insisting that real talks could not take place until the agreement was suspended. Nationalist politicians, though disappointed the agreement did not deliver more reforms, nevertheless continued to regard it as an advance and were adamantly against suspension.

Ian Paisley, leader of the Democratic Unionist party

Both the Irish government and the SDLP strongly suspected that the Unionists were not interested in negotiating a new agreed settlement, but were instead engaged in a wrecking exercise aimed at damaging the accord. Nationalist

198

sources privately made it clear that they believed Unionists were unwilling to contemplate any new deal based on gaining nationalist consent. One senior source said: "The reality of the Unionists is that they don't want a relationship with anybody – not even the British. All they want from the British is to be underwritten, because they won't accept decisions of the British parliament unless they like them."

Thus when Peter Brooke announced earlier this year that he intended to seek the opening of talks, the primary feeling on the nationalist side was one of anxiety. Dublin and the SDLP feared that he might undermine the agreement by giving the Unionists concessions to tempt them to the table. A Dublin source said in March: "Brooke obviously feels that the Unionists are at a point where they are prepared to parley in a realistic way. To be honest, we have seen nothing to substantiate that. We haven't seen a clear articulation that the Unionists are serious. We have grave doubts: efforts of the type the British are seeking to make could be very injurious to the agreement."

It took a series of meetings to reassure the Irish that Mr Brooke was not about to make rash concessions to Mr Molyneaux and Mr Paisley. He was not able to convince Dublin that the Unionists were genuine about talks, but he did succeed in allaying the Irish concern that his strategy might damage the agreement. Mr Brooke has personally never been overoptimistic about success. In May one close observer noted privately: "There is an element in the NIO who have got bright shining eyes and think this is all going to work like magic. That does not apply to Peter Brooke, who is just pragmatically seeing this particular exercise through to its proper end."

Within weeks of that observation, however, came the meeting that has raised the present expectation that the logjam might yet be broken. There were broad smiles on the faces of Mr Molyneaux and Mr Paisley when they emerged from their meeting with Mr Brooke in London on 22 May to declare themselves "well satisfied". Those smiles set nationalist alarm bells ringing, since they suggested the Northern Ireland Secretary had made significant concessions to Unionism.

The two Unionist leaders had recently hardened their position on the secretariat, declaring that only a caretaker could be left inside if talks were to start. Mr Molyneaux in particular had taken a tough line, declaring earlier in May: "They [the Maryfield staff] can't stay there. It's got to be closed down completely because it would just be a pretence otherwise. They would have to withdraw back to their respective bases. It wouldn't be honest to do anything else."

The sight of the Unionist smiles on television caused a flurry of nationalist concern, but when an SDLP delegation met Mr Brooke two days later they too emerged to say they were happy that his proposals met their concerns. An ingenious approach devised by the Northern Ireland Secretary had achieved what most people thought impossible.

Although the proffered deal goes some way towards meeting the stated conditions of the Unionists, a great deal of uncertainty continues to surround the motives of Mr Molyneaux and Mr Paisley in giving their general agreement to it. Their action took by surprise many who had regarded it as axiomatic that substantive talks were highly unlikely to take place so long as the two men remained joint leaders of Unionism.

Mr Molyneaux's is not a devolutionist agenda: his primary demands centre on points of parliamentary procedure, such as the establishment of a select committee on Northern Ireland matters and legislation by bill rather than orders in council, which allow only limited debate. He also presses for the establishment of one or more regional councils with limited powers. Taken together, his policy amounts to one of advocating measures which tend to preclude devolution.

The SDLP and the Alliance party have accused him of "manoeuvring to do nothing" and criticised his "ingenuity for dreaming up excuses for not talking". Such statements may well have embarrassed the Ulster Unionist leader – he has certainly complained several times to Mr Paisley about criticisms from DUP sources – and played a part in changing his anti-talks tactics. There is much speculation about other factors which may have helped effect a change: one theory is that the relentless Mr Brooke may have simply dissected his position to the point of destruction. There is also the competence factor. Mr Molyneaux has proved himself expert, in his decade as head of the largest Unionist grouping, at seeing off policy and personal challenges from within Unionism. But he has been conspicuously less successful in his dealings with outside agencies, in particular the British government. Mr Brooke, surreptitiously aided by second-tier Unionists such as Peter Robinson, may have outflanked him.

What is clear is that there has also been a significant change of mind on the part of his partner, Ian Paisley. Sources within Mr Paisley's Democratic Unionist party say it was around mid-April that he appeared to change his mind and decide that talks were desirable.

The last five years have not been kind to the DUP leader. He vowed that the Anglo-Irish agreement would not last, but it has. His party, which 10 years ago was threatening to overtake Mr Molyneaux's, has lost support. Many of the bright young men who joined the DUP in the early 1980s – the so-called "Duppies" – have been forced out of politics by economic circumstance or disillusion. The current low level of political activity does not suit the DUP leader, who has built a career on the politics of protest and the rhetoric of resistance. His pact with Mr Molyneaux has been useful in helping both of them fend off challenges from ambitious lieutenants, but Mr Molyneaux's party has been the clear beneficiary of the arrangement. Mr Paisley needs action: temperamentally, he would welcome the drama and excitement that a major conference could provide. Whether he is now prepared to make the kind of compromises he has spent his life opposing is, however, an entirely different matter.

Years ago, in his role as Moderator of the Free Presbyterian church, he spelled out his philosophy to his flock in the following terms: "You've got to take your stand, you know. There's not going to be any compromise. If you compromise, God will curse you. If you stand, God will bless you. That's why God has blessed this preacher and this church." The success of the present enterprise may in large measure depend on whether or not this remains Mr Paisley's political attitude, for any new arrangement hammered out in negotiations must, in practice, be acceptable to the SDLP and the Irish government. Mr Paisley has, in fact, acted pragmatically in the past, though he has never brought himself to enter office with the daily compromises which that would entail.

If Mr Brooke's scheme works and the talks begin, the Northern Ireland Secretary will be faced across the table by one Unionist leader who almost certainly wishes he were not involved in talks at all. Opponents of James Molyneaux, a number of whom are in his own party, believe he will be pushing for a small-scale regional council; they also think he would shed no tears should the talks collapse completely.

Also involved will be politicians such as Peter Robinson and Ken Maginnis, MPs whom Mr Brooke believes are ready to consider making a deal with nationalists. Mr Robinson's image has not always been quite so moderate: he has made common cause with some shady characters in the past. But many people – Catholics as well as Protestants – hope that he has learnt his lesson and has become a genuine advocate of the compromise which Mr Paisley railed against.

A great many hurdles remain to be cleared. At this moment Mr Brooke and Mr Haughey are in disagreement over the stage at which northern parties will talk to Dublin. Both appear to agree that inter-party talks should start first; the Unionist position is that substantial progress should be made towards agreement on a new devolved institution before north–south contacts take place. Mr Brooke says the talks will develop organically, and argues that arrangements should be left flexible. The Irish, however, want an assurance that the Unionists will not be able to put off such contacts almost indefinitely. The Irish also do not care for the Unionist stipulation that north–south talks should take the form of a "United Kingdom team", including Mr Brooke and the various Northern Ireland parties, though this is regarded as less of a sticking point.

Evident in some Dublin circles is a continuing suspicion about Unionist motives: few believe that Mr Molyneaux's shift of attitude was voluntary, and no one thinks he will give anything further except under considerable pressure.

The Irish will be watchful for any sign that the Unionists are not genuinely seeking a deal, but are, rather, involved in a stratagem designed to damage the agreement.

If, however, the cynics are wrong and there has been a sea change in Unionism, then it may be argued that the Anglo-Irish agreement has succeeded in one of its purposes, that of compelling Unionists to acknowledge what they never have in the past — that there is a southern dimension to the Northern Ireland problem. Mr Brooke intends the negotiation period to be a time of intense activity; by the end of the year we should know whether his exercise is pointless, or whether there really has been a historic shift in attitudes.

Many more months of painstaking effort were required before the parties finally came to the table in April 1991. They opened with a fund of good will, but as the weeks wore on it became ever clearer that no breakthrough was on the cards. There were many disputes and rows over secondary issues such as venues and chairmanship. Hope gradually turned to disillusion and disenchantment, little momentum developed, and in July they came to a close.

4 JULY 1991   THE INDEPENDENT

Unionists held responsible for collapse of talks

The Brooke talks were quietly wound up in Belfast with no new measure of agreement among the parties, after a year and a half of effort by the Northern Ireland Secretary. All the parties involved expressed disappointment,

Orangemen on the march: the insecurity of Northern Ireland Protestants is on the increase

though many said that failure had for some time seemed inevitable. A number of sources said they hoped the talks might be resumed at a future date.

The talks have both demonstrated and deepened the weakness of the Unionist position. The parties led by James Molyneaux and the Rev Ian Paisley were isolated before they began, and are doubly so now. Both in Britain and in Ireland they will be singled out to bear most of the blame for the failure of the talks. In the space of a few months they have dispelled much of the small element of sympathy they had fostered in the Republic, alienated some of their dwindling band of sympathisers in England, and by their conduct irked much of the British media.

The progress of the discussions confirmed the pre-talks analysis that the Unionists would be the odd men out at the conference table. The other elements involved – the British and Irish governments, the nationalist SDLP and the moderate Alliance party – all envisaged giving nationalism a significant input into government, whether through a north–south link or through the exercise of power shared by Protestants and Catholics. There were clearly different approaches and disagreements among these groups during the talks, but these

203

were rarely pressed to the point of division. On most major points at issue it was a case of the Unionists against the rest.

These elements did not, however, face a Unionist monolith. Within Unionist ranks there was considerable confusion, with factions and individuals differing not just on tactics but also on the wisdom of even being at the talks. It was an open secret, for example, that Mr Molyneaux would have been happier had the whole thing never taken place at all. Having reached the table, he made

GLYNN GRIFFITHS

The leaders of Unionism: James Molyneaux and the Rev Ian Paisley outside 10 Downing Street

it plain he was opposed to devolution. Other Unionists favoured devolution, but seemed opposed to having it on a powersharing basis. Still others were pro-devolution but never specified whether they would or would not share power. Some never clarified their position while others varied in their opinions. Mr Paisley was all over the place; some members of Mr Molyneaux's delegation are intensely bitter about the DUP leader's performance, in particular his penchant for making televised statements committing both parties to positions which had not been formally agreed.

Thus the Unionists found themselves in a high-powered, high-profile negotiation, without agreement on what they wanted to get out of it. In many instances bluster took the place of considered comment; in others the leaders, in the view of senior members of their delegations, were less than frank with their own teams about what they were up to.

Peter Brooke was not just aware of the differences within Unionism: he was depending on them. The theory was that younger and more amenable elements in the two parties, in particular MPs Peter Robinson and Ken Maginnis, would unofficially coalesce, build up momentum, and propel their reluctant leaders towards compromise. In fact, these elements did not form an effective partnership, and showed no signs of having the skills needed to outmanoeuvre the Molyneaux–Paisley axis. They could not, for example, prevent the Unionist teams painting themselves into a corner by insisting that the talking would end when preparations began for the next Anglo-Irish ministerial meeting.

That stipulation represented one of a number of unsuccessful attempts by Unionists to lift the talks out of their Anglo-Irish context. Throughout the exercise the two governments made it clear they were in continual contact at both ministerial and official level, emphasising the point with a meeting between John Major and the Taoiseach, Charles Haughey. At no stage did the Unionists manage to expose any gap between Dublin and the SDLP or drive a wedge between the two governments. The anti-Unionist consensus remained intact.

Nationalists have already begun to argue that British ministers should abandon efforts to do serious business with Unionism under its present leadership, and concentrate instead on strengthening links with Dublin through the Anglo-Irish agreement. Nationalists hope, and Unionists fear, that this will emerge as the new direction of British policy in the aftermath of the failed talks.

The talks process put pressure on local parties, and the Irish government, to clarify their positions on the future. But it tended to obscure another question: what exactly did Britain want?

What is the plan
for Ulster?

Most people in Britain, watching the television pictures of the British soldier standing guard at the white tape after the latest Northern Ireland atrocity, presumably see a symbol of patience and forbearance. The belief is that he is performing an invaluable, highly dangerous job and receiving precious little thanks for doing so. He is, in this view, holding the ring between two totally unreasonable warring tribes and fulfilling an exemplary peacekeeping role.

It is a fair bet that most people in Northern Ireland believe, whether or not they acknowledge it publicly, that the presence of the troops serves a real function and that the level of violence, terrible as it currently is, could be much higher without them. Certainly, any move to remove the troops would result in panic, not just among Unionists but among nationalists as well, and not just in the north but in the south, too.

But the story does not end there. The fact that Britain may be carrying out some commendable functions does not absolve it from all elements of responsibility for this tangled situation. It can often seem that the British stance is that nothing they have ever done could possibly have contributed to the present difficulties. This exasperates both Unionists and nationalists, and helps create the gulf in understanding across the Irish Sea.

The Brooke talks are an example of the British projection that it is a disinterested well-wisher rather than an active player. In England, Peter Brooke's efforts were seen as a gallant attempt by an honest broker to bring the tribes together. What was not recognised was the fact that his own skilful affectation of neutrality might have contributed to the failure.

One of the important factors behind the interminable haggling over preconditions was the suspicion of the parties concerned not just about each other but also about British intentions. Once into talks, would the British have leant towards the Unionists or the nationalists? What was the British agenda? This huge unknown factor lurked in the background all the way through, as Mr Brooke not only concealed Britain's exact interests but did not even acknowledge that it had any. His approach chimed exactly with the general British belief that

206

none of the mess could be their fault. Such a projection may help to conceal Britain's long-term strategy. More likely it hides the fact that there is no such strategy, and that there exists no settled view on whether the union should continue or at some stage be broken.

A key feature of British policy has been that it is changeable and based on no fixed principle. At one stage the British presence was colonial and influenced by the need to safeguard the western approaches against French frigates and Spanish galleons. Those considerations have gone, but there is no agreement on what Britain's interests now are. It was a senior IRA figure who said: "The argument could be made that there has never been a cohesive British policy in Ireland in 20 years. They have stumbled from crisis to crisis: they have never had the political will to face the problem." Leading Unionist politicians have used almost identical words to make precisely the same point.

Many Protestants consider Britain to be chronically soft on terrorism, and fervently believe it is determined eventually to propel them into a united Ireland. Some Catholics characterise Britain's rule as repressive, and think it will fight like a tiger to maintain a foothold in Ireland. Many others are simply unsure, even after more than two decades, what Britain's ultimate aim is.

Since direct rule from Westminster was introduced in 1972, 46 ministers – Northern Ireland Secretaries and their deputies – have proclaimed Britain's commitment to Northern Ireland. The British army has been here in strength for more than two decades. Huge amounts of money are poured in to prop up a grievously damaged economy. Yet there are many other signs – the Anglo-Irish agreement for one – which can be cited as evidence that Britain regards Northern Ireland as a semidetached part of the United Kingdom. The constitutional relationship is highly ambivalent, as, indeed, it has often been in past centuries.

What history shows is that British policy can change unpredictably, sometimes for the worst of reasons. This is a crucial factor in the continuation of the Troubles, for the minds of those who control the gunmen contain a deep-rooted belief that the British sometimes give in to violence. Historically it is difficult to argue that this is not so. Lloyd George sat down and hammered out a treaty with Michael Collins, whose men had killed many of his soldiers and policemen. On the other side of the coin, the Tory party openly encouraged Edward Carson and the Unionists when they threatened to fight the forces of the crown.

The gunmen and their bosses may not be familiar with all the historical details of these and other episodes, but they believe they have the gist of it. The men who are splashing Belfast with blood may have hatred in their hearts, but not all of them are mindless. They do it for a reason. They see themselves as politicians with guns, and it is Britain's record in Ireland which leads them to believe that murder can work as a means to a political end.

It is also understood that policy is prey to various passing pressures. One example is international influence, particularly from the US. The Irish also know that concessions can be wrung from shaky British governments, particularly with hung parliaments. O'Connell benefited from Whig weakness, while Gladstone courted Parnell when he needed the votes of Irish MPs. The Unionists remember, as though it were yesterday, how Jim Callaghan wooed James Molyneaux and Enoch Powell in the late 1970s when he needed support for his minority Labour government. Unionist prayers are currently being offered up for another hung parliament and a rerun.

Such episodes can produce great cynicism in Ireland, for they show how easily the British can drop one set of policies, and allies, and find others. For 50 years they gave the Protestants free rein, but during the Troubles they have also, on occasion, talked to the IRA. Policy at the moment is uncomfortably spread-eagled, with a developing political alignment with the constitutional nationalists but a continuing dependence on the Protestants for security manpower.

Britain has difficulty coming to terms with its mistakes in Ireland. Anything which does not fit easily into the perspective of the honourable overseer of the warring tribes tends to be ignored or denied. It has become practised at ex-onerating itself both for the errors of history and for its various mistakes during the present Troubles. What is missing in the British perception is the sense that its own track record contains inglorious episodes.

The standard British response to such points is to wave a hand airily and complain that the Irish are obsessed with the past. This dismissal of history is a useful mechanism for denying there has been a British contribution to today's problem; but it should never be imagined that the Irish, either nationalist or Unionist, forget these things. History here, for good or ill, is a living thing. Ignoring it makes the search for a solution more difficult.

More talks took place in 1992, but by the summer it was obvious that no real sign of consensus was emerging from the discussions. In this interview a senior Presbyterian clergyman appealed for a move away from traditional attitudes, and a more forward-looking outlook from Protestants. He is the Right Rev Dr John Dunlop, who in June 1992 was elected

Moderator of the Presbyterian church,
Ireland's largest Protestant denomination.

28 JULY 1992   THE INDEPENDENT

Churchman seeks
to break siege

John Dunlop projects self-confidence, tolerance, thoughtfulness and good humour: qualities not normally included in the world's general image of Ulster Protestants. They have been described as a pariah community, receiving a consistently bad press from an outside world which associates them with anti-Catholicism, a lack of give-and-take and an obsession with the past.

The one million Protestants are normally viewed as a majority in Northern Ireland, but Dr Dunlop puts them in a different context. It is a context that he clearly sees as one of the keys to understanding their behaviour. "What many people do not realise is that Unionists and Protestants are much more aware of their minority status in the whole of Ireland than they are of their majority status in Northern Ireland," he says. "I maintain that there is a story to be told inside the totality of Ireland, which is the story of the Protestant minority in Ireland. It has not been persuasively articulated but it is there to be told. So far it's been buried inside the other story, that of the Catholic minority inside Northern Ireland. I say sometimes to my political acquaintances in Dublin: 'Your primary political problem is us – not London, not Sinn Féin, but us, the Protestants. How do you deal with the minority of people on this island who do not associate themselves with your aspirations?'"

John Dunlop is a noted ecumenist, a breed heartily disapproved of, criticised and, indeed, on occasions picketed by the Rev Ian Paisley and other hardline loyalists. He is firmly in the Presbyterian tradition, but is markedly less distrustful of the Catholic church, Dublin and London than are many of his co-religionists. This more open attitude leads him to urge his church to move away from the siege mentality so deeply ingrained in the philosophy of the northern Protestant. According to Dr Dunlop: "We live behind spiritual, political and ecclesiastical ramparts. The siege mentality is defensive, anxiety-ridden and preoccupied with

209

danger rather than opportunity. I think the Unionist position politically is weaker now because it is rooted in such a profound sense of insecurity that it has been incapable of being as generous, or even as flexible, as it required to be in its own interests in the past 25 years. That inability to articulate something which can accommodate diversity is rooted in insecurity.

"I believe there are good historical reasons why this sense of siege exists, going right back to the 17th century, when the 1641 rebellion almost wiped Presbyterianism out. And today there is undoubtedly in some areas a sense of explicit siege, where people are obviously continuously under threat.

"So there are historical and contemporary reasons why people should feel this. But my argument is that getting yourself locked into this does not serve your community well. It prevents you understanding the nationalist or Catholic community. Defensive policies politically or ecclesiastically are not good for the community. There are other realities which ought to enable us to address the situation in more positive terms."

The siege mentality is not just an abstract concept, but can be physically seen in population movements, which Dr Dunlop views as both saddening and ominous. He and others have noted the steady movement of Protestants out of some border areas and from some large areas of Belfast.

"The Presbyterian population on the city side of Derry now hardly exists, because there has been a radical Presbyterian withdrawal over to the Waterside," he says. "This is also happening in congregations in border areas: Strabane congregation is much smaller than it was, and one congregation in Newry is half the size it used to be. In the mid-1950s north Belfast was described as the most Presbyterian part of Belfast, but now many of the Presbyterian churches there have question marks over their continuing existence. In my own part of north Belfast, hardly a house here has been bought by a Presbyterian in the last five years. It's not that Presbyterians are being driven out, it's just that the vast majority of houses which come on the market are being bought by Catholics. Something similar is happening in parts of south Belfast. The Presbyterians are moving out of the city to satellite towns on the periphery.

"Within my congregation, 50 per cent of the university students are studying in Britain, and I know most of them won't be coming back. When you look at all this together, what you are seeing is a community which looks to be in retreat.

"What I want to see is Presbyterianism freed from its intellectual preoccupation with being besieged so that it can make its contributions in a wider way, so that I am not simply to be a chaplain to an imprisoned community. It is in everybody's interests that these bridges of understanding and friendship be built. One wants to see increasing politics of mutual understanding, elements of co-operation rather than hostility and discord and bitterness."

210

In many countries such words would be seen as uncontroversial generalities. But although Dr Dunlop argues that his is not an overtly political stand, there are many in Ireland who will take his words as an attack on Unionism's political performance.

Last month, when he was installed as moderator, he urged his church: "Let us patiently and carefully explain who we are." Yet when he himself is asked the hard question – whether he is British or Irish – his answer is not a straightforward one. "I think I suffer from the same identity crisis as nearly all Northern Ireland Presbyterians," he replies. "In some senses you're Irish and in some senses you're British. I can identify myself with being Irish if the Irish identity is sufficiently wide as to be inclusive of people like me. But if on the other hand the Irishness is Catholic and Gaelic, it is hard to know where I fit into that.

"My orientation tends to be east–west rather than north–south. I would read the *Independent* much more than I would read the *Irish Times*. I watch BBC 1 and BBC 2 and listen to Radio 4 rather than RTE from Dublin. Even though I live in Ireland I feel I don't have an enriching and appreciative understanding of Irish culture. I would, therefore, feel that, to a degree, I am culturally impoverished.

"Two things are required here: first, that I move out across the frontiers to understand that; and second, that people in that culture move across the barriers to try and understand me. With most Catholics I meet on church business I find there is no overt hostility to me at all. But there is a lack of understanding there."

The Catholic church looms large in Presbyterian thinking, for it is, of course, the largest church in Ireland and one which Protestants view as wielding considerable social and political power. Dr Dunlop believes the Catholic attitude towards Protestantism has changed since Vatican II, but he acknowledges that many Presbyterians view Rome as an unchanging and generally hostile institution. He observes: "The experience of living within the Catholic tradition is of living within an institution which is large and secure, and your identity is shaped and formed within it, and in religious terms is not shaped and formed against other people.

"On the other hand, the Protestant theological traditions tend to be shaped not only by their own internal authentic element but also in terms of where they differ from the predominant religion of Ireland, which is Catholicism. So there is a Protestant preoccupation with Catholicism which is not reciprocated."

He sees important changes in the way the Republic of Ireland views the northern state. "There has been a moderation of Irish nationalism, in that I think both of the principal parties in the south have come to understand that Ireland cannot be united other than by the consent of the majority in the north.

211

It can't be done any other way. That has been a slow process which has caused the parties in the Republic to come to a more realistic understanding of the realities of those people who resist the unification of Ireland. The main sources of resistance are not, in fact, in London, as the IRA think they are, but inside Northern Ireland.

"London would grant Irish unity tomorrow if it were not for the resistance to it among the majority of people in Northern Ireland. But the IRA think the problem is located primarily in London. Their analysis is, therefore, flawed, and they then proceed on a campaign of violence based on a false diagnosis of the problem. So it's wrong on two scores: it is immoral and it is misplaced politically. Killing Presbyterians does not advance the republican cause, it impedes it and builds resistance to it. They cannot unite this country by killing their Presbyterian neighbours."

John Dunlop's message was that Protestants and Unionists should be more outgoing. Some Unionist councillors in Belfast seemed to take him at his word.

---

1 MARCH 1992 THE INDEPENDENT ON SUNDAY

Council helps Unionists to go far

There may be no real evidence that travel has broadened the minds of the Unionist councillors of Belfast, but their globetrotting activities have had a marked effect on the city council's bank balance. Their Sinn Féin critics have, after much effort, extracted the fact that sending councillors and officials to conferences and study trips overseas has cost the council a cool £97,000 in a year.

It turns out that the burghers of Belfast managed, in the financial year 1990–1, to range all over the world. From Amsterdam to Toronto, Antwerp to Barcelona, Rotterdam to Paris, Stockholm to Milan, Berlin to Padua, the Unionists of Belfast have been explaining to fascinated foreigners how they have made such a success of Belfast. Next stop, for the chairwoman of the parks committee and an official, will be Hong Kong, to spend a week discussing recreation administration. In addition to such exotic locations, visits to venues in Britain are commonplace.

In 1990–1 there were 44 visits overseas, with places for 95 councillors. Ninety-three of those selected to go came from the Unionist bloc, which has a narrow majority on the council. The 1990–1 record-holder is Jim "Junior" Walker, a councillor with the Rev Ian Paisley's Democratic Unionist party, for whom his Unionist colleagues approved 11 separate trips. He visited Antwerp, Paris, London, Glasgow (twice), Brighton, Bournemouth, Gateshead, Durham, Rotherham and Torbay.

Asked for an example of the benefits which can flow from such visits, Councillor Walker volunteered: "While you're away, you'd see something and perhaps lift a wee card about it. Now, if someone then comes along with an idea and says, you know, blah, blah, blah, you say, look, hold on a minute, I remember such and such, and then you can find a piece of paper or find a name or do something about it.

"One of the things that I seen, which I thought was quite simple, a problem we have in a lot of our parks is dogs fouling. Now at a conference they had, one of the exhibitors had a wonderful little device, which was like a wastepaper bin, and at the side of it a roll of miniature black plastic bags. And the idea is, you take this black plastic bag, you put your hand inside the bag, lift up the dog's mess, turn the plastic bag inside out, and put it in the wastepaper bin. I thought that would be really, really useful.

"But we came back and spoke to the people who deal with it day and daily, and they said, 'No, that won't work.' And when it was explained to me, I went, 'Right, okay, that's fair enough.'"

Sinn Féin have tabled a motion complaining at the number of "junkets" and pointing out that there is no reporting back to council on the vast majority of trips abroad. The motion will be defeated, since Unionist policy on the council is to defeat all Sinn Féin motions regardless of their content. One Unionist, who has made three dozen trips abroad in three years, said: "I don't take any notice of any objections that come from the like of the rubbish that represents Sinn Féin." He was speaking after he and eight other Unionists returned to Belfast after a visit, which cost almost £10,000, to learn how to keep down council costs.

Political and media condemnation
did nothing to deter the globetrotting
city fathers.

5 SEPTEMBER 1992   THE INDEPENDENT

Belfast councillors shrug off junketeering criticism

Unionist members of Belfast's controversial Unionist-controlled council are once again packing their bags for foreign parts. So many Unionist councillors are due to be abroad over the next two months that Sinn Féin has, in a sarcastic little jest, asked the government to appoint a commissioner to handle the city's affairs in their absence.

One symbol of the alleged extravagance which has been much criticised by nationalists is the planned visit of the chairwoman of the parks committee, Mrs Margaret Crooks, to Hong Kong for a week-long conference on the environment. The conference will feature lectures on subjects such as the traditional influence of Fung Shui in oriental landscapes and the restoration of the Malaysian rain forest. According to the programme, Councillor Crooks will be invited to board a "luxurious air-conditioned vessel for a cruise through the harbour while the night falls over the South China Sea. Unlimited free drinks and relaxing live music are available on board."

Critics say such visits are inappropriate when the council is facing a round of cutbacks and redundancies. Eyebrows were raised when Councillor Crooks told a local newspaper: "I work hard as a chairman of a committee, so there is nothing wrong with playing hard." Asked about this remark, she told the *Independent*: "I said it in a joke. It has been repeated so often that it really is no longer relevant. It's not relevant to that at all. It has no relevance to that. I can't see the point in asking all these questions because people have been going on conferences for years and years, so why is all the controversy centred around me? I just happen to be the chairman of the parks committee at the moment. If I decided not to go, someone else would go anyway."

Councillor Crooks, asked about the relevance of rain forests to Belfast, replied:

"Well, I think it is a good thing for people to know what has happened in other parts of the world. It can be a lesson to the rest of us not to make any mistakes. Any information that we can pick up is certainly worth while bringing back. Our own government has sent money to help restore the rain forests in South America, for example. Everyone is interested in global problems now, so why not? Why should we not be as well informed as anyone else?"

Councillor Crooks is a seasoned traveller as a representative of Belfast. In the past two and a half years she has visited Rotterdam, Manchester, Southport, Preston, London (twice), Torquay, Glasgow (twice), Birmingham, York, Reading, Cardiff and Brighton on council business. Critics of the trips abroad complain not only that there are too many of them but also that Unionists maintain a near-monopoly on such visits. Of the eighty-eight places on trips outside Northern Ireland in the last financial year, only five were allocated to non-Unionist members. Apart from the Hong Kong conference, up to seventeen councillors are to visit Brussels, while five will fly to Seville and Barcelona next month. Last year the trips cost £86,000. Councillor Crooks, asked how much her visit to Hong Kong would cost, said: "I don't know. I didn't ask."

Belfast City Council is held up by nationalists as a symbol of Unionist intransigence, while many Protestants are also dismayed by its recurring sectarian wrangles. The Catholic *Irish News* fulminated recently: "Of all the councils in Northern Ireland, Belfast's has become the laughing stock. Its monthly meetings are a source of constant embarrassment. The antics of some of its members would disgrace the monkey enclosure in the city zoo."

The affairs of the council, Northern Ireland's largest, have a special political significance. It has become such a byword for acrimonious disagreement that many doubt the wisdom of giving more power to local politicians, and thus wonder whether there is any real chance of the present political talks succeeding.

The political talks, meanwhile, were dragging on in unproductive fashion. But what messages, behind the scenes, was the Protestant business community sending to the Unionist negotiators?

Protestants haunted by British withdrawal

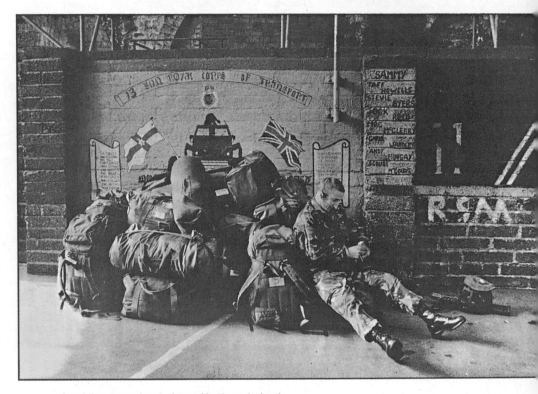

A soldier preparing to leave Northern Ireland

"What business people are scared of," according to a senior figure in the Belfast financial world, "is a British withdrawal – if Britain pulled out in disgust and lack of patience with us. Many business people would say it's a miracle it hasn't already happened – I've heard that so many, many times. There's a very clear feeling that our efforts have helped to keep this place going. But that is built, without any shadow of doubt, on an enormous British government subvention."

Conversations with more than a dozen senior business figures in the Protestant community show they share many of the general preoccupations, and fears,

216

of Unionism. But there is no single view within that business world, beyond a fairly general feeling of good will towards the talks.

One of the most striking features of the business community is the way its members have insulated themselves from many of the effects of the Troubles. The quality of middle-class life is particularly high, with businessmen in general living far from the violence. One senior economist said: "There are people I meet who speak of Northern Ireland as a paradise. They live well, their children go to fine grammar schools, and there are hardly any drugs around. They play their golf and they sail their boats and drink their wine, and they abstract out of it."

The business classes have shied away not only from the violence but from politics as well. Until the late 1960s they were immersed in Unionist politics, but when the Troubles began they, almost to a man, abandoned politics and baled out. Today they have only limited local political influence, many of them privately speaking of Unionist politicians with contempt.

Their critics would say that their own record has been inglorious, in that they first of all helped preside over a sectarian system and then later washed their hands of it. This is not, of course, their own perspective. A prominent businessman who was once involved in politics declared: "We're always being pushed for more, as though we've got the chest of gold and we have to give it away a bit at a time. That drives Protestants absolutely mad, because they don't see themselves as bigots en masse.

"When middle-class Protestants get together around the dinner table, and there's nobody except Prods there, they will ask – what are we going to be asked to swallow next? – what's the next thing going to bloody well be? They don't see themselves as guilty men. They see themselves as misunderstood, as people who have very badly represented their own case. They don't see themselves as people who are to be punished, and if there's any suggestion of that kind of thing from these talks the whole thing could come totally off the rails."

A Unionist representative involved in the talks says he gets two distinct messages from the business community: "One signal is: 'Get in there and stay with it and make sure you're not the first to walk away.' But the other is: 'For God's sake, whatever you do, don't sell us out.'"

There is another strand of opinion, which would shed few tears if the talks did not work. This argument, which is advanced by quite a few, is that the current system of direct rule, with its appearance of stability and its enormous subsidies, works pretty well as far as business is concerned. The direct rule apparatus consists of a Northern Ireland Secretary, a number of junior ministers and a reasonably compact Northern Ireland Office, together with a separate civil service. This system offers the Belfast businessman unparalleled access to the levers of power. The system has had the useful effect of depoliticising and largely removing from the political arena areas such as housing, which once aroused intense controversy but are now regarded as equitably run. There is certainly a fear that any new devolved administration could reopen many old sores.

Those who hold such opinions tend towards the fatalistic view that things cannot be expected to get a great deal better. The alternative school of thought, which includes some in the upper echelons of business and finance, holds that real improvement is possible and that the talks could bring substantial progress. One business leader said: "A lot of people aren't really looking at devolution as offering great possibilities, but I think that if we can get an agreed set of devolved institutions, then the potential for mobilising the latent energies are enormous. It could reflect talent right across the board, while if the talks collapsed, it would be a dreadful admission of failure and inadequacy."

The northern business community has in recent years paid increasing attention to north–south trade, and there have been important cross-border initiatives recently from the local CBI and from the banking industry. While Unionists are traditionally insistent that such moves have no political implications, this trend may well have a long-term effect. To be acceptable to nationalists, the talks will have to result in a significant north–south linkage, together with a sharing of power between Protestants and Catholics. Would such arrangements be acceptable to the Protestant business community?

The answer, from almost every quarter, was yes. A number have reservations, but most say that they, and the people they associate with, now accept that the structure of any agreement will be along such lines. One said: "Some of the old types still have a lot of hang-ups, but the newer generation recognise the shift of power that has occurred. There's now a much more equitable society, and they have come to terms with that." Two other sources said they believed the business class ready to accept far more than the Unionist negotiators would ever accept.

There were warnings, however, that too radical a settlement could drive businessmen back to traditional Unionism: "If it's constitutional adventurism," said one, "they will see that as highly destabilising and as something that's only going to increase mayhem and uncertainty. They would prefer something quieter, low-key."

The business world, like the population in general, regards the talks with varying measures of hope, apprehension and cynicism. In general, expectations are low, for there have been so many false dawns in the past. The former Unionist politician, however, had one observation which crystallised the views of many business people. He said: "There's a view about, it's very well rehearsed, that both sides here have taken so much hammering that at the end of the day

218

you've only got yourselves. The rest of the world doesn't give a damn about you, and at the end of the day the only way forward is to get on with your neighbour and get on and do the bloody thing."

The replacement of Peter Brooke by Sir Patrick Mayhew in April 1992 brought no new momentum to the talks. Unionists went to Dublin for some sessions, but neither side moved appreciably from their initial positions, little trust developed, and no breakthroughs were made. Unionist and nationalist neighbours found no new way of working more closely together.

The ending of the talks caused some in London to pose the question: what policy options were left?

28 JANUARY 1993   THE INDEPENDENT

Should Britain keep soldiering on?

In March 1922, Protestant gunmen burst into a home in Belfast and killed every male Catholic they found there. Two weeks ago in Co Tyrone their descendants did the same thing, leaving two men dead and another badly injured. The IRA was bombing 70 years ago and is bombing still. There is a grim continuity, as if it is forever ordained that a steady stream of people must die in disturbances which never quite erupt into sustained open warfare.

At the moment little is moving on the political front. Last year's talks involving the UK and Dublin governments and the constitutional parties failed to reach agreement, and all is now in abeyance. But with a new Irish government in place and a new Clinton administration professing an interest in the Irish problem, the time has perhaps come to consider whether there might be other alternatives to the current approach of military containment and political negotiation, or if patiently soldiering on is indeed the best option.

Some ideas which attracted attention in the 1970s have faded. The idea of an independent Northern Ireland once had both nationalist and loyalist advocates, but now has none. The weakness is that an independent state would be dominated by loyalists and therefore racked by republican violence, or else run on a basis of Protestant–Catholic consensus. But if there was consensus, then independence would not be needed.

Moving the border and effecting a repartition was also examined at one stage, and might have won some support had it been more practical. It foundered, however, because well over 100,000 nationalists live in Belfast. No redrawing of the frontier, however ingenious, could manage to include them in an enlarged Republic without huge population movements.

Another option, continually urged by republicans, is for the government to talk to the IRA through its political wing, Sinn Féin. The government's attitude to this, which in essence is endorsed by almost all Irish and British parties, is that the IRA would first have to renounce violence. That is to say, it would not only call a ceasefire but would also declare and demonstrate that its campaign of violence was at an end. Common sense suggests that this is not a hard-and-fast position. If there were clear signs that the IRA and Sinn Féin were actively seeking a way to get off the hook of violence, many would stretch a point to help them to do so. But there is no indication that they are considering ending their campaign.

The other main purpose in talking to the IRA would be to inform them that their central demand, for a British declaration of intent to withdraw from Ireland, was being seriously contemplated. There is a deep-seated British instinct to have less and less to do with Northern Ireland, but enormous difficulties face any government inclined to sever the link.

Opinion polls in Britain show that a large section of public opinion favours withdrawal, yet there is a battery of arguments against such a course. It would break the solemn promise that Northern Ireland can remain part of the UK so long as a majority of its residents wish it; it would be seen as a major victory for terrorism; and it would be against the wishes not just of Unionists but also of constitutional nationalist opinion.

Most of all, it could be a leap from the frying pan into a much fiercer fire. The conclusion of most politicians, and most academics who have written on the subject, is that withdrawal under present circumstances could – some say would – lead to violence on an unprecedented scale. The fear is that with no single group strong enough to provide an alternative central authority, Northern Ireland could be plunged into disorder on the scale of Lebanon or the former Yugoslavia. The nightmare scenario is one of Catholic areas controlled by the IRA, Protestant districts controlled by loyalist gunmen, of forced population shifts, of outbreaks of ethnic cleansing. The late Professor John Whyte wrote: "For civil war to break out it is not necessary for a majority of inhabitants to desire it. Quite small numbers of extremists on each side can force a situation where, by reprisal and counter-reprisal, the peacefully inclined majority are obliged to seek protection from, and then give support to, the paramilitaries of their own community."

The IRA argument is that, faced with a British declaration of intent to withdraw, Unionists would abandon ideas of resistance and negotiate rather than fight. Short of putting it to the test, this contention cannot actually be disproved. But most observers – including, tellingly, many nationalists who would ideally like to see a British departure – believe the risks involved are so huge that the gamble should not be taken.

All of this has narrowed Britain's options, bringing it to the current situation where it affirms that Northern Ireland is presently part of the UK but will cease to be so if and when a majority of its people vote to leave. This is in itself a reasonable reflection of much British public and political opinion: it recognises the singularity of the region in British constitutional terms by conceding that unusual right of secession to it. Within these parameters one possibility would be a Unionist tack. This could either take the form of restoring Protestant majority rule or working towards integration with Britain. The former is generally regarded as a recipe for disaster and has long been discarded as a viable option. Moving towards integration would entail a drastic change of direction from the present Anglo-Irish approach and would mean forfeiting Dublin's good will. The inveterate British instinct against deeper involvement in Ireland will probably prevent it.

Constitutional nationalism is currently divided on the advice it offers to the government. One faction believes the inter-party talks were premature and should be quietly laid to rest. It advocates instead a vigorous strengthening of the Anglo-Irish agreement, with more concentration on an agenda of bettering the position of Catholics. Other nationalists believe that talking is worth another try, and the government is inclined to agree with them. Previous negotiations have not succeeded but they have clarified many points, and the essential elements of an agreement are now clearer. It would entail powersharing within Northern Ireland, a link with Dublin, and a more explicit recognition by the Republic of the constitutional status quo. What is not so clear is whether the various interests involved are ready to sign up for such a deal, and whether

221

its vital points can be successfully hammered out in detail. But the government's policy is to pursue such an agreement.

Success would be a historic development, though it could bring its own problems. For example, the IRA, and possibly the extreme loyalists, would see it as a fundamental challenge, and would try to give any new accommodation a baptism of bloodshed. Failure in the talks, on the other hand, would presumably lead to a reassessment. But so many of the apparent options, as we have seen, are not really options at all. The government could at that point decide to place more emphasis on the Anglo-Irish accord, with perhaps another attempt at talks in a couple of years' time.

The idea that nationalists can be forced to become loyal British citizens has largely gone; so, too, has the notion of forcing unwilling Protestants into a united Ireland. What remains is the conviction that Northern Ireland will probably be run on a mixed model of some kind.

PART
TWO

●

THE
PEACE PROCESS

10

STIRRINGS IN THE
REPUBLICAN MOVEMENT

In the early 1980s, when Sinn Féin burst into electoral politics with some spectacular initial gains, most republicans regarded its emergence as a valuable new addition to the IRA's "armed struggle". It did, indeed, prove a thorn in the flesh of the British government in the years that followed.

But even amid the euphoria of Gerry Adams winning a Westminster seat and the party taking more than 10 per cent of the total vote, there were republican purists who worried about the long-term implications of this foray into politics. They were concerned that what they disdainfully referred to as "electoralism" could suck the republican movement into the system it opposed. An old-timer, Ruairí Ó Brádaigh, made an impassioned plea to a Sinn Féin *ard-fheis* (annual conference) not to get drawn into politics: "The destabilisation of the state, we are told, will result, and the movement will be strengthened. Always it was otherwise, the movement suffered and the state was strengthened – four times since 1922 it happened. All ended in failure and ended ultimately in the degradation and shame of collaborating with the British."

But the early 1980s were heady days for the republican movement, as continuing political and propaganda gains were chalked up. Its members ignored the old-fashioned Ó Brádaigh and listened instead to designer-stubbled Danny Morrison, who spoke of taking power in Ireland with an Armalite in one hand and a ballot paper in the other. Sinn Féin decided, with IRA approval, that involvement in politics was a proper weapon of subversion.

As the years have gone by, there is little doubt that the development of Sinn Féin has helped change the character of the republican movement. The violence has gone on without respite, but the party's existence meant that a growing culture of debate was grafted onto the IRA's inherent militarism. There was always a large penumbra of republicans who were sympathisers, but not members, of the IRA, and the emergence of an openly organised republican party gave opportunities for a wider input into policy-making. They included many intelligent and articulate men and women: Sinn Féin has extraordinarily talented middle ranks who can hold their own against any other party in Northern Ireland. These were not peaceniks, but the debates and discussions began to produce a discernible shift away from the simplistic ''Brits out'' line.

Sinn Féin policy became more complex as, for example, attempts were made to find a place in republican theory for northern Protestants who had traditionally been despised and dismissed as "pseudo-Brits" with no real national rights. At the same time, it became apparent that by the mid-1980s Sinn Féin had passed its electoral peak and had lost momentum.

Although many groups and individuals refused to talk to Sinn Féin, a whole series of private contacts took place with politicians, community workers, clerics and others. As the years went by, Sinn Féin policy documents had become thoughtful, intricate, and often tediously lengthy. Often their titles included the word "peace", and often Gerry Adams and other republican leaders made appeals to the British government to open talks with them. These developments led to a spate of media speculation in 1989−90 that an IRA ceasefire was in the offing.

The following interview with the IRA was conducted in the autumn of 1990, and is interesting in that it contained little of the rhetoric of peace and much in the way of menace. It is, therefore, revealing in retrospect to compare the republican style in 1990 with the more conciliatory language that has since been adopted.

227

The men of war promise third violent decade

The question about the assassination of Ian Gow and the wounding of Sir Peter Terry [Sir Peter, a former governor of Gibraltar, was seriously injured in an assassination attempt in September 1990] drew a barely perceptible shrug from the representative of the IRA's "general headquarters staff". He replied: "The grief of Mrs Gow is no different from the grief of families of IRA volunteers who are killed. The suffering of the Terry family is no different from the suffering of the McCann or Savage or Farrell families [the families of the three IRA members killed by the SAS in Gibraltar]. But it is wrong to personalise this conflict. We are at war with a coalition of interests. Ian Gow was an integral part of that coalition. I'm not going to get into a discussion of the specific criteria for targets. To do so would only aid the British to develop countermeasures. We want to stretch the enemy, both materially and in terms of their nerves."

The main points he wanted to project in the lengthy interview were, clearly, that the IRA had both the means and the stamina to continue its violence into a third decade. The impression came across that the organisation was pleased with the progress of its campaign in Britain.

"The war which Britain wages in Ireland has inflicted a very heavy price on all sections of our people," he said. "The IRA have quite forcibly told the British establishment, those who legislate for the war in Ireland, that they too will have to pay a price. It's our intention, and we have the means, to continue to exact that price from the British establishment. We will increasingly bring the war to the attention of the British public, and to the doorsteps of those who sustain the conflict. And their life styles will not stand the strain that our life styles do, for we have nothing.

"When one hears Tory MPs having to repeat 17 times that the IRA are not going to rattle them, it's fairly easy to see that they are hollow words. They are rattled, and so long as they persist with their illogical and illegal claim to Ireland, we will not only continue to rattle them but will rattle them harder."

The words of menace were delivered in a flat near-monotone, the words of someone for whom death has become a way of life, as he calmly described the thinking behind the IRA's killing patterns: "The strategy of waging war is also directly linked to the British desire to Ulsterise the conflict. We are quite aware that the perception in England, when an RUC man is killed, is, 'There are the Paddies fighting each other again.' The RUC and UDR are important parts of the war machine and we must therefore wage war against those forces. But it has been our aim for a number of years, whilst not limiting the scope of our operations, to concentrate our efforts on British military personnel."

For more than a year some newspapers have been speculating about the possibility of an IRA ceasefire, and the IRA spokesman clearly wished to make a definitive statement on the issue. "It's a tired old subject and it's one that comes up with predictable regularity. But the only debate within the IRA is on how best to prosecute the war against the British. We can state absolutely, on the record, that there will be no ceasefire, no truce, no cessation of violence short of a British withdrawal. That, as blunt as that, is our position. Having said that, should the British government at any stage genuinely seek dialogue, then we are more than willing to engage in dialogue with them.

"The principal aim of the armed struggle is to sap the will of the British government to remain in Ireland – to impress upon them that sooner or later they will come to accept the futility of their armed campaign, and will grant the internationally recognised right of self-determination to the Irish people. It's important for people to understand that; short of the removal of partition and the British presence, there will never be peace in Ireland."

An event as momentous as the break-up of the Warsaw Pact has had little apparent effect on the republican conviction that Britain regards Ireland as a country of strategic significance. The IRA spokesman outlined their position: "When you have United States planes refuelling at Shannon, I don't think you need to look any further to see that Ireland is still strategically important to these people with global political designs. Events in eastern Europe will have a bearing, of course, but I think that in general terms Ireland still remains strategically important to Britain. The last thing they can accept is a landmass just off their western shore that is not under their control.

"There are also those people who still believe that Britain is a world power. They think they have an absolute right to be here. Expressed at its simplest, it's 'You can't let the Irish run the country, sure they'd make a hames of it.'"

But where, after two decades of terrorism and death, where was the evidence that Britain had been brought any closer to withdrawal? The answer was ready: "There is no specific evidence to demonstrate that the campaign, in Britain or elsewhere, has brought tangible evidence of withdrawal. But there is the irrefutable case that, 21 years into this conflict, the British are fast running out of solutions. There is only one solution that they haven't tried, and that's disengagement.

"When things begin to move, they move fairly rapidly. What evidence was there in Afghanistan, even a few months before Mikhail Gorbachev took the troops out, that it was going to happen? That evidence wasn't there – the Russians were increasing the tank and helicopter patrols around Kabul just a short time before.

"There was a similar situation in Vietnam with the Americans. I think a reassessment under Margaret Thatcher would have been fairly unlikely; but then anyone can be brought fairly quickly to deal with political realities, just as F.W. de Klerk was. A few years ago Thatcher was condemning the ANC and Umkhonto We Sizwe in the most strident terms. But then there was the spectacle of her almost falling over herself to meet Nelson Mandela. That showed very clearly that there is no such thing as an absolute in politics. You should never take at face value what British politicians say. History has taught that.

"In personal terms she has obviously suffered quite a lot since 1984, and I don't think she's all that rational in dealing with IRA operations. She was almost killed, and I think that our words after Brighton still haunt her: 'Today we were unlucky. But remember, we only have to be lucky once. You will have to be lucky always.' At her age you should be looking forward to retirement, sitting back on her laurels. It'll be very hard to enjoy your retirement with a permanent bodyguard."

Was the IRA looking forward to the election of a Labour government with a policy of aiming for Irish unity by consent? Another shrug: "I think Gerald Kaufman, throughout the present American and British intervention in the Middle East, has shown he's every bit as much on the military bandwagon as any Tory.

"As far as Ireland goes, bipartisanship is still the order of the day: the policies of the parliamentary Labour party are a fudge. I don't see that either a Labour or Tory party in power makes any difference to the British determination to remain in Ireland. I think that determination is only as strong as the politicians' ability to repress the demand for withdrawal in England, and to keep a lid on their war in Ireland through censorship, media manipulation and naked propaganda.

"There isn't a very strong consensus on remaining in Ireland. It's a fairly fragile one, and it exercises the minds of the British establishment to keep that consensus intact. Every time an IRA bomb explodes in Hampshire, or any time the IRA comes within a hair's breadth of wiping out the British cabinet, the cracks in that consensus appear. We immediately have Robert Maxwell weighing in with an editorial calling for withdrawal; Peregrine Worsthorne saying we should be put outside the pale; Churchill-Coleman [Commander

George Churchill-Coleman, then head of the Anti-Terrorist Squad] calling for another security review, and howls from the backbenchers for more direct action against the IRA. They show the level of desperation that is there."

And what of the efforts of the Northern Ireland Secretary, Peter Brooke, to open a new round of political talks? This was denounced: "I think what he is about there is attempting to give a positive side to British strategy. The most hopeful scenario for Peter Brooke is that he involves the SDLP in a public endorsement of British military policy.

"I believe he is engaged in illusions, in selling the idea that Britain has a solution. All he's doing is perpetuating the agony. There is no incentive for Unionists to shift their position while Britain remains.

"After partition [in 1921] the British simply failed to take any meaningful interest in Ireland. And when the cesspit erupted in 1969 it was almost inevitable that they would be sucked into the conflict, that they would have to prop up the Orange state.

"The argument could be made that there has never been a cohesive British policy in Ireland in 20 years. They have stumbled from crisis to crisis: they have never had the political will to face the problem. There is a very clear military policy – for repression and for smashing the resistance of the Irish people to British rule. But they haven't thought beyond that. The only political policy that they have pursued, consistently, is stabilisation and containment."

But if Britain's concern is with stability, how could it contemplate the potentially totally unstable situation which withdrawal might create? Many analysts, after all, have argued that a pull-out would, or could, lead to a breakdown of order and new conflict on an unprecedented scale. His response: "I can accept what you're saying. The dilemma which faces the British is a very real one. I can accept that. But what they have to realise is that if they don't disengage, then their aim of stability is also defeated. They need to realise that the quest for stability in the six counties [of Northern Ireland] is futile. Their presence is the catalyst for instability."

And what of the possibility that the Unionist community, or a large part of it, would opt to fight rather than negotiate their way into a united Ireland? "What are the Unionists going to fight for? Are they going to fight to bring the British back? The dynamic for violence within the Unionist community stems directly from the British presence.

"I think the British government has one simple role in this: to convince those Irish people who at present subscribe to some hazy idea of Britishness that the British connection is going, and that they have to come to some sort of accommodation with the other people with whom they share the island. The British must work hard to convince the Unionists: they must have the will to lance the Orange boil. The Unionists cannot exercise a veto over democracy in Ireland."

So: the IRA hoped Unionists would one day realise they were Irish. How did he feel, in the meantime, about the organisation killing so many Unionists who were members of the UDR and RUC? "Those people who join a part of the British war machine, be it RUC or UDR, are an integral part of the British war machine. I don't think people in Britain during the Second World War would have had any qualms about killing English people who went to fight for the Waffen SS.

"I understand that the awfulness of this conflict means that for generations to come there will be bitterness. The Unionists, too, are victims of partition. There are Protestant families in Tyrone who have had six in one family killed. I understand that they will remain bitter for a long time: they will probably never fully integrate into a unitary Irish state. But I think Protestants will gain because they will cease to be victims of the British presence. They wouldn't be shackled and tied any more. I can't see that as losing. I see that as liberation.

"An irrevocable declaration of intent to withdraw, within a fixed timetable, would inject a dose of reality into the situation. In one fell swoop it would remove the biggest problem in Ireland, which is the British presence. The removal of the British presence would force the Unionist people to enter into meaningful negotiations."

But Britain, he made clear, would be expected not just to desert the Unionists but to disarm them as well. "Part and parcel of the demand for withdrawal is the disbandment and disarming of the British forces in Ireland, which includes the UDR and RUC. These partisan militias are unacceptable forces."

But would not the departure of the army and the disbandment of the UDR and RUC mean that the two armed groups left would be the IRA and any privately armed loyalists? A pause, and then: "Because the principal responsibility for the conflict lies with Britain, they must take steps to begin a process of convincing the Unionists that they're going. How they do that, that ball lies in their court. The dilemma facing them is huge, but it isn't insurmountable."

But how would the average Protestant UDR man feel and react, having been abandoned by the British army, disarmed, and left at the mercy of those who have killed so many of his colleagues and co-religionists? "The UDR man's feelings don't come into it. If the British have the will to break the loyalist veto, then they take the practical steps necessary. Once the UDR is disbanded, the UDR man becomes simply another member of the community. His interests in the island of Ireland will be represented by the person for whom he votes.

"It's for an all-Ireland conference to give guarantees to convince Unionists that their lot lies in the island of Ireland, to make them accept the political reality that Britain has gone. Unionists have to come to realise that they share this island with the rest of us, and it is in their interests to work out structures which guarantee the rights of all the children of the nation.

"There is no community which seeks conflict when negotiation is possible:

I think that holds true generally, and it holds true for the Unionist community. We are offering to Unionists and Protestants the first chance, in Ireland's long, tortured history, of genuine and lasting peace."

The City of London, April 1993:
the IRA fulfills its 1990 threat to keep up its campaign in Britain

Security sources are in no doubt that the IRA's threats to step up its campaign of violence in Britain are more than empty rhetoric. The intelligence assessment that the organisation now represents a greater menace than at any time in the past two decades has been borne out by a string of attacks on government and establishment figures. Like the terrorists, the security forces are committing themselves for a long haul.

There is no real sign of any shortage of recruits to IRA ranks, nor of any lack of volunteers willing to operate in England and thus risk very long jail sentences in the most hostile of prison conditions. Government attempts to squeeze its finances have so far met with, at best, partial success. In other words the terrorists have, over two grim decades, managed to construct a self-perpetuating and ruthlessly efficient killing machine. The point made most persistently by the organisation's spokesman was the threat that violence would continue so long as Britain remained in Ireland.

At the moment the IRA must consider that its shift in emphasis away from Northern Ireland itself towards Britain and the continent has paid dividends in terms of securing the attention of British politicians and public. The fact that the Ministry of Defence is spending over £100 million on measures to protect military bases in Britain and West Germany is a telling indicator of the level of official concern. In December last year the Northern Ireland Secretary, Peter Brooke, publicly warned that British servicemen and their families were at greater risk from the IRA outside Northern Ireland than inside it. The accuracy of his observation has been borne out by events since then, for only one regular soldier has died this year in Northern Ireland.

The security forces have yet to penetrate the structure of those carrying out attacks in England, though it must be assumed that more and more resources will be put into doing so. No one is in any doubt that the IRA will try not just to sustain the present level of attacks but to step it up.

The picture is very different in Northern Ireland, where the security forces have had a number of striking successes this year and increased their arrest rate significantly. In Belfast in particular, the IRA has for much of the year been largely, though not completely, pinned down.

The IRA spokesman's blunt dismissal of any possibility of a ceasefire will come as no surprise to the security forces, who have been aware for some time that such a move was not in prospect. The impression remains that republicans went through a period of introspection following the 20th anniversary of the beginning of the Troubles, but there is no real indication that any of the internal IRA – Sinn Féin debates ever focused on the possibility of an end to the violence.

For the IRA, the choice is stark. Continuing the campaign keeps alive, in the minds of its leaders, the possibility that Britain will some day throw in the towel, prompted, perhaps, by some change of political circumstance, or by an IRA action of particular enormity. Stopping the violence, to their minds, would amount to abject surrender, throwing away any gains made over the years. They would view it as a betrayal of those who have worked, and died, for their cause

234

over the years, and as condemning a future generation of Irish republicans to start their fight all over again.

The present northern-dominated IRA leadership came to power, in fact, because the ceasefire agreed to by the previous leaders in the mid-1970s was seen as a tactical disaster for the organisation. They have ever since rejected the idea. Furthermore, the existence of the huge Libyan-supplied armoury has its own imperative: to give up now, while so well equipped, would earn them a place of infamy in the republican annals. Thus a cessation of violence would mean total defeat, while a continuation carries the possibility of success.

In the meantime, in their carefully constructed theory, their supporters need not feel discouraged by the absence of any indicators of impending British withdrawal. They affect indifference to the lack of such signs, citing the analogies of Vietnam and Afghanistan. They believe they will one day hit the jackpot: that the fruit machine will, after many unsuccessful tries, some time, suddenly and without warning, disgorge its prize. The argument also has the convenient effect of absolving the IRA from having to provide its supporters with evidence that it is making headway.

SINN FÉIN

From the republican point of view, Sinn Féin, the political wing of the IRA, provides a useful political and propaganda adjunct to the terrorist campaign. Its presence in political life is a standing embarrassment to the authorities and a continuing affront to Unionists, who continue to lobby for the banning of the party.

Sinn Féin has become a fact of life in Northern Ireland. It has a Westminster representative in Gerry Adams who holds West Belfast [Mr Adams lost his seat to Dr Joe Hendron of the SDLP in 1992]. It has 43 councillors who sit on 14 of the 26 district councils.

Unionists – in particular, loyalist councillors – regard Sinn Féin as a major irritant in the body politic and denounce its spokesmen as mouthpieces for terrorism. Sinn Féin makes no secret of the fact that it sees its role, not as taking part in the political process, but in subverting it, though some of its councillors regard their positions as incidentally useful in giving them access to statutory agencies.

The government is uncomfortable with Sinn Féin. On one level it is a legal political party, standing for elections and representing its voters. But on another it is clearly attached to the IRA and is, to most intents and purposes, subordinate to it. The government has not sought to ban Sinn Féin (which was legalised in 1974), and civil service departments routinely deal with its members. At the same time, however, ministers will not meet Sinn Féin personnel, and its representatives are, in general, banned from appearing on television and radio.

In its heyday, in 1983, Sinn Féin collected 102,000 votes. In last year's European elections this fell to 49,000, its poorest performance for years, though this was in a contest in which its constitutional rival, the SDLP, traditionally excels through the large personal vote for its leader, John Hume. The Sinn Féin vote has clearly slipped and tended to contract into the republican heartlands. Early hopes of displacing the SDLP as the main nationalist party have disappeared. Sinn Féin lost seats in many councils last year, but actually increased its vote in Belfast, where it lays claim to being the second-largest party. Sinn Féin leaders say that in all they have a baseline support of around 70,000.

Even more disappointing than the slippage in Northern Ireland, for party activists, is the fact that it has failed to establish a parliamentary foothold in the Republic. There it takes less than 2 per cent of the vote and has no real chance of a Dáil seat.

Nonetheless, the existence of Sinn Féin, with the public support it offers to the IRA, is a reminder that the IRA has a substantial community base. The republican community exists as a series of concentric circles, with a comparatively small IRA at its centre. Around that core, however, exists a much larger body of nationalists prepared to lend support to, or simply acquiesce in, the IRA's campaign of violence. It may be in a decline, but it is not going to disappear.

SCENARIO FOR WITHDRAWAL

The second part of the interview concentrated on the IRA's scenario for a British withdrawal. This subject is necessarily highly conjectural, since to begin with there is no consensus on why Britain remains in Ireland. Various factors and combinations of factors have been suggested as to why this should be. These, in no particular order, include the following: a belief in the union; sheer imperialism; loyalty to the people of Northern Ireland, in particular the Unionist population; an unwillingness to confront the possibility of a loyalist backlash; a desire not to give in to terrorism; a belief that Northern Ireland has an internationally strategic significance; a desire to keep the island of Ireland under British economic dominance; and a fear that withdrawal would lead to a blood bath.

While there is no agreement on how these factors rank in importance, it may safely be assumed that the last-mentioned is a major consideration. Any country acts primarily in accordance with its own interests, and a departure which led to a civil war would result in international condemnation and an uncertain outcome. Any British government considering withdrawal would, therefore, wish to leave a stable administration behind, a point taken by the IRA spokesman when he said the only consistent political policy pursued by Britain was that of seeking stabilisation and containment. Thus, even if a government was intent on withdrawal, it would have to satisfy itself that its departure would not lead to conflagration on a horrifying scale.

The problem at that point would be that none of the elements left behind, with the possible exception of the Protestant community, has the military clout necessary to impose order and establish a new central authority in succession to Britain. The IRA may be a formidable force on a hit-and-run basis, but it is not strong enough to control Northern Ireland; nor is the Irish Republic, which has only 12,000 soldiers in its army. The million-strong Protestant community, by contrast, is one which has little tradition of negotiation and a long history of placing its faith in military methods. Its members make up the vast bulk of the various military elements: the 20,000 members of the RUC and UDR, the 38,000 former UDR members, 3,000 members of the prison service, 4,000 Territorial soldiers, and perhaps 5,000 others in various security-related occupations. They also control most of Northern Ireland's legally held firearms, which number in excess of 126,000.

The IRA proposal is for Britain to disarm the RUC and UDR before leaving. Their proposition is that, in the circumstances, Protestants would conclude that resistance to Irish unity was pointless, and for the first time would feel they had no option but to negotiate with the rest of the island. This analysis is rejected by, among others, leaders of constitutional Irish nationalism. But it is accepted, either in detail or in principle, by thousands of IRA members and supporters, and is thus important in sustaining the organisation in its violence.

The opposite view has been set out by John Hume, leader of the SDLP. In an exchange of views with Sinn Féin in 1988, he argued: "Each section of the community would seize its own territory and we would have a Cyprus/ Lebanon-style formula for permanent division and bloodshed. Is it not likely and natural, in the emotionally charged atmosphere that would obtain, and in the absence of any acknowledged authority, that the 20,000 armed members of the RUC and UDR would simply identify with the community from which most of them come and become its military defenders?

"And what would happen to the Catholic community in such circumstances, particularly in those areas where they are most vulnerable? Is the risk involved in such a military policy not an awesome one and likely to ensure that the peace and unity of Ireland will never come?"

Mr Hume's view has been echoed from the Republic by the former Taoiseach, Dr Garret FitzGerald. He wrote, of the prospects of such a breakdown of order: "No one can say with certainty that this is what would happen, but the danger is seen by most of us as sufficiently grave – the loss of life that might take place could be on a far greater scale than anything that has happened hitherto, or is likely to happen for many years ahead, and the situation left by a repartition would be far worse and less capable of ultimate resolution than the present situation – to preclude taking this risk."

In the end, the IRA's argument is that Ireland with the British presence will always suffer from violence; and most will accept that, for the foreseeable future at least, they will have the capacity to fulfil that prophecy.

The counterargument, even in the event of a government which wanted out, is that withdrawal could lead to a blood bath; and furthermore, that such an escalation of the conflict could not easily be controlled, since in the absence of Britain there would be no central authority with the strength to impose order. The IRA can argue that this would not happen, but it cannot guarantee that it would not. Thus it can promise Britain that staying in Ireland will lead to continuing violence, but it cannot promise that a British withdrawal would lead to peace. It cannot say for sure that withdrawal would not mean a leap from the frying pan into the fire.

In the end, Britain is essentially faced with a balance of instabilities. The price of staying may carry the penalty of violence, but the cost of going could be much higher.

In the mid-1980s the annual Sinn Féin *ard-fheis* was often a vibrant, lively affair with intense debates. But then, with the party seemingly past its peak, most of the excitement faded away. The 1991 *ard-fheis* was markedly downbeat, though behind the scenes something was stirring.

Sinn Féin faces future besieged by self-doubt

This was the most subdued Sinn Féin conference for years. Debates at the Mansion House in Dublin started late, speeches were lacklustre and many delegates did not bother to vote. Self-doubt and questioning were evident in a way that has not been visible before. At one stage the party proposed banning journalists from the tea room, apparently because they might eavesdrop on conversations between disgruntled delegates.

Sinn Féin is in the process of redefining its relationship with the IRA, though the conference showed little enthusiasm for openly debating the question. That relationship remains an organic one, but there are problems. Some types of IRA violence are bad for political business, and a certain distancing is thought helpful. The doubts seem to concern the prospects for Sinn Féin, though they have been misinterpreted — republicans at the weekend alleged deliberately — as raising the possibility of an IRA ceasefire.

Sinn Féin's leaders convincingly denied that any ceasefire was on the cards. The IRA may not have had a good year, but its capacity for violence remains clear. The organisation is heavily armed and still collects the recruits it needs: Belfast's Crumlin Road prison currently holds 146 republicans arrested and charged within the past year or so.

But Sinn Féin, the other part of the "Armalite and ballot box" strategy, is faltering. The impetus and drive of the early 1980s has gone. In the north it has lost councillors and assumed a defensive posture, concentrating on holding Gerry Adams's parliamentary seat in West Belfast and preserving as many council seats as possible. All idea of expansion has disappeared. In the south Sinn Féin has been marginalised and has a derisory share of the vote. The peace picket outside the conference was larger this year — another sign that Sinn Féin is now largely a northern phenomenon.

During the three-day conference, republican leaders repeatedly emphasised their willingness to open negotiations. There is, however, no sign of readiness by the British government to talk while the violence continues. In such circumstances, a ceasefire would be seen as a sign of weakness. In republican terms, it would amount to something close to surrender.

The mood of the conference was sombre, but not quite defeatist. The hope of many will be that this will lead to republicans thinking seriously about calling off the violence.

POSTSCRIPT

We now know, following the later disclosures about contacts between the British government and republicans, that a meeting had taken place between Sinn Féin leader Martin McGuinness and a British government representative several months earlier, in October 1990. The revelation shows that in Ireland things are not always exactly as they appear on the surface: some would say they never are.

An unusual by-election in Co Londonderry, brought about by a violent death, showed how politics and violence intertwine. It also showed the resilience of Sinn Féin.

13 DECEMBER 1991   THE INDEPENDENT

Sinn Féin makes gain at ballot box

There were only a couple of dozen of us at the counting tables in the Meadowbank recreation centre to hear Patsy Groogan's victory whoop as he became the latest Sinn Féin councillor. Nearly everybody from the other parties had already slipped away a few minutes earlier when it became clear that a Sinn Féin success was on the cards. Mr Groogan, a spare, elfin, mountainy man, was left to make his delighted little speech to the only available
240

audience, the row of young women who had done the counting. They watched him with studious impassivity.

Nonetheless, more than 4,000 citizens, a 57 per cent turnout, had felt it worth while braving Wednesday's freezing fog to register their choice at the ballot. They chose the Sinn Féin man in preference to Damian Sweeney, the downcast SDLP candidate. The margin of victory, after transfers under the proportional representation system, was only 2 votes, Sinn Féin collecting 2,157 votes to the SDLP's 2,155. But the result was a striking advance for the republicans, whose share of the vote went up from 31 per cent to 48 per cent. In a similar by-election just three months ago the SDLP had comfortably taken the seat, polling 2,600 first preferences to Sinn Féin's 1,400. This time round the comparable figures were: SDLP, 1,800, Sinn Féin, 2,100.

A number of local factors produced the different patterns, but the key reason lay in the cause of the by-election. On 16 September another Sinn Féin councillor, Bernard O'Hagan, had just arrived at the local college where he taught business studies, computers, and statistics, when a loyalist gunman ambushed and killed him. Mr O'Hagan was a Belfast man who had lived in England for many years and moved into the district only six years ago, quickly building a reputation as an energetic political worker. His widow, Fiona, has an unexpected English accent, with traces of both Birmingham and Liverpool in her speech.

According to Mrs O'Hagan: "I used to give him a bit of stick about all the time he spent on council work, but at back of it all I would have been very supportive. I've been very annoyed that there has never been any mention of Bernard's death by the council. There's been no sign, it's not mentioned in council minutes. It's never been acknowledged that he was ever there, that he did anything – good, bad or indifferent. I thought that would be just common courtesy.

"I've been following the election, trying to help out, getting involved in canvassing. It's a sort of a medicine for me – I have been so busy, I nearly don't want it to stop. I get some satisfaction from following Bernard's interests. When I do these things I think he would be pleased with me for continuing his work. I feel in some ways that he was removed because he was successful and articulate, not the mindless type some people like to portray Sinn Féin as being.

"People say I must be bitter. I suppose I'm angry that things are the way they are here, and people who have power and responsibility just don't feel strongly about it. People in England feel people can die here and it's no odds to them – they're just indifferent."

This by-election was essentially a political sequel to an act of violence. But in the past year Sinn Féin has now pulled off three unexpected victories in council by-elections, sending the unmistakable message to its many opponents that, while perhaps past its overall peak, it still has its strongholds.

What the outside world generally does not appreciate about republicans is the fact that they genuinely feel the IRA has morality on its side when it kills. They have traditionally seen themselves as a demonised community under attack from a hostile world, with no other option but recourse to force.

What the republicans lack is any sense of responsibility about the killings. What chills is their facility for self-absolution. All those deaths, they would say, are the responsibility of the British government alone. They see themselves as the real victims and appeal for recognition of this. At the same time they seem to have been fitted with a mental erase button which blots out the memory, and the humanity, of their own victims.

Their community and the rest of the world can sometimes seem to exist in mutual exclusion zones which intersect only in acts of violence, each blaming the other, each unwilling or unable to concede that the other side might have an iota of right.

Backdrop of violence
lies behind Sinn Féin vote

Sinn Féin press conferences are something of a ritual. We ask Gerry Adams and his colleagues about their attitude to violence, and they reply that Sinn Féin does not advocate violence and so has no need to renounce it. The IRA has the right to oppose "the British military occupation", the line goes. The British should not have a presence in Ireland, and the ultimate responsibility for violence, therefore, rests with them. We cantered round this familiar course at a leisurely pace, as Mr Adams introduced the 14 candidates who hope to retain Sinn Féin's Westminster seat and maintain its vote in the general election.

And then suddenly, an unexpected question took us to less familiar ground: how many of the 14 had been personally touched by violence, and how many had themselves been to prison? Matter-of-factly, the candidates, one by one, gave us their potted histories, which provide a glimpse of the culture which produces people like them, and organisations like Sinn Féin.

Brendan Curran said he had been to jail and had survived attempts on his life. Another Brendan Curran (the party has two candidates of the same name) had been to jail and had twice been injured in murder attempts by loyalists, one of which had also injured his father. Pauline Davey-Kennedy is standing in place of her father, who contested the last election but was since shot dead by loyalists. Joe O'Donnell said he had been in prison and that loyalists had tried to kill him and attacked his family on various occasions. Sean Fitzpatrick had been officially warned that his security details had fallen into the hands of loyalists and he was thus at risk. Paddy McManus had been interned without trial in the 1970s. Barry McElduff said he had been in prison for eight months and was now on bail on a charge of false imprisonment. He said he was trying to change the date of his trial since it would disrupt his election campaign. Martin McGuinness said he had been to jail on a number of occasions, stalked by a loyalist assassin, "and fired at by the British army on countless occasions over the last 20 years".

Gerry Adams said he had been shot a number of times, and heard of various plots to kill him. The British army had shot dead his brother-in-law and shot and seriously injured his brother. "I had a cousin picked up, tortured and stabbed to death by loyalists. Most of my immediate family have been in prison. I've a brother in prison at the moment." Nine of the fourteen candidates have been behind bars.

Sinn Féin will be contesting the election on the same basis as everyone else, but it is a party like no other. Most of the people who will support it – probably more than one in ten of all voters – will scarcely need to read its manifesto or listen to its arguments. The words will be less important than their communal perception of having been under violent attack for more than 20 years.

The result of the 1992 general election brought a severe blow for Sinn Féin – the loss of Gerry Adams's West Belfast seat, which he had held since 1983 and which his party had treasured so much. The Sinn Féin vote actually held up, but Dr Joe Hendron of the SDLP overtook Mr Adams by collecting some tactical votes from several thousand Protestants who were anxious to keep the republicans out.

Sinn Féin was crestfallen, having made intense efforts to keep the seat.

10 – 11 APRIL 1992   THE INDEPENDENT

Irish fiddle may still be on the cards

The entrance of the big polling station at Whiterock looked like a Sinn Féin carnival in the sunshine: a mass of green, white and orange flags, bunting, posters, and people festooned with stickers.

The journey to the station takes the visitor past army patrols of 16 men, along roads imprinted with tyre tracks left by joyriders practising their handbrake turns, past the betting shop where undercover troops killed three hoods. Then suddenly the drab landscape was alive with colour, the graveyard walls festooned with posters for Gerry Adams. Two dozen Tricolours, augmented by bunting, made it very clear that this is like no other part of the United Kingdom.

A dozen or so Sinn Féin men and women milled around the entrance, some of them with clipboards, some handing out green slips marked "Adams, Gerry, Sinn Féin". A caravan sporting Sinn Féin posters and flags sat nearby. Many of those who voted went over to its open window, where two cheerful women noted their names and addresses for their records. Sinn Féin cars and black taxis zoomed up and down the road, plastered with Adams posters, flags fluttering from windows and sun roofs, rebel songs blaring through loudspeakers.

There were four other candidates in the constituency, but at Whiterock there was no sign that anyone else apart from Gerry Adams was standing: no posters, no people, nothing. A poster for the Workers' party had been fixed to one wall, but an Adams poster had been carefully sellotaped over it. Two RUC men were there but were tucked away well inside the polling station.

At the Sinn Féin caravan the two friendly women told another journalist and myself that things were going well. Then we noticed that propped on a shelf behind them was what looked like a batch of new medical cards. The first in the sheaf was certainly a medical card, and the edges of what appeared to be others could be seen behind it. This was of some interest, since there have been allegations that in west Belfast in particular the ancient Irish arts of personation and vote-stealing may yet live on, despite all the authorities' attempts to eradicate them. The chief allegation has been that forged medical cards were being used. The women told us the medical cards must belong to voters who would be picking them up later on, and gave us balloons marked "I love west Belfast".

Later in the day we ran into Gerry Adams as he visited another polling station on the Falls Road. Word had already reached him about our questions, he said. He had no knowledge of any medical cards; it could be that a medical card had been left in for somebody coming in later, but that was entirely speculation on his part. Any suggestion that false cards were being used was completely untrue, he said. He bounded into the station, ignored by, and ignoring, the police and troops who were delivering meals to election staff. In other parts of the country the food is probably sent in small vans and cars. But in west Belfast it took a little convoy of three armoured Land-Rovers of troops and armed police to get the chicken and chips to those involved in the democratic processes in this most peculiar place.

For Sinn Féin the loss of Gerry Adams's seat was a telling blow, deposing, as it did, the party's single MP, with a consequent loss of local and international status. In addition, the overall Sinn Féin vote showed a drop of 5,000 compared to the 1987 Westminster election, its share of the vote falling from 11.4 per cent to 10 per cent.

At this time a change was being consciously introduced into republican rhetoric. Gerry Adams and other republican leaders began to speak continually about peace, and the word was used in the titles of important Sinn Féin documents such as "Scenario for Peace". Even against a background of continuing IRA violence, many found the use of such language very interesting.

---

11 AUGUST 1992   THE INDEPENDENT

Sinn Féin leaders raise hopes with talk of peace

Sinn Féin produced a symbol of longevity in west Belfast at the weekend for its annual commemoration of the introduction of internment: Joe Cahill, a veteran republican whose involvement with the IRA goes back a full half-century. Cahill's IRA career almost ended in 1942 when he was sentenced to death for the murder of a policeman. Reprieved, he was arrested 30 years later on board a ship bringing arms from Libya to Ireland and was jailed.

He was welcomed to the platform with the same affectionate reverence as British Labour party conferences accord those elderly socialists who knew Keir Hardie. And Sinn Féin has one thing in common with Labour these days: it is still hopeful of ultimate victory, but aware that it is some distance away.

In Labour the talk is of change while in Sinn Féin there is much more emphasis on continuity. It believes the solution to the Irish problem is British withdrawal, and that this can only be accomplished by force. Yet there has also been some intriguing language from the party which hints at some fresh thinking among its leaders. Speeches and statements have mentioned the need for a period of peace before British withdrawal, indicating that party thinking is evolving. Party figures have also paid some attention to the question of the rights of others with different opinions, such as Protestants and constitutional nationalists. Such statements have brought a cautious welcome from Protestant and Catholic clergymen and indeed, most unusually, from the paramilitary Ulster Volunteer Force. The UVF welcomed the "departure from republican dogma" and said Sinn Féin had entered the real world. Sinn Féin denied that the comments represented any significant shift, but it is fairly clear they were designed to catch the attention of the authorities and other sections of opinion, and to create speculation on the value of opening a dialogue with Sinn Féin.

Senior Protestant and Catholic clergymen, and probably others, have been in contact with the party, spurred mainly by the hope that the IRA might be persuaded to give up its campaign of violence. But all the public signs are that the British government sees no value in opening contacts, probably believing there is no point and that such moves would break up the political talks involving Dublin and the four main constitutional parties. Certainly the RUC and army show no sign of believing the republicans are contemplating any ceasefire.

There are, for the IRA, reasons for and against ending the violence, but there is no sign that any "doves" have ever come close to persuading any "hawks" that the time has come to stop unilaterally. In any event, the formidable armoury at the IRA's disposal in itself may represent the clincher, for with such large amounts of hardware around, ceasefire becomes virtually unthinkable.

The hope for many is that some in the ranks will at some stage conclude that the violence has not worked, and will not work. But it is also a fact that for many republicans the campaign has become an article of faith and that the use of force has ceased to be a tactic and has been elevated to a principle; and that after almost a quarter of a century violence has become a way of life.

Note again the assumption, which was then general, that the British govern-ment was not in contact with the republicans. In fact, regular messages were passing back and forward between them at this stage.

Even as the IRA attacked courts and judges, Sinn Féin was making increasingly effective use of the legal system.

---

3 MARCH 1993   THE INDEPENDENT

Republicans exploit the system they oppose

A recent feature of the Northern Ireland legal system has been the increasing readiness of Sinn Féin to appeal to the courts for justice. The practice, which at first seemed bizarre, has become a familiar part of legal and political life. Sinn Féin members and supporters have voluntarily been to court more than half a dozen times in the past three years, and more actions are in the pipeline. Their applications have enjoyed a strikingly high success rate.

In particular, they have scored a series of successes in obtaining High Court judgments against the Unionist-run Belfast City Council. Four cases either taken or supported by Sinn Féin have all been upheld by the courts. In each instance the council has been forced to reverse its policies. Furthermore, since such actions can be taken under legal aid, the whole exercise has not cost Sinn Féin a penny. But perhaps £50,000 of ratepayers' money has been spent in unsuccessfully defending the council against Sinn Féin complaints.

Even opponents of Sinn Féin concede that their cases have been well chosen and carefully prepared. Last November Lord Justice Murray was so impressed with the Sinn Féin evidence that he complimented its councillors on their "genuine interest and enthusiasm" for the welfare of their constituents. In only one case have Sinn Féin's hopes been dashed, when an attempt to unseat the MP for West Belfast, Dr Joe Hendron of the SDLP, failed last month. The republican hope had been to force a by-election in which Gerry Adams of Sinn Féin could have regained the seat. The court ruled that while Dr Hendron had acted illegally, he had done so inadvertently and should not be penalised.

Nonetheless, Sinn Féin's regular use of the legal system has made other parties noticeably nervous about the prospect of being taken to court by the republicans. When a new Unionist lord mayor of Belfast, Herbert Ditty, was chosen last year, Sinn Féin sent him a solicitor's letter warning of legal action. "That did the job," said one republican source. "Ditty treats us like the crown jewels now." Some Unionist councillors are known to be nervous that they could face personal surcharges if they persist in contesting cases where they have little chance of success.

Sinn Féin has clearly moved a long way since the days when republicans turned their backs on judges and refused to recognise the court. No one believes, however, that the new tactic amounts to a sign that republicans are coming to accept the legitimacy of the court. Its opponents regard the phenomenon as the height of cynical hypocrisy. "It's more than hypocrisy, it's a downright cheek and an abuse," according to Belfast loyalist councillor Sammy Wilson. "They use the courts while the IRA forces judges to go round in armoured cars with a police escort. IRA bombs have cost millions of pounds of damage to courts, then Sinn Féin go to the same courts to ask for their rights. They actually appeared before one judge whose house had been attacked by a rocket. It's ridiculous. The government should declare that Sinn Féin is linked to the IRA and ban them outright."

Sinn Féin representatives lose little sleep over such points. Máirtín Ó Muilleoir, one of the councillors whose diligence was commended by Lord Justice Murray, spelled out the pragmatic approach: "As far as I'm concerned, what the IRA's attitude is towards the courts is neither here nor there. We are in city hall to represent our constituents and if somebody puts an obstacle in your way, you have to get round it or over or under it." He would not concede that his party's successes in the courts suggest that the legal system might be fairer than Sinn Féin accepts. "The cases we brought have been so obvious and so blatant that there could have been no other judgment. It's also been suggested that the courts make political decisions. I would hate to go back to the people of Upper Falls and say, 'Oh sorry, I could have done something but I preferred to remain aloof with the green flag wrapped around me.' I'd much rather go back and say, 'Yes, we did that, we got the change, we got the gain.' It makes sense and it's something we will continue to do."

Many of the cases arose from Unionist attempts to exclude Sinn Féin councillors from council activities. In one instance Unionist councillors had attempted to avoid holding committee meetings, since Sinn Féin members were on the committee. Under threat of legal proceedings from Sinn Féin, they were obliged to hold committee meetings, but they then set up subcommittees from which the republicans were excluded. Sinn Féin members could not be barred from subcommittee meetings but they were not given the dates of meetings or the agenda or any documentation, and were not permitted to speak. Sinn Féin argued that the subcommittees had been set up, not to improve council efficiency, but for the unlawful purpose of excluding them. No Unionist councillor appeared in court to contradict this. The judge accepted that the system was "tainted with illegality", and found in favour of Sinn Féin.

In another case a judge found the council guilty of discrimination in its decision not to provide play equipment or a safety surface in a playground in a Catholic area of west Belfast. In a third case a High Court judge ruled that Unionists had breached procedures by barring Sinn Féin councillors from a special meeting following IRA incendiary bomb attacks in Belfast.

Lord Justice Murray summed up the legal position: "The extreme hostility of the Unionist councillors towards the Sinn Féin councillors in their midst is completely understandable in view of Sinn Féin's policy of giving unqualified support to the Provisional IRA. However, parliament has not seen fit to ban the political activities of members of Sinn Féin, and while this is the legal position, a duly elected Sinn Féin councillor is entitled to take his seat on the council and to enjoy the same rights and protection under the law as any other duly elected member. Unionist councillors may find this statement of the law very hard to accept, but accept it they must if they are not to fall foul of the law."

11
ON AND UNDER
THE SURFACE

The issue of whether or not politicians
and others should talk to representatives
of paramilitary groups has always been
one of the most vexed questions in Irish
politics. Some say terrorists and their
representatives should be shunned; others
say contacts should be made if there is a
chance of advancing the cause of peace.

After some years when little contact appeared to take place, the spring of 1993 brought sudden movement when it was disclosed that Presbyterian ministers had met leaders of the paramilitary Ulster Defence Association. The revelation aroused great interest and much comment – surprisingly little of it critical – and there was speculation that the largely favourable response might pave the way for more contacts involving churchmen and others. There was a sense that the Presbyterian initiative had created a new option and opened up a new avenue for exploration.

The Rev Jack Weir, one of the senior Presbyterians who met the UDA, said: "Some of these people, directly or indirectly, may have been involved in devilish things, but they are not devils. They are flesh-and-blood men and women like ourselves. Part of the problem is that people are living in fantasy worlds, dream worlds. When Irish people begin to dream, so often the result is killing. We do not get rid of them by pretending they are not there."

The contacts were the latest in a long line of surreptitious meetings between churchmen and terrorists, as one Protestant cleric recalled.

Clergyman recalls meetings with gunmen

For one minister, now retired and preferring to remain anonymous, the news of clergymen meeting terrorists brought back memories of his own experiences with both the IRA and the Ulster Defence Association. His story shows how such contacts can come about.

One example was in 1976, just after the loyalist assassination of a senior Sinn Féin leader, Maire Drumm. There were fears in the Protestant community that the IRA planned to retaliate by killing a major loyalist figure, possibly the Rev Ian Paisley. The clergyman contacted the late Dáithí Ó Conaill, who was then a senior figure in the IRA. He recalled: "I had been asked to intervene to try to persuade the Provisionals not to kill Paisley, because there were fears that that would plunge the whole community into a civil war situation.

"In the event I had no negotiating to do. Ó Conaill just simply told me: 'There's no way we would kill Ian Paisley. Paisley is the best recruiting sergeant we've got.' He said that after some IRA bombings and shootings Paisley would say there had to be better security or else the Protestant people would take the law into their own hands. He said: 'When the Catholic community hears that, a chill goes down the spine of every Catholic in west Belfast. And after that we have no trouble getting volunteers, safe houses and money.'"

The clergyman also had dealings with the UDA. When a UDA commander went missing it was thought he had been kidnapped by the IRA, and the minister was asked to convey to the IRA that the UDA intended to abduct 12 prominent Catholics from the legal and educational worlds and hold them until their man was released. In the event, it turned out that the UDA man had been taken and killed by a rival loyalist group, so the threat was not carried out.

The most striking example of clerical intervention came in December 1974, when seven senior clergymen met IRA and Sinn Féin leaders in a hotel in Feakle, Co Clare. The meeting, which took place at the request of the churchmen, broke up suddenly when it was learnt that gardaí were on their way to the hotel. This was despite the fact that contact had been made in the strictest secrecy. According to one of those involved, the participants never used the telephone or put anything in writing. On one occasion one of the ministers disguised himself as a priest, travelling under the name of "Father William James".

The Feakle contact bore fruit in that the IRA subsequently declared a short ceasefire. This led on to contacts between British government officials and republicans, which in turn produced a longer ceasefire in 1975. An IRA bombing campaign was going on in England at this time, and one of the main threats used by the IRA was that it would place bombs in the London underground.

The anonymous clergyman was involved in this episode, which he remembers now with some discomfort. He received many threats to his life, had to move home, and was given a police guard. Some people, including other clergymen and even members of his family, would not speak to him.

The episode has had a lasting effect on the republican movement, for the ceasefire was seen as disastrous for the IRA. Ó Conaill and his associates lost their authority and were pushed aside by more militant northerners, including Sinn Féin president Gerry Adams. Mr Adams has since said that the British government "probably came as near at that time to defeating the republican struggle than at any time during the last 14 years". Ever since then, the IRA and Sinn Féin have ruled out the idea of ceasefires.

The anonymous clergyman recalls Dáithí Ó Conaill speaking of this with some prescience. "Ó Conaill told me at the time that we would have one bite at the cherry, no more. He said: 'That's because behind every one of us on the army council there's a young man with a gun in his hand who still has to make his name for Ireland and write his name in the history books. And when they take over, there will be no more ceasefires.' Those were certainly prophetic words: they haven't given an inch on it since."

One of the saddest of the meetings which took place in the early 1990s was that between the IRA and Gordon Wilson, the Fermanagh businessman who lost his daughter Marie in the Enniskillen Remembrance Day bombing in 1987. Mr Wilson, who was described both as naïve and as an outstanding example of Christian charity, took away from his secret meeting with the terrorists the sombre message that Northern Ireland could face another 40 years of suffering and violence.

His action generated much controversy. He was praised as courageous by nationalist sources but condemned by Unionists, who said he had handed a propaganda coup to the terrorists.

He said he had met two unmasked IRA representatives, a man and a woman, for two hours of talks, which he described as friendly. But they did not succeed in persuading him that the IRA did not set out to cause civilian casualties, and he did not succeed in moving them from their opening statement.

The meeting took place not long after an IRA bomb killed two children in Warrington, Cheshire. Mr Wilson was a deeply disappointed man as he reported to a news conference: "I got nothing."

---

9 APRIL 1993   THE INDEPENDENT

Wilson swallows bitter pill of futility

"I had a copy in my hand all the time I was there of the Marie Wilson book, if nothing else to reinforce me and to give me the strength of mind and body to go through with it.

"We had a friendly meeting. I was given a statement from the IRA, which seemed to me to be simply saying no to my request for peace. They were saying to me that they would not abandon the armed struggle, that the armed struggle was not their initiative, it was their response to the British presence in Ireland.

"We had a discussion, and in all honesty I have to say it was friendly. Voices were not raised. I spoke at some length, as Marie Wilson's dad, as one who had suffered at their hands. I told them about the suffering that is Northern Ireland. I told them what I found in Warrington and what those people were suffering. I said there was no excuse for the killing of innocent civilians, including Marie Wilson and the two innocent little children in Warrington and dozens of others. I made it very clear that I was aware that they had their losses. I was very aware, and said so, that they were not the only ones who were in the business of shedding blood and killing and shooting people.

"They apologised once again for Enniskillen and for Warrington. They said they do not condone, nor, indeed, do they set out to kill innocent civilians, men, women or little children. I said, 'I am sorry, I cannot accept that. You do not convince me, and I cannot accept, that the bomb you placed in Enniskillen was intended only for the security forces – which in itself was wrong, in my opinion. Because you knew that there would be civilians there and that 99 per cent of the people who were there would be Protestants. I do not believe your statement when you tell me that you placed two bombs in the middle of Warrington that killed two children, where there were no security forces.' That was what my heart and mind moved me to say.

"I tried with all the sincerity and honesty and integrity I could muster to get over my simple request with as much conviction as I could. They listened, but they made no change in their position. Perhaps it was naïve of me to imagine that, because it was me, they would. That word has been used: I have to live with that.

"I left disappointed and, indeed, saddened. It seemed to me that nothing I had said had in any way moved them. I made the point: 'Are you then telling me that we in Northern Ireland have to go on for another 20 or 30 or 40 years, suffering as we have suffered, and that is your response?' In effect, they said, that is it.

"There are those who have said that my talk to the IRA cannot do any good, and can only do harm. I went in innocence to search for what my heart told me might be a way forward. I was disappointed I didn't get more. I got nothing, so in that sense perhaps I was duped.

"I appealed to them, as one human being to another, to try to spread a little of the love of God. But my talk with the IRA was quite pointless, in relation to what they said to me. I do not believe the discussion has brought us any closer to peace, not an inch.

"They told me that history is on their side. They seemed totally convinced of that. I said: 'Could we forget about the past? Could we think about now? Could we think about the future of this lovely land?' And they said: 'We will not change our ideals or our struggle. We feel we must do, and continue to do, what we are doing.'"

The various meetings and contacts formed part of a hectic cycle of political activity which began in the spring of 1993 and mounted in intensity throughout the year. Most of the action took place on the nationalist side, but Protestants regarded, with growing unease, developments which they saw as unsettling and worrying. One sign of increasing Unionist insecurity was an escalation in loyalist violence.

14 APRIL 1993   THE INDEPENDENT

Unionist psyche unsettled by change in status quo

In the early 1980s warnings that Catholic alienation was reaching a dangerous pitch helped give rise to the Anglo-Irish agreement, which established a new relationship between Britain and constitutional Irish nationalists.

A decade further on, there are unmistakable signs that a major inversion has taken place. It is now Protestant alienation and disquiet which is reaching dangerous new heights. The most obvious indication of this is the alarming rise in loyalist violence. The killing rate has doubled in recent years, to the extent that it now outstrips that of the IRA and republican groups. Recruitment to paramilitary groups has gone up, with the organisations becoming steadily more ruthless and vicious. One opinion poll carried out earlier this month by a Protestant Belfast newspaper, on the admittedly unscientific basis of telephone polling, came up with the disturbing result that 42 per cent of Protestants supported loyalist paramilitaries.

A former loyalist prisoner living in a hardline area confided that a great many young men in the district admire him and the acts of violence he has carried out. This man now disapproves of violence but, he says, the general mood is so militant that it is simply not possible for him to speak out and say so. He has thus become an unwilling role model for youths who are now joining the paramilitary groups.

While most Protestants disapprove of such violence, observers say they detect a dismaying rise in its toleration. According to Chris McGimpsey, a senior Ulster Unionist politician in Belfast, Protestants who a year ago were expressing "absolute disgust" about loyalist violence are now much more muted in their comments. He said: "When people are, if not supporting it, at least saying nothing about it, you realise that the temper of the community is rising. In other words the preconditions for violence are increasing, so the opportunity for loyalist paramilitary groups is increasing, and that's going to lead to even further sectarian killings."

A similar warning came from an unexpected source – the Alliance party, which as a nonsectarian middle-of-the-road grouping usually tends to seek common ground rather than to highlight differences. But its leader, Dr John Alderdice, said: "Things have changed, and the change is that the boot is on the other foot. The British government now says very clearly that it is neutral on the question of Northern Ireland's future. Nationalists find themselves in a position of considerable success politically, and I think they have the scent of success in their nostrils. When that happens it creates a frightened, humiliated minority who turn to violence because they see no other way forward."

Some nationalist observers accuse those who make such statements of exploiting and exaggerating Protestant unease for their own purposes. One said: "This is a highly opportunistic approach by Protestant politicians. For some of them the borderline between prediction and incitement is becoming very blurred. Some of this is basic sectarian animosity finding a socially acceptable expression in terms of alienation."

But a survey of general Protestant opinion, together with the rising graph of loyalist killings, leaves little doubt that much of the escalation in violence stems from a widespread sense that nationalism is making progress and Unionism is losing out. This is confirmed in conversations with a number of moderate Protestant churchmen in the Belfast area. One in the north of the city said: "Everybody condemns loyalist violence, then they say, but . . . Certainly when an obvious republican gets shot many feel, well that's one person we can happily do without." A former moderator of the Presbyterian church said: "I'm afraid there is a growing toleration of violence within the Unionist community. The view is that democratic politics doesn't work, that political negotiation doesn't get anywhere, and the only thing the powers-that-be understand is violence. People feel they can't articulate their longings and aspirations, that there's no ability to influence policy. Young people feel they have nothing to lose – they have no stake in society, no motivation. That vacuum is being filled by the paramilitaries, who give them an alleged cause, a purpose for living." A third senior cleric added: "It's the old axiom: violence begets violence. We're seeing that. The sad fact is that where people feel at risk, they're not very rational, and that's when aggression and anger come out."

Much of the increased violence stems from a deep-seated Unionist unease, which in turn arises from a fusion of political, psychological, demographic and economic factors. Taken together, these have produced a community which thinks its allies are unreliable and its opponents are prospering: a community chronically unsure of itself and its future.

Ulster Protestants have always had a siege mentality, springing partly from the sense that they were in an unfriendly land and partly from an ingrained lack of confidence in British politicians. The suspicion of Britain increased dramatically in the late 1960s and early 1970s as Westminster and Whitehall moved away from a pro-Unionist stance and instead laid emphasis on the rights of the Catholic minority. It reached new heights in 1985 when Britain and the Republic of Ireland signed the Anglo-Irish agreement, forging a new London–Dublin relationship which excluded – and appalled – Unionists. The accord strengthened Unionist fears that Britain saw no long-term future for itself in Ireland.

Seven years after the signing of the agreement, that uncertainty is still there. One political leader, in fact, said bluntly: "All of politics in Northern Ireland is centred around British intentions." The gap between Britain and the Unionists is still evident, and many of the latter feel it is growing wider. A senior Protestant clergyman summarised the views of many when he said: "I detect a growing feeling that the British government would like out. We feel that probably we are an embarrassment to them. If they could get out decently, with pride and world respect, they would do it."

A prominent banker put it this way: "The IRA, the SDLP, the Irish government, Kevin McNamara and the British Labour party – they're all working for Irish unity. Where's the balance? Who's on our side? Nobody. People get annoyed when the British keep saying they're neutral, even-handed."

The current Northern Ireland Secretary, Sir Patrick Mayhew, may himself be instinctively pro-union, but he has noticeably failed to soothe Unionist fears.

The atmosphere of mistrust is such that when Sir Patrick made an unexceptionable speech, which was clearly aimed at detaching any waverers from the fringes of Sinn Féin, he attracted a torrent of Unionist criticism for allegedly wooing the IRA.

Last year's political talks had the unforeseen by-product of increasing the mistrust in many quarters. A large number of Protestants had hoped the British team would somehow align itself with the Unionists, and were disappointed when this did not happen. Britain's professed neutrality was viewed by Unionists as worrying.

Another source of frustration was the nationalist approach to the talks. Some Unionists had the unrealistic expectation that they could, by making modest offers on Catholic participation in a new administration, have Articles 2 and 3 removed from the Irish constitution and dismantle the Anglo-Irish agreement. As one of the nationalist negotiators put it: "They wanted to get rid of Dublin influence and put nationalists back into their old box. The contest in the talks was essentially about whether the nationalists would occupy the place that Unionists want to give them: the answer was no. The realisation of that bleak reality has certainly been unsettling for Unionists."

Northern Ireland has in the last two decades undergone a series of fundamental economic and demographic changes which are having profoundly disconcerting effects on the Unionist psyche. Although anti-Catholic discrimination and inequities linger on, the system has changed a great deal since a Unionist prime minister was able to describe Stormont as a Protestant parliament for a Protestant people.

Within a generation Northern Ireland has almost lost its Protestant-dominated industrial base, gaining in its place a public sector economy in which Catholics are playing an increasingly prominent role. More and more jobs, including some of the top positions, are now going to Catholics. At the bottom end of the scale Catholic unemployment remains high, but more Protestants are now joining the dole queues as well. One churchman said: "Protestants are now facing unemployment in a way they have never faced it before."

Some of the changes come from the fair employment policy that is being pursued by the British government: and here some nationalist observers say that what is happening is the inevitable consequence of the loss of traditional Protestant privilege. The more unsympathetic describe it as a Thatcherite-style "shake-out". Underlying these changes are even more unsettling trends. The state of Northern Ireland was traditionally based on a 2:1 proportion of Protestants to Catholics, but the latest census shows that the Catholic population has risen to 41 or 42 per cent.

The west of the state is now majority Catholic, while Belfast will probably have a Catholic majority before the end of the century. Catholics used to be readier to emigrate than Protestants, but there are indications that this trend has been reversed, and there is certainly a brain drain to Britain of bright Protestant students. Within Northern Ireland many Protestants are leaving areas with growing Catholic populations to cluster, in a striking geographical illustration of the siege mentality, in Protestant-majority districts, mostly to the east.

Politically and economically, many Unionists feel their back is to the wall. More of their number are resorting to violence, or emigrating, or showing signs of defeatism. Unionism is behaving as a frontier community whose frontiers are steadily contracting, and whose world is changing too fast for comfort.

Much of the rise in loyalist violence was directed specifically at members of Sinn Féin and other republicans. When Sinn Féin people were killed, little political or official sympathy for them was evident.

10 AUGUST 1993   THE INDEPENDENT

Sinn Féin death
part of sustained assault

The loyalist assassination of a Belfast councillor's son means that 18 people with Sinn Féin connections have been killed by Protestant extremists in a period of just under five years. This amounts to the most intense and sustained assault ever seen on a particular political grouping. Three of the dead were Sinn Féin councillors, while there have been dozens of other attacks on party representatives.

Sinn Féin has reacted with calls for the authorities to supply some of its members with personal protection weapons. A number of councillors from other parties are allowed to carry guns but, so far as can be established, no Sinn Féin member is permitted to do so. In addition, it seems that no Sinn Féin

261

representative has been given financial assistance to fit strengthened doors and windows to their homes. By contrast, the authorities have installed metal doors and bulletproof windows for members of other parties and other individuals considered to be at risk.

In the most recent incident loyalist gunmen poured automatic gunfire through a window of the north Belfast home of Councillor Bobby Lavery, killing his 21-year-old son Sean. Councillor Lavery's brother was shot dead in a similar attack last Christmas. Republicans said Councillor Lavery was warned by the RUC that loyalists intended to attack him, but that a request by him for permission to carry a legal weapon was refused.

The authorities are unlikely to issue personal protection weapons to members of a party which is the political wing of the IRA. An RUC spokesman said: "All applications are considered on merit and on the particular circumstances of the individual case." A senior Unionist politician commented: "You cannot possibly start giving weapons to people who are advocates and apologists of violence. It would be absolute folly."

Many loyalist politicians have noticeably refrained from condemning the killings of Sinn Féin personnel, and some have come close to commending the actions of the loyalist gunmen. Many observers draw a distinction between the deaths of uninvolved Catholics and those of Sinn Féin people, arguing that joining such a party carries well-known risks. Party president Gerry Adams responded that the party had a right to mobilise and organise, adding: "Membership of Sinn Féin should not mean the death penalty."

The offensive against Sinn Féin is part of a general increase in loyalist violence in recent years. Many of the other loyalist victims had no republican connections and, indeed, have often been chosen at random, while this year there have also been a number of attacks on the SDLP.

Many political activists and others now take considerable security precautions, with or without the help of the authorities. Homes often feature steel front doors, metal cages at the bottom of stairs, and windows with thicknesses ranging from 11 millimetres to 30 millimetres. A number of personalities wear body armour while Mr Adams, who has been the subject of several assassination attempts, travels in an armoured black taxi.

At the top of the security range are MPs and judges, some of whom have permanent police escorts, armoured saloon cars and homes protected by both guards and sophisticated electronic equipment. When a councillor or other representative asks for protection, the RUC makes a threat assessment. This may result in a conclusion that no specific threat exists, in which case no measures are paid for, or it may mean that protection is provided.

Lethal loyalist attacks on Sinn Féin members, their families and associates:

1
OCTOBER 1988
Phelim McNally shot dead in Tyrone in mistake for his brother, a Sinn Féin member

2
FEBRUARY 1989
Councillor John Joe Davey shot dead outside his Co Londonderry home

3
MARCH 1990
Sam Marshall, former Sinn Féin member, shot dead in Co Armagh

4
OCTOBER 1990
Tommy Casey shot dead in Co Tyrone

5
MAY 1991
Councillor Eddie Fullerton shot dead in Co Donegal

6
AUGUST 1991
Patrick Shanahan shot dead in Co Tyrone

7
AUGUST 1991
Thomas Donaghy shot dead in Co Londonderry

8
SEPTEMBER 1991
Councillor Bernard O'Hagan shot dead in Co Londonderry

9–11
FEBRUARY 1992
Paddy Loughran, Pat McBride and Michael O'Dwyer shot dead at Belfast Sinn Féin office by RUC officer who later killed himself

12
APRIL 1992
Danny Cassidy, Sinn Féin election worker, shot dead in Co Tyrone

13
OCTOBER 1992
Sheena Campbell shot dead in south Belfast

14
DECEMBER 1992
Malachy Carey shot dead in Co Antrim

15
DECEMBER 1992
Martin Lavery, brother of Sinn Féin councillor Bobby, shot dead in north Belfast

16
MARCH 1993
Peter Gallagher shot dead in west Belfast

17
MAY 1993
Alan Lundy shot dead at west Belfast home of Sinn Féin councillor

18
AUGUST 1993
Sean Lavery, son of Bobby, shot dead in north Belfast

The high political temperature rose even more when word leaked out that SDLP leader John Hume and Sinn Féin president Gerry Adams were engaged in a series of confidential contacts. News of the move seemed to emerge by accident.

---

2 MAY 1993　　　　　THE INDEPENDENT ON SUNDAY

Hume steers for peace in risky waters

On Saturday last Eamonn McCann, well-known left-wing journalist and activist, was selling copies of *Socialist Worker* outside a shop in Londonderry's Shipquay Street when a neighbour approached him. "Here," he

John Hume, leader of the SDLP

said, "you'll never guess who I just saw going into John Hume's house."

Mr McCann rang the Dublin *Sunday Tribune*, breaking the story of the latest meeting between John Hume, the leader of constitutional nationalism in Northern Ireland, and Gerry Adams, the most important figure in unconstitutional republicanism. Ever since then, the speculation has raged. What is Mr Hume up to? Why is he issuing agreed statements with Mr Adams? What's going on?

Mr Hume himself is reluctant to be drawn into detail about the talks. "Look," he said, "it's a highly sensitive process. I am working for a lasting peace. There are only two possible outcomes: one is that it will fail, and the other is that it will succeed. If it fails, nothing has changed, but if it succeeds, the whole atmosphere has changed. I am prepared to explore that possibility with Mr Adams, and I think it is my duty to do so."

Reaction to the meeting has ranged from furious Unionist denunciation to warm endorsement of his actions, but between these two poles there is considerable bewilderment about the significance of it all. There is no talk of immediate IRA ceasefires, but Mr Hume clearly hopes that at some stage the republicans will stop using force, with the loyalists and the security forces following suit.

Mr Hume repeatedly refers questioners to the agreed statement he and Mr Adams issued. Critics have seized on the phrase that "we accept that the Irish people as a whole have a right to self-determination", one Dublin politician branding it as "Provo-speak". Mr Hume is particularly insulted by this characterisation, and indeed he can point to instances in the past when his party has used exactly the same phrase.

And certainly the statement, read as a whole, contains language of a type not usually associated with Sinn Féin. A key section declares: "We have told each other that we see the task of reaching agreement on a peaceful and democratic accord for all on this island as our primary challenge. We both recognise that such a new agreement is only achievable and viable if it can earn and enjoy the allegiance of the different traditions on this island, by accommodating diversity and providing for national reconciliation."

As both supporters and critics pore over the statement, Mr Hume is aware of the difficulties and dangers of the enterprise. What sustains him in the face of so much criticism and puzzlement is his international reputation as an opponent of violence. Many observers who are worried about it are nonetheless prepared to trust his judgement, finding it deeply improbable that he would give comfort to men of violence.

The risks go beyond the merely political. Some loyalist politicians, hamming it up in the local election campaign, have been particularly inflammatory, speaking of an SDLP–IRA coalition and denouncing "Mr Hume and his IRA–Sinn Féin friends". This is dangerous talk. The UDA, the main loyalist terror group, regularly tells journalists of their hatred for the SDLP in general and Mr Hume in particular. The homes of SDLP councillors have been firebombed and security sources say a carload of armed loyalists who were arrested recently were on a mission to assassinate an SDLP politician.

The talks, and the loyalist political accusations, increase the likelihood of such attacks, since the violent loyalists see them as confirming their simplistic belief that all Catholics – SDLP, IRA, the church, everyone – are locked together in a conspiracy against the Protestant cause.

The idea of nonviolent nationalist politicians maintaining contact with underground republican movements has historical sanction in Ireland: O'Connell did it, and so did Parnell. Mr Hume's sporadic attempts to talk republicans into giving up the gun date back as far as 1972, and in 1988 he

266

and Mr Adams met regularly over a period of months and exchanged a series of detailed documents.

After two decades the IRA campaign shows no sign of abating, either in Northern Ireland or in Britain. Events such as the City of London bombing [in two attacks in April 1992 and April 1993 large IRA bombs caused massive damage in the City] have borne out the judgement of Peter Brooke, the former Northern Ireland Secretary, that the IRA will not be stopped by military means alone.

The bombings go on, but over the years there have been significant changes in republican thinking. It is not much of a caricature to say that in the early days the philosophy was one of "the Protestants don't count, just get the Brits out". Sinn Féin today presents a very different picture. Mr Adams and other republican theorists can outline and defend a philosophy which, though abhorrent to many, is nonetheless closely detailed, thoughtful and cohesive. They pride themselves on their theory and analysis. That theory is also evolving and developing: republican leaders are now, for example, prepared to say that the British presence is not actively colonial, and that Britain has no economic or defence interests in remaining in Ireland. They have also been reflecting much more on the question of the Protestants and, as the Hume–Adams statement showed, think more in terms of agreement and the accommodation of diversity than they once did. At least some of this may be due to the influence of John Hume.

It may seem fanciful, as the bombs continue to go off, to point to such developments as signs of progress. But if the republicans cannot be defeated militarily, then it makes logical sense to tackle them not just by military means but by force of reason as well. This appears to be the tortuous and hazardous process in which John Hume is engaged, in the belief that it might inch Ireland along the road to peace.

Something was stirring in the republican undergrowth, but it was unclear just how significant it was. The question was whether, in a changing world, Sinn Féin and the IRA might at some point come to believe that resorting to violence was no longer necessary.

Details of the Hume–Adams talks remained secret but, in an attempt to highlight the differences, and similarities, between the two nationalist parties, important strategists in each were interviewed. Mitchel McLaughlin of Sinn Féin and Mark Durkan of the SDLP, both from Londonderry, are close to their respective leaders and are important thinkers within their parties. The following interviews, distilled from hours of separate conversation with them, compared their positions.

Unsurprisingly, they differed most sharply on the issue of IRA violence. Mr McLaughlin argued it was the dynamic that brought about change, while Mr Durkan's view was that IRA bombs were counterproductive, distracting the British and alienating the Republic from the north.

They thought alike, however, in their analysis of how Britain viewed Ireland today. Both said Britain's traditional defence and economic arguments had gone, Mr McLaughlin attributing the continuing British presence to "inertia". Both men felt Britain held an ambition to disengage. The SDLP saw this as a gradual process which was dependent on the development of agreement between the various interest groups, since withdrawal without consensus would lead to worse violence. Sinn Féin, on the other hand, envisaged a sudden jackpot win for the republican cause, with a British administration, perhaps in five years, arranging withdrawal terms with the IRA. Any British government contemplating such a course would wish to be reasonably certain that it would leave behind a stable situation. Mr McLaughlin was unable to offer much assurance, however, that this would be the case, or to show how it might be effected with little risk of conflagration.

At the same time, the extent of the change in the republican analysis of Britain was striking: the imperialism and colonialism cited in the 1990 IRA interview (*see* "The men of war promise third violent decade", pp. 228–38) had turned into nonmalevolent apathy.

Nationalists remain split over bullet or the ballot box

MITCHEL MCLAUGHLIN,
NORTHERN CHAIRPERSON OF SINN FÉIN

Violence

Warrington didn't help. It didn't help in any shape, form or fashion: no republican would argue that. The IRA have explained what they did, or attempted to do, in terms of clearing civilians away, and the Samaritans say they received a warning. There was confusion after that and we might never know exactly what happened.

The IRA bomb in the City of London, as well as clearly having a major economic effect, also had a political effect. People, particularly from the business community, are saying that this is an intolerable situation.

British policy

There are signs within the British government itself, and certainly within the British establishment, that people are starting to ask questions – what's it about? why are we still involved? That debate is going on, but my hard view is that the British government haven't changed their policy and aren't about to change, that we're in for another maybe five years of it. But I believe that the pressure is actually building up for change – we're talking about green shoots, to quote Norman Lamont.

The changing strategic parameters have an effect, and the IRA campaign and the existence of Sinn Féin separately have effects, and the Unionist reaction to those changes does also. All of this means that the British, if they're not examining their policies now, then they certainly will be.

I don't believe that republicans would sincerely argue now that the British have an active colonial policy. The old kind of colonial imperatives that were there, in terms of Ireland as the back door, needed for their own security, and dominating the domestic market and all of that, those reasons have actually changed quite significantly. The advent of the open Europe has changed the economic reasons for Britain wanting to dominate Ireland. In military terms modern technology has absolutely rendered all those military strategic reasons obsolete.

I think it's actually more inertia. They're not exercised about the issue. There's very little evidence that they even agonise over the failure of their policies. It's a situation of "out of sight, out of mind". It sometimes takes horrific instances such as Warrington to throw a focus on the day-to-day reality of British government policy. But then maybe within a day or two something else crops up and Ireland slips back to its normal, fairly low priority. So it's inertia more than a stubborn conviction that their policies on Ireland are right.

It has to be down not to any kind of malevolence or ill-will or whatever. And although it may sound like being a warmonger to say it, if it wasn't for the IRA, Ireland wouldn't feature at all.

British withdrawal

We're trying to break the log jam, and I actually don't believe the British government and the IRA are that far away from it. I think they can actually arrive at an understanding that would allow for a cessation of hostilities. For instance,

270

if the British, privately first of all, concluded that they were going to end this conflict between the IRA and themselves, it might not necessarily require from them a unilateral declaration which might be difficult to explain in the international arena.

If there was a willingness there, if people were prepared to be imaginative and flexible, a way forward could be found. If there was a change of attitude on the British part, then lines of communication could be set up.

Scenario for withdrawal

The threat of a loyalist backlash is a factor: the British are thinking that a bad situation could get worse. First of all, it has to be said that that's not the IRA's responsibility. It may even be true — whether it is a full-scale loyalist backlash or one limited to a section of the loyalist community — that it's unavoidable. We may all be victims of decisions that were made in history, which have created a particular conflict scenario that can only be contained and minimised.

But we're arguing that in circumstances where you achieve a cessation of hostilities between republican and British forces, you're then left with one source of violence against a background of constitutional negotiation. So if the British government were to announce next week that they were going to get out of Ireland, and they set a time limit on it, then you have a basis for starting a process of reconciliation, starting constitutional negotiations, and getting immediately as a reward an end of the IRA campaign.

There's a very sizeable group of people within the Unionist community who will immediately begin to open up negotiations and discussions. If the British and Dublin governments were operating on a joint programme to end partition, and the IRA campaign had ceased as a result, then I believe loyalist violence can be contained because it would be isolated. I'm not talking about the immediate knee-jerk, which might be quite savage and dangerous. But when the dust settles and they're thinking about it in the long term, they have to ask themselves — what is the point of this? where is this going to take us? Can they force the British government to change its mind and to re-engage in Ireland again, with a prospect of starting up the IRA campaign?

I think in those circumstances loyalist violence would have no project whatsoever. As a result it will attract very limited support from within the loyalist community, and will be containable and will very quickly fizzle out. I do actually have a great faith in people's pragmatism and common sense and ability to make decisions in their own self-interest.

Representatives of all of the Irish people would then sit down and work at whatever comes up. That would require imagination and flexibility, and it might well produce structures which are not the same as Sinn Féin policy. But the democratic integrity of the exercise comes from the fact that it would be submitted to the Irish people and voted on in an all-Ireland referendum. If it's ratified, then it's binding on all parties, including republicans, whatever that arrangement would be.

MARK DURKAN,
CHAIRPERSON OF THE SOCIAL DEMOCRATIC AND LABOUR PARTY

Violence
The effect of IRA violence is to deepen division and fear. All that people feel is the hurt of violence and all they hear is the din of it. It causes direct economic harm to everybody in the north and it clearly handicaps our economic and social development. Violence galvanises the British presence. Every time you're about to get the British to look sensitively at the full political dimensions of the problem, violence from some quarter or another – not unusually IRA violence – means that they revert simply to a security agenda. IRA violence is self-defeating. Ending it would mean that people could entertain new possibilities, and I strongly believe it would alter the profile of the British presence quite dramatically.

In the south IRA violence is making people sick of the north, scared of it and ashamed of it. It makes them feel they must dissociate themselves from IRA violence, and so it has actually diminished the nationalist ideal and made people increasingly self-conscious and apologetic. The supreme irony of the IRA campaign is that it is mounted on this notion that it will create a British psychological disengagement from the north. But what it has actually achieved is a psychological disengagement by large elements of the south from the north.

The SDLP has improved the self-confidence of the nationalist community. It has encouraged people to face up to the practical and the real, rather than just be obsessed with the symbolic or the rhetorical. We have succeeded in getting a very clear realisation by the British government that it's not simply an internal Northern Ireland problem or even an internal UK problem. We have made them realise that we're not to be treated simply as a freestanding internal minority and that people of the Irish nationalist tradition in Northern Ireland are part of the body politic of the island as a whole. We have contributed more to the Europeanisation of the outlook of people here than any other party. We have achieved much international sympathy, not just for our position, but for everybody who's trying to grapple with a complex situation which to outsiders often looks more simple than it actually is.

British policy
I have the firm impression that people in the British establishment would quite

happily want to be out of their involvement in Northern Ireland, if they could. It's the security requirement, as they see it, that keeps them here, and what they would see as the responsibility to respect the current wishes of the majority. The British establishment has quite clearly drawn those conclusions, and they have been percolating their way into British government thinking as well.

The traditional arguments were that Britain was here pursuing several self-interests, principally economic and strategic. The strategic self-interest – history has passed that by. The nature of relationships within Europe itself are very different from what they were when Britain was first motivated to treat Ireland in the way that she did.

The more modern strategic interest has been overtaken by the end of the cold war: that's all out the window. In terms of the economic interest, to suggest that Britain is in Northern Ireland for economic interests is quite bizarre – it's costing them a fortune.

Scenario for withdrawal

I can't see the IRA winning, I really can't. But if it did, I can't see that it would bring any great peace. It would outrage those of us who have pursued change without resort to violence. It would also outrage the Unionist community, who would see themselves as the main victims.

I think the British stay because the basic position is: how can they leave without being seen to abandon the majority in Northern Ireland without being accused of giving in to terrorism? How can they leave in the absence of actual agreement on new structures? Everybody would say to them that the last circumstances in which you leave anywhere is in a vacuum, that would be quite irresponsible. The British feel there would be more violence if they left in advance of securing agreement. My own hunch would be that withdrawal in a vacuum would lead to more violence. There would be a rush for territory in different parts of the north. Who would exercise authority over the security forces, and where would their loyalties lie? In those circumstances police and locally recruited soldiers would feel that all they could do was defend their own community.

Various people have talked about creating another Bosnia or Lebanon or whatever. It wouldn't necessarily get to those terms, but that particular dynamic – of a territorial rush stemming from fear, from real or imagined threats – that would happen. You don't deliberately walk yourself into a scenario where all sorts of people are going to feel an impulse to violence as a means of protecting their position or advancing their position.

The only way to get a British withdrawal is in the context of agreement on new arrangements in Ireland. That means agreement that is wide enough to ensure that those new institutions are going to be sustainable on their own without the need for British security or military backup.

273

We believe in the unity of the people of Ireland, and that can mean political arrangements that can be different in different parts of the island. If members of the Unionist community still want to have a direct point of allegiance with Britain, including maybe the crown or whatever, we should find ways and means of respecting that. It's not a question of Brits out and Brits no more, any more than we are prepared to bow to Unionist demands that it should be Dublin out. I wouldn't have any particular hang-ups that a new political dispensation has to be made purely in the image of 19th-century Irish nationalism.

It seems clear to me that if there was agreement on some form of Irish unity, the British would honour and respect that, and do what they could to help deliver it, helping to contribute to stability and disentangling themselves from an involvement that they've got rather tired of and confused about.

Another taboo was broken when the president of Ireland, Mary Robinson, visited west Belfast. Despite the disapproval of the British government, she had a fleeting encounter with Gerry Adams. This generated much controversy but, interestingly, an opinion poll in the Republic showed strong support for her action in shaking hands with the Sinn Féin leader.

19 JUNE 1993   THE INDEPENDENT

Robinson guest of honour in Belfast

Mary Robinson, president of Ireland, sat in the place of honour in the west Belfast hall as Sean Maguire, virtuoso on the violin and pipes, led a group of traditional musicians in some stirring jigs and reels.

274

Behind her stood her minders, tallish policemen in conspicuously good suits, each facing in a somewhat different direction, each flicking their eyes slightly anxiously around the hall. If they were searching for Provos, they did not have far to look. Gerry Adams, president of Provisional Sinn Féin, stood a little way away in his best blue jacket, tapping his foot to the infectious airs. Close by was his own minder, in his accustomed place a few feet behind him, eyes hidden by tinted glasses.

On this day, however, all the minders were completely superfluous, for the atmosphere in the hall could not have been more friendly, welcoming and good-natured. While the two sets of minders did not actually shake hands and exchange tips on the finer points of bodyguarding, there was no tension in the air.

Photographers jostled as they contrived to get a picture of the two presidents together, but the media were, courteously, asked to leave before Mrs Robinson mingled with the guests, shaking Mr Adams's hand and holding a short conversation with him. Those present said that in the brief encounter "she greeted him like everybody else, with no more and no less attention".

Such tension as there was appears to have been in Downing Street, where John Major, in uncharacteristically Thatcherite style, reputedly took angry exception to the idea of the Irish president staging a visit to Sinn Féin's strongest area. Mr Major's concern that the republicans would exploit such an occasion was probably unfounded, for nobody in the hall turned a hair at Mr Adams's presence. His party is the largest one in the area and is, like it or not, part of the west Belfast community. In this context it is impossible to ignore. To demonstrate that this was a community-oriented occasion rather than a political one, however, Mr Adams appeared on the guest list as, improbably, "founder of west Belfast community festival". Some of those in the hall wholly support Mr Adams; some, like the Protestant clergymen who were there, presumably heartily disapprove of him.

Mrs Robinson has carved out a unique niche for herself as the people's president, establishing links with all sorts of groups and people, including northern unionists. Yesterday was the turn of the nationalists of west Belfast. Some of them have felt that this new style of president has paid too much attention to unionists and not enough to northern nationalists, but almost all feel that this reservation is outweighed by her other qualities. The tone was set when Mrs Robinson walked into the reception to be greeted with spontaneous applause and cheering, her presence providing a rare moment of uplift, and even joy, in one of the most deprived districts of western Europe.

August 1993 brought one of Sinn Féin's leaders, Martin McGuinness, into the full glare of publicity. Central Television's *Cook Report* claimed he was "Britain's number one terrorist" and the man in charge of the IRA. Mr McGuinness denied the allegations, saying the programme contained lies, smears and black propaganda. Months later it emerged that he had been the link man in the republican movement's secret talks with the government, but this was not known at the time.

26 AUGUST 1993   THE INDEPENDENT

Bogside fighter turned to politics

For more than 20 years Martin McGuinness has been viewed as a living symbol of the IRA's unflinching determination to expel the British presence from Northern Ireland, and to do so by the use of force. Whether Mr McGuinness is or is not a member of the IRA is almost by the by. The fact is that he is almost universally perceived as one of the pivotal figures in the republican movement, a usefully nebulous term often employed as a euphemism to encompass both the legal Sinn Féin and the illegal IRA.

As a young man in the early 1970s, he was regularly described as leader of the IRA in Londonderry, building up a reputation as one of its most prominent street fighters in battles with troops in the Bogside and Creggan. In those days he was perceived as a straight militarist, with no hint that he might be interested in other forms of activity. In 1972 he was again described as an IRA leader when he and other republicans were flown to London for secret talks with government ministers. He remembers that experience vividly: "Gerry Adams and I went to London – it's like a lifetime away, 21 years ago, when we were only children really – and we talked to William Whitelaw." He appears convinced that he will one day meet British ministers again, this time, in effect, to accept Britain's surrender.

What was slightly surprising was that a man with his reputation for straight militarism should have developed into such an enthusiastic advocate of building up a political party, Sinn Féin, alongside the IRA. It was in the late 1970s that he, Mr Adams and other younger northern elements wrested control of the republican movement away from the southern-based old guard. In the early 1980s they brought Sinn Féin into the political arena. Since then he has stood in a series of elections.

He has had a particularly important role to play in the Sinn Féin strategy. Many republicans have worried that what they term "electoralism" might eventually soften the leadership's line and nudge it in the direction of a ceasefire. Mr McGuinness, with his particularly hawkish image, has essentially acted as an important guarantor to any doubters that Sinn Féin will not betray the IRA. A republican source said: "Gerry is articulate, that's his strength. Martin has the respect and confidence of the volunteers. He's seen as their man. They trust him." This was particularly important in 1986, when the disgruntled older guard split away from Sinn Féin. Mr McGuinness assured the party *ard-fheis* that the IRA went along with the Sinn Féin strategy. His crucial intervention was described thus by a Dublin magazine: "McGuinness's speech was only thinly disguised as the authentic statement of the IRA army council."

The security forces regard him, in the words of one source, as "a very key player", while loyalists have acknowledged his importance by plotting to kill him on at least one occasion. Last year he himself summed up his eventful career by saying he had been to jail a number of times, stalked by a loyalist assassin "and fired at by the British army on countless occasions over the last 20 years".

Interviewed in his home city the following month, Martin McGuinness reminisced about his 1972 contacts with the British. He did not reveal, however, that he was once more secretly in touch with them.

Republican mixes hope with menace

Martin McGuinness of Sinn Féin poses by a Bogside mural

The outside world may regard Martin McGuinness as a flint-eyed godfather of terrorism, but as he strolls through the Bogside passers-by greet him with unfeigned warmth and genuine smiles. No one treats him as a celebrity and no one seems afraid of him. He has spent most of his 43 years in the Bogside, a close-knit little urban village which has seen much violence, and which was scarred most of all when British troops shot dead 14 people on Bloody Sunday.

Though clearly a busy political activist, he is technically unemployed, drawing the dole, as do a majority of men in the Bogside. He has four children and

278

lists his hobbies as fly-fishing and chess. His last employment was working in Doherty's butcher's doing prepacked meats in the bacon department. His last day at work, he says, was "8 August 1971, the day before internment". At that point he appears to have become a full-time street fighter.

Today he is a key figure in the republican movement. His importance is that he is regarded, by both security sources and republicans, as a guarantor that Sinn Féin will not go soft. The IRA volunteers who are out there doing the bombings and the shootings need to be assured they will not be sold out. This is one of Mr McGuinness's jobs, for nobody has ever detected any doveish tendencies in him. If Martin says there is no sellout, then even the most militant are reassured.

He was clearly annoyed by the recent *Cook Report* programme that portrayed him as Britain's number one terrorist. But he does not deny the generality – that he is a senior member of the republican movement, jailed twice in his younger days for IRA membership. He says: "The reality is that I am not a member of the IRA. But the story of my involvement in republicanism and the struggle, none of that bothers me at all. Everybody in Derry knows what I've been in the past – everybody in Ireland knows. I'm not ashamed of it. Everybody knows I was always involved in opposition to British rule in Ireland and the British occupation forces."

So what were his formative experiences? "They happened in this city when I was 18, 19 years of age. I joined Sinn Féin in 1970, after a period of watching brutal assaults on civil rights marchers by the RUC, raids on homes in the city, the battle of the Bogside, and all that. Like everybody else, I threw stones and whatever else was to hand at the RUC. People saw me as someone who was prepared actually to be within 10 feet of the RUC and the British army and throw stones.

"For decades the Unionist community treated the nationalist community abominably, and we didn't have too many statements from Protestant archbishops and clergymen condemning that. The nationalist community eventually could take no more and in 1968 they marched on the streets. When they did they were attacked and beaten by the RUC, who were acting at the behest of the Unionists. We saw our fathers and mothers humiliated like that, and we were not prepared to take it any more. Things changed. People decided they would struggle against what was wrong in this country."

That struggle led Mr McGuinness to a couple of jail sentences and in more recent years into the leadership of Sinn Féin. In 1972 it also led to a secret visit, as a member of an IRA delegation, to a plush house in Chelsea. His memories of that event are still vivid.

"I was 22 years of age, and I couldn't be anything but impressed by the paraphernalia surrounding that whole business, and the cloak-and-dagger stuff of how we were transported from Derry to Cheyne Walk in London.

"I was on the run at the time. There were contacts with the British government and we insisted on a written note from them which would guarantee our safety in the event of us agreeing to go to London. That we were given, and it was held by a lawyer acting on our behalf.

"We assembled here in Derry, six of us, and we were taken in a blacked-out van from a back road in Shantallow to a field in which a helicopter landed. We were put in the helicopter and brought to the military end of Aldergrove airport near Belfast. We were then brought on by RAF plane to a military airfield in England, where we were met by a fleet of limousines. They were the fanciest cars I had ever seen in my life: it was a most unreal experience.

"We were escorted by the Special Branch through London to Cheyne Walk and there we met Willie [now Lord] Whitelaw. We were offered drinks at the meeting and we all refused." Mr McGuinness chuckles at the memory: "Willie was Willie," he recalls. "Singularly unimpressive, I must say. All of us left the meeting quite clear in our minds that the British government were not yet at a position whereby we could do serious business."

Today Mr McGuinness believes, or hopes, that that position may have changed. There are people within the British establishment and elsewhere, he says, who now accept that there will be no resolution "until republicans are involved in the search for a peace process". Asked whether there have been feelers from the government to Sinn Féin he replies: "No, there haven't been." [An answer which, it turned out, was less than frank.] But he adds: "Everybody you meet says it's quite obvious that the British are going to talk. The important thing is that important elements to the conflict are coming to a position where they now accept that there has to be inclusive dialogue. I think it's clear the British are going to talk to us. The logical next step in the whole process is for a meeting to take place." If not, he adds, in a tone which somehow manages to be both casual and ominous, then the future will be bleak and violent: "We're going to face, for the next 20 years, continuing strife on this island, which will affect all the people of the island and the British people as well."

The hint of menace is followed by the hint of pragmatism. "Every party to this conflict is going to have to be prepared to apply new thinking, not just to their own position, but to how they view the position of others and the fears of others. We in recent times have attempted to come to grips with the reality that there are Unionists out there who are in trepidation as to the future intentions of the British government.

"The end of the process for us means a British withdrawal from Ireland at some stage in the future. There's an awful lot of work to be done before we can arrive at that position, and the British government are the key to the whole thing."

280

On Unionism, he pulls few punches: "There's so much bigotry involved in it, it's accurate to say there is the most unbelievable anti-Catholic bigotry and prejudice. Catholics are being slaughtered wholesale in Belfast, yet look at Derry. Protestants are not being slaughtered wholesale on the streets of Derry, where there is a nationalist majority. I think that's because you don't have the same degree of bigotry and prejudice in the community that I come from."

But could moves towards a British withdrawal produce even greater loyalist violence? "No doubt there would be uproar and a certain convulsion within Unionism. There would be people within the loyalist paramilitary world who would attempt to kill more Catholics even than they're killing now. But I honestly believe that could be handled if we had a situation where the British government, in conjunction with the Irish government and supported by the international community and the United Nations, actually decided to move along that road."

So if he was involved in talks with Unionists, how would he go about addressing their concerns? He would, he says, make the economic argument that Ireland would be better off as one unit. "Our life styles would be better, Ireland would be more prosperous, it would be more inviting for people to invest their money, to build factories. Tourism would be a massive industry, in the context of peace.

"Nobody craves peace more than republicans, because nobody has suffered as much as republicans. We have lived totally abnormal life styles for the last 25 years as a result of the political disturbances. We would like to live normal lives just like everybody else, but we'd like to live lives of dignity, of being able to walk around our own streets without being harassed."

And what would he be doing, if and when this idyll came to pass? Martin McGuinness, the one-time Bogside stonethrower who now says the time has come for all to talk, smiles and replies without hesitation: "I'd be fly-fishing in the Cranna river in Donegal."

The fifth of October 1993 brought yet another anniversary: it was exactly 25 years since the RUC used baton charges to break up a peaceful Catholic civil rights march in Londonderry, focusing world attention on Northern Ireland for the first time.

Two people who had never really known
peace talked of what they had learnt, the
hard way, and spoke of their hopes for
the future.

25 OCTOBER 1993   THE INDEPENDENT

Children of the Troubles

THE LOYALIST'S STORY

"I was born into the Troubles. I come from a predominantly loyalist area
and we just had Protestant friends. We knew of Catholics but we wouldn't
run about with them.

"I got into trouble when I first started drinking, at 14, 15. It made me
aggressive – I would fight with people, fight with the police, get done for riotous
behaviour around the Twelfth, do burglaries to get money for drink, everything.
In 1985 there was a riot at the time of the Anglo-Irish agreement, and I was
involved. We were skinheads at the time. I was supposed to be protesting against
Dublin rule, but I'd so much liquor in me, I'd have protested against anything.
I hadn't really a clue, I was only 16. All I knew was what they were telling
me on the news.

"I was involved on the fringes of the loyalist paramilitaries. I know people
now who're in their 40s, who've spent 15 years of their life in jail. They were
just the same as me, but they got more deeply involved.

"I wouldn't have associated with Catholics in the old days but I met them
when I started doing the Duke of Edinburgh award, through the Probation
Service. At the start we thought it was for pansies but now I'm all for it, it's
super. We went away on an expedition and lived together, Catholics and
Protestants mixed together, we all mucked in. We had a good laugh about my
tattoos. As well as these ones on my hands, I've got them on my arms, too,
and I've one on my arse. It says, 'Kiss my Orange ass'. We had a real laugh
about that one.

282

"I would still be against republicans but I wouldn't be against all Catholics. A few years ago I thought they were all the same, but I don't think they are now. We should live and let live. I got the Duke of Edinburgh gold award, it was the best thing ever happened to me. I'm trying to get into voluntary work now."

THE REPUBLICAN'S STORY

"I was a kid of 10 at school when it all started. I wouldn't have been in trouble without the Troubles, I'd never been in jail, had no previous criminal record. I got involved with the republican movement and I ended up doing over 10 years in jail.

"I am still a republican. I just feel it's unfortunate that I had to get involved, that someone had to die. I'm sorry that it happened, I'm sorry for the person who was killed and the suffering that was caused, but I still am a republican.

"Coming from a nationalist area, we had very little to do with Protestants. I didn't really have anything to do with them. It's only meeting them in jail that you realise they're human beings too – they have their beliefs, we have ours.

"Since coming out I have got involved in youth work. Being in jail helped me understand young people, their hardships and what they're going through. I work in a very deprived area, trying to get them off the street corners. There's nothing for the kids in the area at all. I feel hurt when I see that.

"We were away on an expedition, Protestant and Catholic kids, and not once was there any sectarianism. There was a bit of banter about Celtic and Rangers – one fella had 'Kiss my Orange ass' tattooed on his bum – but there wasn't one bit of trouble. Those young people were brilliant ambassadors for their country. That's what makes me say there is hope for this country. Some day we're just all going to have to live together. I believe it's possible and we all can do it, and the sooner it comes the better.

"I just hope these Hume–Adams talks, something might come out of it, I really hope so. Give these talks a chance, let them talk, let's see what's coming out of there and let everybody talk and get together."

To the outside observer, 25 years ago Northern Ireland had all the appearances of a tranquil backwater. Many people in Britain were, in fact, pretty well unaware of partition, assuming wrongly that Ireland was one political entity. To the casual visitor, it also presented a placid appearance. It had its own little assembly, Stormont, nestling in hills just outside Belfast, which had been set up on the British model, complete with Speaker and mace. Old industries such

283

as linen and shipbuilding were in decline, but a flow of inward investment was establishing a new artificial fibre industry and other plants to provide new jobs. The little backwater seemed to be successfully modernising itself: unemployment was falling and a new era of prosperity was in prospect.

Just below the surface, however, a potent mixture of resentment, mistrust, suspicion, fear and hatred was quietly simmering. The entire state, the entire system which had been set up in the 1920s, was the product of northern Protestant determination not to become part of a united Ireland. It was a monument to the fact that Unionists could not come to terms with nationalists. They feared they would lose their British citizenship, their British subsidies and their religious rights in a nationalist-dominated island. The new technocratic Unionist rhetoric of the 1960s masked the fact that those fears were still intact. The border around the six counties of Northern Ireland provided a form of defence against most of the nationalists, but the state had within its frontiers half a million Catholics. Successive Unionist administrations regarded these as a potential fifth column within the walls, fearing they might some day link up with the Catholic south. Today this same fear of a "pan-nationalist front" makes Unionists fear the development of a talks process which might include Sinn Féin, the SDLP, the Irish government and Irish-American elements.

The Unionist party ruled Northern Ireland, almost entirely untroubled by interference from London, with two main approaches: maintaining the border to keep out the southern nationalists; and excluding the northern minority from power. The strength of the built-in Unionist majority was augmented by underhand devices such as gerrymandering and discrimination. In many areas Protestants routinely received preference in jobs and housing. Political boundaries were massaged to produce Unionist majorities, even in areas where Catholics were in a majority. One peculiarly shaped constituency, designed to maximise the Protestant vote in Fermanagh, was known as "Ferguson's sausage".

Nationalists, in effect, faced a double exclusion: trapped in a state which denied their Irishness, they were also treated as second-class citizens. The patently unfair system survived for so long because of the indifference of London and, to a lesser extent, Dublin.

October 1968 marked the point when a new, articulate and educated Catholic leadership emerged, employed fresh tactics, and exposed the reality of the Stormont system to a scandalised world. The system could not cope with the simple demand for equality with Protestants. Television pictures of the RUC using batons to break up a peaceful march produced a tremendous wave of condemnation which marked the beginning of the end of Unionist domination. Three and a half years later, after some unsuccessful attempts at reform, Stormont was abolished and replaced by direct rule from Westminster.

Direct rule, which was supposed to be a temporary expedient, has lasted more than two decades. Since October 1968 the story of Northern Ireland has been that of a debate, conducted by both political and violent means, on how, and by whom, the state should be governed. Twenty-five years on, after much argument and much bloodshed, that debate remains unresolved.

The violence which since 1968 has been a constant feature of life has masked enormous changes – social, economic, demographic and psychological. Many of these have not been seen by Unionists as beneficial and have served to increase their traditional sense of siege.

The Catholic population has increased from one-third to more than 40 per cent. Upwardly mobile Catholics now hold important posts in areas of life which were once Protestant preserves. John Hume's SDLP wields great influence in London, Dublin, Brussels and Washington; it no longer needs to go on marches to make its voice heard. The IRA, once something of a joke, has evolved into one of the world's most brutally efficient terrorist groups.

Unionists are doubtful about Britain's ultimate intentions, worrying that the British might some day pull out and leave them to their fate. They see London and Dublin drawing closer together. The angst and the alienation have resulted in an alarming rise in loyalist violence in recent years.

On the Catholic side there are two starkly different pictures. An expanding middle class and upper working class has escaped from the ghettos and is prospering under direct British rule. This contrasts sharply with the life experience of a large section of the Catholic working class. On all the major social and economic indicators, Catholics are worse off than Protestants: more likely to be unemployed, in poor housing and in poor health. In other words, the reforms and improvements of the last quarter-century have provided many with a ladder out of the ghetto: but the ghettos themselves are still there, with conditions which help provide the IRA's endless supply of recruits.

The IRA itself, together with its political wing Sinn Féin, may be at a crossroads. The key hope is that the republicans have come to realise that Unionists, however their political representatives may have misbehaved in the past, nonetheless have their intrinsic rights. The Hume–Adams talks will provide a crucial test of whether republicans cling to an absolutist position or are at last trying to come to terms with the idea of Unionism. If this initiative fails, the bleak prediction must be of an indefinite continuation of the present violent stalemate.

The Unionist–nationalist divide is the kernel of the matter in Northern Ireland, but it has been obvious, since the events of October 1968 shattered that hermetically sealed little world, that the problem has many other dimensions. Some of these dimensions have themselves changed: the south, for example, is busy modernising itself and revising many traditional attitudes.

And at the core is Britain, which over the years has been exercising an increasingly reluctant sovereignty over this troubled area. Britain is always in two minds about Ireland: never quite letting go, but never quite committed, either, to staying for ever. Some elements of the establishment seem to favour eventual disengagement while others envisage staying, but neither tendency seems strong enough to settle the matter one way or the other. The result is that after 25 years of debate, argument and the clash of arms, Northern Ireland seems fated to remain in a state of perpetual uncertainty.

Almost 3,400 people have died as a result of the Northern Ireland Troubles. Most have been killed in Northern Ireland, though there have also been fatalities in Britain, the Irish Republic and continental Europe.

The following allocation of responsibility for the killings is based on a project which will produce a database of all Troubles-related deaths. Since the project is not yet complete, the figures should be regarded as having an error level of perhaps 5 per cent.

TOTAL KILLINGS	3,361	

Killings by republicans	1,940	(58 per cent)
Provisional IRA	1,592	
INLA	86	
Official IRA	35	
IPLO	22	
Unclassified	205	
Killings by loyalists	900	(27 per cent)
UVF	354	
UDA	257	
Unclassified	289	
Killings by security forces	361	(11 per cent)
Regular army	239	
SAS/undercover troops	59	
RUC	55	
UDR	8	
Others and unknown	160	(5 per cent)

12

DEATH ON THE SHANKILL

While speculation continued on whether Sinn Féin was genuinely moving towards politics, the Ulster Unionist party had entered a new phase in its relationship with the Major administration. John Major, who had a small majority and a troublesome right wing, was anxious to enlist Unionist support in the Commons lobbies. It first emerged in July 1993, in votes over the Maastricht treaty, that he had reached an accommodation with Ulster Unionist leader James Molyneaux. Unionists were excited by the prospect of wielding new influence.

The annual Unionist party conference illustrated several points, including complete disapproval of the Hume–Adams initiative, and the hope that the parliamentary weakness of John Major's government would lead to ever-greater Tory reliance on Unionist MPs.

Ulster Unionists pour scorn on Sinn Féin talks

The Ulster Unionist party, the electoral voice of a large majority of Northern Ireland Protestants, demonstrated at the weekend that it has no time whatsoever for the Hume–Adams talks process. The initiative was treated with a mixture of dismissiveness and disdain at the party's annual conference, with party leader James Molyneaux attempting to dispel any impression that it had softened its line on the question of Sinn Féin's eventual participation in talks.

One Ulster Unionist MP last week appeared to suggest that Sinn Féin could be at the table following a cessation of violence. Mr Molyneaux, in his leader's address, made it clear that this idea was accompanied by a formidable battery of qualifications. Sinn Féin could only be considered for access to the democratic process, he said, when the IRA had been extirpated, when there was a total cessation of terrorism and when all arms and explosives had been surrendered. Sinn Féin would then have to go through a "quarantine period" lasting at least five years, he added.

Although Mr Molyneaux did not rule out the possibility of meetings between his party and Irish government ministers, it was clear at the conference that the key relationship his party is hopeful of developing is that with the Conservative party. The party has obviously drawn considerable satisfaction from the arrangement which Mr Molyneaux is said to have made with the Prime Minister in exchange for support in the Commons lobbies from the nine Ulster Unionist MPs. Mr Molyneaux was repeatedly complimented on his performance: "He has brought us in from the cold," one speaker commended him.

One sign of a new warmth in Unionist–Tory relations was a conference fringe meeting addressed by the director of the Conservative Political Centre, Alistair Cooke. He stressed that he was appearing in a personal capacity, but his advocacy of closer co-operation between the parties and a renegotiation of the Anglo-Irish agreement endeared him to the well-attended meeting.

However, the feeling that this is a promising relationship ran alongside a strong strain of dissatisfaction with the administration of Northern Ireland. Running

288

through the conference was a frequently voiced sense that Protestants are being officially discriminated against and Catholics favoured. The Fair Employment Commission, which monitors religious discrimination, was described as anti-Protestant and as "pursuing a hidden agenda of positive discrimination against Protestants". There was prolonged applause for a speaker who described it as "blatantly bigoted and discriminatory" and called for its abolition. The conference unanimously called for a reassessment of its role.

The conference also unanimously rejected proposed educational reforms after speakers complained they contained favouritism towards the Catholic church and unfair treatment of Protestant churches. One declared: "The losers are going to be the Protestant councillors, Protestant churches and the Protestant people."

A debate on urban regeneration centred on allegations that Catholic areas were receiving more money than Protestant districts. A Belfast councillor said that of £124 million in government spending, only £44 million had gone to Protestant areas, adding: "It's discrimination of the worst kind." Another councillor declared: "The years of whining and whingeing by nationalist politicians have indeed paid off." This current of thinking was summed up by the party president, Josias Cunningham, who said he hoped the world would hear "the strength of our feelings about our disadvantaged position". Veteran observers reflected that over the years the culture of complaint has moved from the nationalists to the Unionist tradition.

J ust when people were wondering whether they might dare hope that peace could be drawing closer, appalling tragedy struck. An IRA bomb went off in a fish shop on the Shankill Road, Belfast's working-class Protestant heartland, on a busy Saturday afternoon. Ten people were killed and scores injured.

The IRA's intention had been to blow up the headquarters of the UDA. But the bomb went off prematurely, killing an IRA member and nine civilians. Two of the

dead were little girls, aged seven and
thirteen; another four were women.

The IRA explanation that they had not
meant to kill these victims was small
consolation to the relatives of the dead. In
the aftermath, raw, harrowing grief poured
from the relatives as Belfast and the world
stood aghast.

---

25 OCTOBER 1993   THE INDEPENDENT

Atrocity helps to swell
Belfast's fund of bitterness

The Shankill Road bombing has been one of the IRA's most disastrous
mistakes for many years. At a stroke it killed nine civilians, brought
widespread opprobrium down on its own head, and lost one of its own members.
Even if the IRA's own version of events is accepted, the entire concept of the
attack was fraught with extraordinary dangers, both to civilians and to the
bombers themselves.

The IRA said the targets of the bomb were loyalist extremists who were in
the offices above the fish shop. A number of loyalists appear to have been present
at a meeting there, but it ended around 12.30pm, three-quarters of an hour
before the explosion.

It seems two IRA members carried the bomb into the shop, where it exploded
prematurely. The IRA said the intention was for warnings to be given to allow
the shop and the immediate vicinity to be cleared, though it is unlikely that
this could have been achieved without causing a commotion, which would have
alerted the loyalists upstairs. One possibility is that the plan was based on an
assumption that the loyalists would have taken cover in a back room upstairs,
probably on the third storey, since evacuating the building would have meant
them going downstairs and thus closer to the device. A bomb timed to go off

290

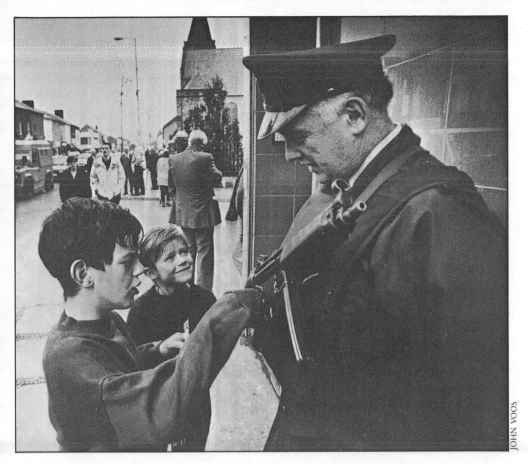

RUC officer on the Shankill Road, several days after the IRA bombing there

perhaps three minutes after being planted would have trapped the loyalists upstairs, while in theory giving shoppers time to disperse. The bomb seems to have been designed to demolish the building, as it did, with the intention of sending the loyalists plunging to their deaths or serious injury.

In the event everything went wrong: the IRA men did not have time to make their escape; nor did people in the fishmonger's; and the loyalist targets had already gone. In the end, the judgement must be that anyone taking a primed bomb into a busy shop is taking an enormous gamble, both with their own lives and the lives of others. On Saturday both the IRA and the civilian population paid a heavy price when that gamble was lost.

The bombing represents the culmination of several months of increasingly desperate IRA attempts to assassinate loyalist paramilitary personnel. Hardly

291

a week has passed without IRA gangs attempting to gun down or blow up those they believe to be associated with groups such as the UDA and UVF.

But loyalist figures have taken more and more precautions as it became obvious that the IRA was intent on waging a sustained campaign against them, and this year the republicans have been frustrated by the failure of literally dozens of unsuccessful murder attempts. One well-known Shankill Road figure, widely regarded as a leading UDA gunman and commander, has been the subject of six republican assassination attempts, several of them in the last few months. Other individuals, in particular three UDA figures in south Belfast, have each escaped death on three or four separate occasions.

This year the IRA has killed three people whom it alleged had violent loyalist connections, and in all, over the last six years, republican groups have killed thirty-nine Protestant men, citing this reason. In some cases the IRA's intelligence on these men has been accurate, and their actual or potential victims have been acknowledged as important loyalist figures and given paramilitary funerals. In other instances those killed seem to have had only fringe associations, perhaps family connections. One man killed was shot when the IRA could not reach his brother.

A number of the IRA's victims have had no known associations with terrorism. One innocent victim was gunned down and his body left with his sons, aged six and seven. One of the boys telephoned his grandmother, saying: "Nana, would you come and mind us, for a bad man has shot my daddy dead."

In a number of cases the families of those killed, often together with the RUC, have strenuously denied those killed were loyalists. One widow said the allegation concerning her husband was "a dirty slur on his good name" and others have made similar comments.

The fish shop bombing was not the first hardship that this tough district has had to bear.

Bigotry and violence
keep city district in isolation

Some of the Shankill Road bombing victims are buried

If ever an entire community could be said to be disturbed and ill-adjusted, it is the Shankill Road district of Belfast. Once a vibrant and prosperous working-class area that attracted many outside visitors, it has in many ways lost its heart. The sense of community has gradually all but disappeared as economic, political and other misfortunes have befallen the district, increasingly leaving it prey to paramilitarism and other problems. Today it has lost much of its status, its employment and its vitality. It is now shunned by most of the rest of the city: too many people have got into trouble simply by straying into the district, too many Catholics have wound up dead in a backstreet simply because of their religion. It is a fair bet that more than half of Belfast's population have never been up the Shankill Road in the last two decades.

293

The Shankill was always a tough community. It had legendary hard men, ever ready to accept a challenge for fisticuffs. At weekends the streets could be hazardous after the pubs closed: even before the Troubles, the police at certain times used to patrol in pairs or in fours, wearing metal helmets.

In the relaxed 1960s some Catholic families lived in the district but 1969 brought serious sectarian disorder and the erection of physical barriers to keep the two sides apart. Today the peace lines are less unsightly, rusting tin having been replaced with brick, but the segregation is complete.

Before the Troubles the Shankill was home to a working-class élite of men who jealously guarded what they regarded as their privileges over Catholics. The housing was only marginally superior to that of the adjoining Falls Road, but Protestants dominated the jobs market, especially in well-paid, high-status engineering work. Such material advantages went hand in hand with the political supremacy which, in the old days, Unionists enjoyed over nationalists. Today the Unionist power system has collapsed, and gone too are many of the jobs. In Belfast terms the area is not among the most disadvantaged: over a dozen Catholic areas are worse off by all the indices of deprivation, and male unemployment, at 31 per cent, is only half that of the Falls. But the Shankill has not come to terms with the new order of things, and its representatives complain constantly that it is the object of deliberate discrimination by the authorities. The complaint that "the Catholics get everything now, we get nothing" is a familiar refrain.

It was, and is, a community of contrasts. The hard-drinking men are still there, though many are today in paramilitary groups and occasionally settle their disputes with guns rather than fists. Side by side with their pubs are dozens of churches and an extraordinary selection of gospel halls, where the faithful go to "wee meetings". Here the puritan element, imported from Scotland centuries ago, define "being saved" as abstaining from drink, cigarettes and women.

This fissiparous proliferation of tiny churches – one had the nickname of "Duff's Chosen Few" – is a reflection of the tradition of Presbyterianism dissent and individualism. Local politics had a similar flavour, for the Shankill has always favoured mavericks and independents to representatives of the larger Unionist parties. But as one community employment worker put it: "The downside of the individualism is a lack of community cohesion. These people had a tradition of standing on their own two feet, but they found it harder to cope when the structures all started to crumble." The result has been a near-collapse of the institution of the family. The more upwardly mobile tended to move away to escape the paramilitarism and look for work elsewhere, leaving behind a community beset with problems which are clearly beyond its own means to solve.

The loyalist violence emanating from the community – of which the notorious

294

Shankill Butchers assassination squads were only one example among many – did nothing to increase external sympathy for the Shankill's descent. This was a community where no one thought it strange to have a terrorist group's head-quarters above the local fish shop. For fifty years its people were told by their political leaders that they were superior to the Catholics in the next district. When the Troubles came, it was, perhaps, hardly surprising that many of them thought they should defend their way of life, and do so by force. Twenty-five years on, with a marked lack of local leadership, with little tradition of self-help, and with little outside sympathy, the district has lost its self-confidence. Saturday's IRA bombing has stunned an already depressed district; and it will do nothing to convince its ill-educated, underprivileged children that they should turn away from violence.

More horror followed, as loyalist groups exacted retribution by killing Catholics, and much controversy attended the funeral of IRA volunteer Thomas "Bootsie" Begley, who was killed by his own bomb in the Shankill Road blast.

There was widespread condemnation of Gerry Adams when he acted as a pallbearer: many assumed his action meant the Hume–Adams initiative was dead. But Mr Adams had no choice but to carry the coffin.

31 OCTOBER 1993   THE INDEPENDENT ON SUNDAY

Why Gerry Adams mourned

Gerry Adams once outlined something of his family history. "I had a cousin picked up, tortured and stabbed to death by loyalists. Most of my immediate family have been in prison. I've a brother in prison at the moment."

The British army had shot dead his brother-in-law and shot and seriously injured his brother. He could have added that his father and father-in-law had both been jailed for republican activities. He has been arrested on numerous occasions and been to jail several times: at one point he was simultaneously a sentenced prisoner and an internee. He was hit by three bullets in a loyalist assassination attempt in 1984. There have been numerous other plots to kill him, one of them involving placing a limpet mine on the roof of his black taxi. In the most recent, a grenade was thrown at his house a few months ago.

It has been an eventful life, yet the extraordinary thing about this record is that it is, in Belfast republican terms, not really extraordinary at all. There are scores, if not hundreds, of IRA and Sinn Féin people whose life experience is very much along the same lines: for a whole class of people this is really the stuff of what passes for normality.

On television Gerry Adams's well-groomed articulacy and sixties-sociology-professor presentation may seem to set him apart from the common run of republicans, but he is an integral part of that world. In private he may well be appalled by some of the IRA's excesses, but he is not in the business of showing that in public: these are his people.

He often uses the phrase "republican family" as a synonym for "republican movement", a term which attempts to encompass that amorphous mass which includes the IRA, Sinn Féin, various other republican organisations and fringe elements. Back in the 1950s and 1960s the republican family used to be tiny and was actually family-based, consisting of a few hundred men and women in Belfast and some rural areas. After the last IRA campaign petered out in the early 1960s its main activity was holding annual Easter parades to republican graves.

In times of tension, or occasions such as royal visits, the Unionist administration would deal with the old IRA with almost contemptuous ease. The RUC was simply dispatched to round up a couple of dozen activists, who were held in jail for a couple of weeks until things cooled down. This happened to both Gerry Adams's father and his future father-in-law, and to a range of various uncles, cousins, neighbours and friends. Up the Falls Road, where the Adams family lived, most people thought it a disgrace that the Unionist government should act in this way; but there was no uprising in protest.

The republican hard core was regarded as a respectable but misguided and slightly quixotic hangover from the past, idealists dreaming an impossible dream. The republican families were well regarded in the district: they were lawbreakers but they were not criminals, coming from decent, upright families.

That old republican movement is scarcely recognisable as the movement of today. The old guard used to debate whether it was legitimate to shoot RUC men, since they, too, were Irishmen; today's terrorists think nothing of strapping people into vans and using them as "human bombs" to blow up army bases. This week I watched mourners at an IRA man's funeral taunting Protestant women by holding up nine fingers to signify the nine victims of the Shankill Road bomb.

The small, scrupulous old IRA has turned into a large-scale machine which has killed more than 1,600 people, often with breathtakingly casual brutality. Furthermore, they have brought large sections of the ghettos along with them and developed a political wing, Sinn Féin, which can rely on the support of three in every ten nationalist voters. In other words, Gerry Adams is leader of a party which commands 10 per cent of the total vote in Northern Ireland. Judging by the large turnout for the funeral of the IRA man who blew himself and nine innocent Protestants to bits, it is a fair bet that the incident will hardly cost Sinn Féin a single vote.

To understand why this should be, it is necessary to try to envisage the life experiences of those who live in the Catholic ghettos of Belfast and elsewhere. When the Troubles blazed up in 1969 much of the IRA leadership was in a Marxist phase and was upset by the sudden outbreak of communal violence: the two sections of the working class should be uniting to overthrow capitalism, they said, not fighting each other. While IRA leaders conducted this theoretical debate in Dublin, hand-to-hand fighting was going on in the backstreets of Belfast. The Falls and Ardoyne areas were invaded by loyalist mobs who firebombed Catholic homes, occasioning mass flight on a scale later described as the largest population movement in western Europe since the Second World War.

The republicans, who were supposed to defend Catholic areas, were hardly in evidence and the bitter slogan "IRA – I ran away" is said to have appeared on a Falls Road wall. Within months the IRA jettisoned its Marxists, styled itself the Provisional IRA, and set about building a military force. Recruits flocked into the ranks in their hundreds as the Falls and Ardoyne swore they would never again be left defenceless against rampaging loyalists. It was not long, however, before defence became attack and the major elements – republicans, loyalists and the army and police – became locked in a three-sided conflict that has dragged on for more than two decades.

The IRA has been sustained for so long because the republican mindset has become the attitude of a majority of people in the Catholic ghettos. In particular, it has to be grasped that they believe they are much more sinned against than sinning.

Thomas "Bootsie" Begley, the bomber who created such carnage last Saturday, was born in 1970, just as the Troubles were beginning. A hundred yards from his home, on a gable wall of a Sinn Féin office, is a long list of IRA members and civilians killed in the immediate vicinity. He must have seen the memorial almost every day of his life. The gable wall does not, naturally enough, list those who have been victims of the IRA, but it gives a sense of how many members this community feels it has lost. There are 121 names on the list, ranging from IRA members to old ladies killed by stray bullets during gun battles.

The overall statistics for the area are stark. In total, north Belfast has seen almost 650 killings: 235 of these were Catholic civilians killed by loyalist gangs, while the army has killed a further 20 civilians. A high concentration of these deaths occurred in Begley's neighbourhood: this is a district where violent death is a common occurrence, where everyone has lost relatives and friends, where everyone has been an eyewitness to appalling events.

Sinn Féin leaders may talk in abstractions such as self-determination and building a new Ireland, but most of the young men like Begley who join the IRA's ranks do so because they view themselves and their district as being involved in a constant struggle against a hostile world. To them, British soldiers are not peacekeepers but the enemy. To them, Protestants are men wearing balaclavas who burst into their homes and open fire with rifles.

Most of his neighbours will remember Thomas Begley as a young man who decided to do something about it, and gave his life in an attempt to strike back at loyalist assassins. Had he succeeded he would have been fêted; but even in failure he is regarded as a hero. He was given a grand sendoff to the republican plot in Milltown cemetery, his funeral taking six hours to get from the house to the grave. He was born into the front line of a vicious little war, and he died taking part in it. In a while his name will be added to the grim list on that gable wall: he will be number 122. Local youths will gaze at it and think of him, not as a mad bomber who killed two little girls, four women, three men and himself, but as a young man who died doing his bit for Ardoyne.

The action of Gerry Adams in carrying his coffin created a major stir in Britain but less in Belfast. A grainy black-and-white picture taken around 1971 shows the future Sinn Féin leader attending an IRA funeral in Belfast. Mr Adams, who was then a clean-shaven young man around the same age as Thomas Begley, was part of an honour guard wearing black jacket and black beret. Since then he has attended perhaps 200 republican funerals, acting as pallbearer at almost every one of them. In February 1992 the *Independent* report of the funeral of an IRA member shot dead by the SAS noted that Mr Adams was "dressed in his standard green funeral coat, whose shoulders must by now be threadbare from carrying the coffins of so many dead IRA and Sinn Féin members". In republican terms it would have been amazing for Adams to refrain from carrying the Begley coffin, amounting to a dramatic renunciation of the IRA. It would have been nothing less than the end of him as a republican leader.

Mr Adams would have been well aware that the powerful image of himself hefting the coffin would be on every television bulletin and in every newspaper;

Gerry Adams carries the coffin of Thomas "Bootsie" Begley, the IRA man killed by his own bomb in the Shankill Road bombing

he would have been aware, too, of the impact of that image on his projection of himself as a man seeking peace. But he had no choice, even if carrying the coffin meant the collapse of the Hume–Adams initiative. Whatever the damage to his political moves, Adams had to shoulder the coffin: for he and Thomas Begley were part of the same republican movement, the same republican family.

The crucial question now is whether that movement might think of dropping violence and attempting to operate through political means. At one level it is almost impossible to imagine that it might, for the name of the IRA has been synonymous with sheer terrorism. Its members have piled body upon body: soldiers, policemen, civilians, judges, politicians, people who work for the security forces, alleged loyalists, alleged informers, other republicans in feuds. It has killed them in Northern Ireland, in Britain, the Irish Republic and on the continent. Two hundred and eighty of its own members have been killed, one hundred of them dying like Thomas Begley in premature explosions. More than 1,000 others have been to prison: they have inflicted a great deal of suffering and grief, but republicans have suffered much themselves. Too much blood has been spilt, too many sacrifices made, the rhetoric has always run, to think of calling it off without achieving total victory.

Three years ago an IRA spokesman told the *Independent*: "We can state absolutely, on the record, that there will be no ceasefire, no truce, no cessation of violence short of a British withdrawal. That, as blunt as that, is our position. Having said that, should the British government at any stage genuinely seek dialogue, then we are more than willing to engage in dialogue with them."

If that remains the case today, there seems little or no room for manoeuvre, which means that any prospect of success in the present moves is dependent on the hope that republican thinking has evolved since then. There has certainly been evolution within the movement in recent years, much of it pioneered by Gerry Adams. The centrepiece of the movement remains the IRA, but Mr Adams and his associates have grafted onto that central culture of violence both a culture of debate and a new pragmatism. A great deal of outdated republican dogma has been pruned away and new avenues explored. Sinn Féin, once simply a mouthpiece for the IRA, has developed an identity of its own: its conferences are frequently marked by lively debates; its leading members often make intriguing speeches. The presentation and the rhetoric have changed: where once the dominant style was threatening bombast, Mr Adams and his associates now speak routinely of peace. The key question, on which many lives may depend, is whether the change goes beyond style and into substance. At the moment it has to be said that the republican movement is so secretive that there is as yet no definitive answer to that question.

The grim fact is that the IRA has sustained itself for more than two decades; that more than 70,000 people regularly vote for its political wing; that security sources say its military defeat is not in prospect. Perhaps republican leaders weigh these facts and conclude that keeping it up for another decade or so will bring victory. Or perhaps they conclude that all the violence does not appear to have brought a British withdrawal closer; perhaps they wonder if there could be another way; perhaps they look at the lists of names on the gable walls and wonder how many more Thomas Begleys are fated to be added to them.

Gerry Adams is steeped in the republican tradition but he has also been an innovator. The questions now are whether he genuinely has the will and the support to strike out for the biggest innovation of all – peace – and whether the two governments will dare to believe that he can take the IRA from terrorism to the table.

In the days after the Shankill Road bombing, Northern Ireland lived in dread of a loyalist retaliation of similar magnitude. It came a week later when UDA gunmen burst into a Catholic pub in the Co Londonderry village of Greysteel, where a Hallowe'en party was in full swing. One of the gunmen called out "trick or treat" before machine-gunning the bar. Seven people were killed, including a 19-year-old girl and a man in his 80s.

1 NOVEMBER 1993   THE INDEPENDENT

Tribal killers drown doubts with hatred

The massacre in Greysteel has once again illustrated one of the most striking features of loyalist terrorists: that for sheer hot-blooded, vengeful savagery they can often leave the IRA standing. The IRA uses murder as a cold-blooded and clinically calculated means to a political end; loyalist assassins often leave the unmistakable impression that they are men who enjoy their work. That "work" has left more than 900 people dead during the Troubles. The fact that the vast majority of these have been uninvolved Catholics demonstrates that loyalist paramilitary groups define the entire Catholic population as the enemy and hence "legitimate targets".

For these groups, killing someone with republican connections is a bonus, since they see their basic mission as attacking Catholics. For public consumption they often claim their victims are republican activists, but at inquest after inquest over the years RUC detectives have testified that the "IRA intelligence officer" killed was, in reality, a man with no paramilitary connections.

After an incident such as Saturday night's attack, no such pretence is possible. In cases like this the loyalists often describe their targets as "members of the

301

pan-nationalist front" or the "nationalist electorate"; but these are simply preposterously grandiose synonyms for the Catholic population as a whole.

Nearly all members of the violent Protestant groups are drawn from the loyalist lumpenproletariat. They tend to live in exclusively Protestant areas, though quite a few say that before becoming involved in paramilitarism they had Catholic acquaintances and, occasionally, girlfriends. Their view of the Catholic population is a completely tribal one. One reformed loyalist terrorist, who nearly 20 years ago took part in an attack which killed six people in a Catholic bar, described his attitude then in the following terms: "Any doubts were drowned by hatred. We dehumanised the other side and branded them animals. We didn't think in terms of them being people. If we couldn't get the IRA, we would have to slaughter members of the Catholic community, who, after all, seemed to support them."

In the early 1970s the ranks of groups such as the Ulster Defence Association contained tens of thousands of members; today they have shrunk to a few thousand at most. Much of the Protestant population at large has little time for groups which have been responsible for appalling killings, and whose leaders have gained a reputation for lining their own pockets with the proceeds of racketeering. But at the same time there have been worrying signs in recent years that the level of approval, or at least tolerance, of these groups has risen steadily, with a deeply ingrained Protestant belief that IRA violence has worked and produced results.

Protestant violence such as the Greysteel attack clearly does no service to the image of the Unionist cause in Britain and elsewhere. It helps ensure that the IRA will plan more retaliatory attacks on loyalist targets in the future. Had loyalist groups opted for inactivity in the wake of the Shankill Road bombing, the pressure of local and international opprobrium would have remained on the IRA. But such considerations never seem to weigh with the loyalist terrorists. Over and over again they demonstrate that they are motivated not by political considerations but by sheer sectarianism, and that they are ever prepared to squander moral advantage to indulge ancient hatreds.

By this stage the atmosphere throughout Northern Ireland was poisonous and close to despair. As trade unions staged peace rallies in an attempt to lift spirits, Terry Carlin, Northern Ireland's most senior trade-unionist, painted this grim picture.

"It's the worst for years... you can see the fear everywhere"

"We are organising rallies, but we have not called for marches because we would be afraid that there are brutal people out there, on both sides, and some of the marches might themselves become the focus for attack.

"It's hard to place it on a scale, but certainly it's the worst for years. I do think they are actually taking us back to the early 1970s. I really don't come across anyone now who doesn't talk about how dreadful it is.

"One union tells me that they have not had to deal with as many reports of intimidation or sectarian remarks and sectarian tension in the workplace for many, many years. Another union official told me he went into a factory the other day and you could have just cut the atmosphere with a knife. Everybody was frankly scared to talk to people of the other community or even talk to people of their own community, in case anything they said might be overheard and give offence.

"A union official told me he was driving to Belfast from Dublin with four others after a meeting when the news came on the radio about the Shankill bombing. The company in the car was mixed, Protestant and Catholic. He said there wasn't a word spoken for the next hour until somebody said, 'Look, can we pull in here and have a break.' That was the only way the silence could be broken.

"We have reports of people leaving jobs because of the dangers. We know of one construction site where a car was seen touring around and passed the site four or five times. The workers just decided, that's not at all healthy, and they went and packed up the job. There was an incident in a hotel with an attack on a member of the staff. After that, some of the other staff decided that was it, that was them finished, they didn't feel safe any longer and they left. Those kind of things are repeating.

"Other officials get word of threats against their members, and the problem is to work out whether it is a serious threat or a nutcase. I have to advise unions on how serious it might be. You have to use your experience and hope you get it right, because you'd feel bloody awful if you got it wrong.

"We have an understanding with the police about personal safety and security and so on, and we've written out to unions with a book from the RUC about how individuals or groups of workers with concerns about personal security should liaise with the RUC. We've facilitated meetings between police and union officials, and sometimes with management, to assess which of the threats are real. We also have some informal mechanisms where we can help to check out threats to see how serious they are.

"I suspect the bulk of intimidation is aimed at Catholics. It runs from very straightforward stuff – things like 'get the Fenians out of there or else' – to various other things.

"You can see the fear everywhere. I was talking to a taxi driver and he told me many of the guys have pulled out of the business. Among those who are left, there is now an agreement that the Prods will only go into Prod areas and Catholics will only go into Catholic areas.

"When I went to mass on Sunday attendance was down by a third and there were armed RUC officers on guard duty in the car park. The priest said at the end of mass that police advice was for us to leave quickly, not to congregate chatting, just to get into our cars and get going. I've been living in Belfast since 1968 and it's the first time I ever heard that.

"There is so much fear and apprehension about. We hope to work out proposals for a community day to involve a spectrum broader than simply the trade union movement. In the meantime the rallies are to reaffirm the right of anyone to live and work where they want without the fear of intimidation or death."

In such black times it hardly seemed possible to think that the peace process might still have life. Yet along with the killings came political developments, some of them highly significant. Chief among these was the fact that the Hume–Adams initiative, which both the British and Irish governments had appeared to reject, was suddenly and unexpectedly revived. That revival began in the Republic.

Why the south changed tune

This has been an extraordinary and possibly historic week in Irish politics, all the more remarkable for the fact that its significance has gone largely unmarked by the Irish media. This week the Irish government was told, quietly but firmly, to reverse its approach to the Hume–Adams talks process; that there was promise in the initiative which should not be thrown away; and that it should make amends for slighting SDLP leader John Hume earlier in the week. By the end of the week it was moving, in an undignified and even slightly panic-stricken fashion, to meet these points. The net result is that in Dublin, at least, the apparently dying Hume–Adams initiative has been given a new lease of life. Whether or not it will be revived in London is a more problematic question, but in the coming weeks the British government must expect steadily increasing pressure not to throw the initiative in the bin.

This week's message to Dublin came from both southern and northern nationalists. The latter, a highly politicised group, took great offence at what has been described as Dublin's "ham-fisted and hurtful" response to Hume–Adams. The result was to send a tidal wave of northern bitterness sweeping south.

Mr Hume had invested enormous political capital, and in effect his personal reputation, in the highly controversial move of talking to Gerry Adams. Against all the odds, he emerged from the enterprise saying he believed there existed the best hope of peace for 20 years.

Dublin's apparent brushoff produced particular rage because Mr Hume's supporters regard the SDLP as not just another political party. Its leaders see themselves as heading a party which has stood out for the democratic processes, and believes the Republic owes it a great deal, since it acts as a bulwark for the south against the terrorists and their sympathisers. It argues it has held the line against Sinn Féin and the IRA, while at the same time producing in John Hume Ireland's most creative political figure.

This week party members watched on television the sight of the SDLP leader weeping in a country graveyard. He had been approached by the daughter of a man who had just been shot dead by loyalists. She told him: "Mr Hume, we've just buried my father, he died in the shooting on Saturday. My family wants

305

you to know that when we said the rosary around my daddy's coffin, we prayed for you, for what you're trying to do to bring peace." Mr Hume nodded, shook her hands, turned away and broke down in tears.

SDLP members and others are daily confronted with the unpalatable but unavoidable reality that republicans are a fact of life in Northern Ireland. The IRA exists, it kills people, and 10 per cent of the electorate consistently vote for its political wing. Since the republican community has withstood, for a full quarter of a century, all the efforts of the authorities to defeat its campaign of terrorism, the SDLP has concluded that the only chance of stopping them seems to lie in the Hume–Adams dialogue. It is, admittedly, a faint hope, but it is seen as the only hope available. Even in her grief, the woman in the graveyard was expressing a deeply held northern nationalist view: that if the British army, the RUC, MI5, MI6 et al. cannot end the violence, then John Hume should be given the chance to try.

Few northerners were particularly surprised when John Major rejected Hume–Adams: the outrage came when the Irish government followed suit, Irish foreign minister Dick Spring suggesting coolly that Mr Hume should step aside and allow the two governments to get on with the real business. A Belfast solicitor said: "Sure we expected Major to do what he did, to humiliate Hume like that. It was the sight of our own in Dublin doing it too that got me so angry." The most common comment was that Mr Spring and Taoiseach Albert Reynolds had "hung Hume out to dry". It was an almost unprecedented breach in Dublin–SDLP relations, which have been among Ireland's most carefully tended relationships, characterised by a close sense of partnership and identity of interest. The way that breach is being mended is assuming the importance of a moment of definition in Irish nationalism.

In the last few years Mr Spring has had two major triumphs. First his nominee, Mary Robinson, swept to victory in the presidential election. Then he led his Irish Labour party into coalition government with its highest-ever vote. There were clear signs of the emergence of a strong new modernising, secularist, feminist element in Irish politics.

One huge question posed by this development was how this new factor would relate to the continuing conflict in Northern Ireland. Mr Spring began his tenure as Foreign Affairs minister, which gave him responsibility for both the north and Anglo-Irish relations, with gestures towards northern Unionists. He thus gave the impression of moving away from the traditional southern view of northern nationalists as "our people up there". In the new scheme of things, Mr Spring seemed to be moving into a new post-nationalist, or even anti-nationalist, phase. Mr Hume was to be relegated from his pivotal position as Dublin's key northern ally; henceforth Unionists and nationalists were to be dealt with on an equal basis.

306

Mr Spring's problem, as he learnt with a shock this week, is that Ireland showed itself unready for any such new approach. All the evidence is that the old Ireland, which is still out there, heartily approves of John Hume and his initiative. So, it seems, does much of the new Ireland: university students at a debating society in Dublin recently gave Mr Hume not one, but two, standing ovations. The same students initially extended a warm welcome to a Unionist spokesman, but were clearly disappointed in his speech. There is in the south a considerable reservoir of good will towards Unionists, but also a feeling that northern Protestants have yet to respond to gestures of friendship.

Mr Spring's problem was that he combined his apparent rejection of Hume–Adams with a new olive branch to Unionists. This increased the northern nationalist sense of abandonment, for their belief is that Unionists will not reciprocate the concessions.

One of the fascinating points of the week was that Mr Hume, though clearly angry, did not publicly voice any sense of betrayal at the rejection of Hume–Adams, opting instead to make his feelings known at a private meeting with Mr Spring and Mr Reynolds. The wave which hit Dublin was all the more effective for being clearly unorganised and spontaneous.

All the signs now are that a major adjustment of Irish government policy is under way. A sudden public volte-face and a ringing endorsement of Hume–Adams would have presentational difficulties, but the concept of this kind of initiative has taken root. John Hume was one of the leaders of the old Ireland: it has now been conclusively established that he is one of the leaders of the new Ireland as well.

Having taken less than a week to begin the business of turning around the Irish government, Mr Hume's next focus of attention will be London, where he will try to reverse John Major's rejection of his initiative. The Prime Minister had a number of obvious reasons for turning it down in the first place: no government wants to receive pieces of paper with Gerry Adams's fingerprints on it. A warm welcome for such an initiative could easily spark off even greater loyalist violence. And any form of welcome could well break up the Conservative party's increasingly close relationship with Ulster Unionist MPs, whose votes it craves.

Mr Hume clearly hopes to respond to these forces with pressures of his own. One would be a united Irish nationalist front, with the Irish government endorsing his approach. His other tactic has been to appeal to the court of public opinion, repeatedly going on television to say that a chance for peace exists. He has plainly intrigued Jon Snow and Jeremy Paxman as to what he has up his sleeve; presumably the viewers want to know too.

The central problem for Mr Major, in countering these pressures, is that he has implied that an alternative peace process exists. If it does, no one in Northern Ireland knows what it is. If he means the old inter-party talks process, he faces the major stumbling block that nobody, with the possible exception of Sir Patrick Mayhew, believes in it. Over a period of years increasingly disillusioned party delegations dragged themselves to Stormont for talks which the community in general now regards as futile.

In the first place, the Rev Ian Paisley has made it abundantly clear that he will not be at any new talks. The same may well be true of James Molyneaux's Ulster Unionists, who have laid down several difficult preconditions. And Mr Hume can hardly be expected to show enthusiasm for what he clearly regards, in present circumstances, as an inconsequential waste of time.

The second point is that there have been no moves which make success likelier next time round. In Northern Ireland waves of violence tend not to make finding agreement any easier; rather, they increase divisions and tensions, and lead to more pressure on the politicians not to compromise.

The third point is that inter-party talks are just that: political talks, not peace talks. Even in the unlikely event that agreement did emerge, IRA and loyalist violence would continue.

The apparent absence of a realistic alternative to Hume–Adams will be one of Mr Hume's strongest cards in the political manoeuvring which lies ahead. But in an important sense the SDLP leader has already changed the agenda, for there is really no market now for the idea of attempting to make tiny incremental advances. Whatever the merits of Hume–Adams, there has been a shift in the discourse of Northern Ireland towards the idea that talks should not be about political minutiae but should be on a grand scale, concerned with the biggest issue of all: that of a peace settlement.

13

THE DOWNING STREET
DECLARATION

Towards the end of 1993 there were persistent reports that the government had been in secret contact with the republicans. The reports were repeatedly and insistently denied by Sir Patrick Mayhew, but suspicions persisted, not least because of the many precedents for such contacts.

Troubles cloak long history of secret meetings

Although the government adamantly denies reports of recent talks with Sinn Féin, the fact is that a succession of British politicians, including government ministers and in one instance a future Prime Minister, have met republican leaders on numerous occasions in the course of the Troubles. The details of a number of encounters are known, but it seems likely that there have been many other contacts which have never emerged into public view. It is certainly the case that contact occurs on a daily basis in contexts such as prisons, interrogation centres and on local council business.

On a more strategic level, however, there have been important talks between republicans and British representatives. When news of these has emerged, there have been protests from Unionists and Irish governments, both of whom have recurring fears of Britain doing a deal with the IRA. For example the former Taoiseach, Garret FitzGerald, described Harold Wilson's action of secretly meeting IRA leaders in Dublin in 1971 as "an act of treachery". Lord Wilson, then leader of the opposition, met the IRA again the following year in England, but his aide, Joe Haines, later wrote: "A meeting of minds was clearly impossible. We were planets apart; words had different meanings. It was completely meaningless." One of the Provisionals present, Joe Cahill, reached a similar conclusion, describing the Dublin meeting as "a waffling session. To me it had been a complete waste of bloody time."

The most direct formal talks between a government and republicans came in 1972, when Lord Whitelaw, then Northern Ireland Secretary, had a group of republican leaders, including Gerry Adams and Martin McGuinness, flown to London for secret talks in Chelsea. More systematic contacts took place in 1974 and 1975 when, under a Labour government, senior officials met Sinn Féin leaders on a regular basis at Laneside, a large house outside Belfast. The meetings helped set up an IRA ceasefire, with the government designating a number of "incident centres" designed to provide channels of communication with local republicans.

There have been many more examples of contacts between politicians and

310

paramilitaries or their representatives. In 1978 Douglas Hurd, now Foreign Secretary, met Gerry Adams when he was a Conservative frontbench spokesman on European affairs. He stressed he was acting in his capacity as an individual MP. In his memoirs Garret FitzGerald voiced southern Irish fears about the effect of such meetings. He wrote: "The contacts that had taken place had had the effect merely of prolonging the violence by deluding the IRA into believing that a British government would eventually negotiate a settlement with them."

Today Martin McGuinness, 21 years on from his visit to Cheyne Walk in Chelsea, is once again said to be involved in talks with British representatives. Clearly there have been many precedents for this; but the precedents for success are, equally clearly, unpromising.

The already seething political scene was thrown into renewed turmoil when a newspaper produced documentary evidence that, in spite of all the denials, the authorities had been in regular contact with the republicans. At a stroke the government's credibility was undermined.

5 DECEMBER 1993 THE INDEPENDENT ON SUNDAY

Mayhew stumbles, the documents don't match, and British credibility in Ireland reaches a new low

The old Sir Patrick Mayhew was a big, bluff character with a genial twinkle in his eye and a ready smile. Some in Belfast thought him, perhaps, a little patronising, but in general he was accepted as a man of rectitude and straight dealing, as indeed befits a former Attorney General.

311

The new Sir Patrick Mayhew made his first appearance at a Stormont Castle press conference last Sunday. Pale, tense and unhappy, he stumbled through his explanations of why he had been in protracted contact with Sinn Féin and the IRA. His audience was not a receptive one, for it consisted of journalists who had repeatedly heard him denying such contacts. Absolutely untrue, he had insisted. His press officer had scoffed at one such report from journalist Eamonn Mallie: "It belongs more properly in the fantasy of spy thrillers than in real life." Sir Patrick, asked by Mr Mallie how he would react if somebody produced evidence of such contacts, had chortled condescendingly, "I should be very interested to see it."

The production of that evidence last weekend – by Eamonn Mallie – introduced us to the new, grim, nonchortling Sir Patrick. The press conference was unimpressed by his performance. "We have witnessed you being extremely nervous," one journalist told him with Belfast directness. "I think we noticed you swallowing, and your syntax has gone to pieces several times." He made a hurried, graceless exit after his ordeal, leaving his glasses behind.

He was, by all accounts, deeply apprehensive about how the House of Commons would treat him the following day. As it turned out he need not have worried, for the House was understanding and there was hardly a breath of criticism. For tactical or other reasons, Labour, the Ulster Unionists and the SDLP gave him an easy ride. The only really outspoken critic was the Rev Ian Paisley, who was escorted out after calling the Northern Ireland Secretary a liar. Afterwards a Catholic woman doctor said: "I never thought I'd feel sorry for Paisley, but I did then. They threw him out for telling the truth."

Sir Patrick justified his actions by emphasising several key points. The context of the contact was that in February of this year Martin McGuinness of Sinn Féin had communicated to the government this message: "The conflict is over but we need your advice on how to bring it to a close." The government had a duty to respond to that message, he said, to loud support from the Conservative benches behind him. In the contacts that followed there had been no talks or negotiations: messages had been sent in written form. There had been two meetings with Sinn Féin, but these were unauthorised. Everything communicated in private had been consistent with the government's publicly stated positions. To demonstrate this, Sir Patrick said he was placing in the Commons library all consequent messages received and dispatched by the government.

Sinn Féin denied each of these substantive points at a series of press conferences, where Gerry Adams's body language, radiating cool confidence, was in marked contrast to Sir Patrick's edginess. Sinn Féin said the present series of contacts had begun, not this year, but in 1990; that Martin McGuinness had never sent such a message; that the meetings had been authorised; and that real negotiations had taken place.

312

But at this stage the issue seemed to be fading. Sir Patrick's secret contacts had been revealed, and while in Ireland there was much head-shaking and talk of perfidious Albion, he had been exonerated by parliament. The IRA and Sinn Féin were contradicting him, but then they would say that, wouldn't they?

Then new points emerged. Sinn Féin issued some documents before Sir Patrick issued his, and comparison of the two versions showed that vital parts had been altered by one of the parties. Someone was engaged in a major deception exercise: forging, omitting and doctoring documents. Each accused the other of fabrication.

One point of central importance was whether Martin McGuinness actually had asked for advice on how to bring the conflict to a close. Sir Patrick told the Commons that he had, but there was scepticism in Ireland that Mr McGuinness, with his reputation as a militaristic hardliner, would have acted in such a way. Furthermore, the message was supposed to have come in February, yet there was no sign that the conflict was over: the killings and bombings continued.

A key paragraph in a document sent by Sir Patrick to the republicans on 19 March touched on this point, but he and Sinn Féin published different versions of the text.

Sir Patrick's version read: "We note that what is being sought at this stage is advice, and that any dialogue would follow an unannounced halt to violent activity. We confirm that if violence had genuinely been brought to an end, whether or not that fact had been announced, *then dialogue could take place* [our italics]." This offered strong support for the assertion that Mr McGuinness had indeed asked for advice.

The republican version said: "What is being sought at this stage is advice. The position of the British Government is that any dialogue could only follow a halt to violent activity. It is understood that in the first instance this would have to be unannounced. If violence had genuinely been brought to an end, whether or not that fact had been announced, *then progressive entry into dialogue could take place* [our italics]."

At first the claim and counterclaim on the issue of advice could not be resolved satisfactorily, but the phrase "progressive entry into dialogue', unexpectedly offered a vital clue as to which version was accurate. Among the material published by Sir Patrick was a later message in which the republicans told him: "We need clarification of the phrase 'progressive entry into dialogue'." This apparently innocuous phrase now assumed major importance, since it did not appear anywhere else in the exchanges. The government said it had published all consequent exchanges: how then did it explain its absence?

When asked on Tuesday to account for this, a Northern Ireland Office spokesman told the *Independent*: "We are checking this out." On Wednesday afternoon, in response to the same query, the spokesman said: "The only thing we can say at this stage is that the matter is being examined carefully." The response, when it eventually came, was unexpected. Late on Wednesday night, too late for *News at Ten* or the first editions of the newspapers, Sir Patrick announced that a number of errors had come to light. There were 22 of these which, he said, had been caused by typographical and transcription errors. Fourteen of them were in the key 19 March document, eight of them in the section mentioning advice and dialogue. He said that "transcription was mistakenly made from a late draft".

One of the amendments he announced was that the phrase "progressive entry" should be inserted into the text. The other amendments meant that Sir Patrick's document was now identical to the republican version; but the forced admission of errors amounted to a success for Sinn Féin. It was another blow to the government's credibility, leading in Ireland to more head-shaking and more talk of perfidious Albion. The Rev Ian Paisley accused the government of falsifying documents, adding: "They made the changes so quickly they made very obvious mistakes that have exposed the fabrication."

There remain serious weaknesses in Sir Patrick's lines of defence. Sir Patrick said the government did not negotiate, but his own version of events contains details of intricate to-ings and fro-ings. Martin McGuinness has given a lengthy account of a web of contacts stretching back to 1990. Of his meetings with officials, he said wryly: "They were unauthorised meetings which became authorised meetings when they were caught out."

What particularly concerned the Irish government was Sinn Féin's assertion that the British government had been passing on detailed briefings about last year's confidential inter-party talks, in which Dublin was involved. The republicans produced a government document to back up their claims, which among other things showed that the Northern Ireland Office hoped to manipulate the independent chairman: "The idea is to ghostwrite his report," it explained. In other words, it seemed Britain had been passing on to Sinn Féin and the IRA confidential information on the Dublin government and the constitutional parties. This prompted Irish government chief whip Noel Dempsey to talk bitterly of the British "dealing from the bottom of the deck". The Taoiseach, Albert Reynolds, made a personal complaint to John Major when they met in Dublin on Friday last.

The hard fact for the government is that the revelations mean it is now widely disbelieved, by both Unionists and nationalists, in both north and south. A great deal of damage has been done to its credibility and worse may be to come, for Sinn Féin has more documents up its sleeve. Mr Paisley, who in his own way is a master of exegesis, is promising a pamphlet underscoring the inconsistencies in the government documents.

314

The fact is that, even after 22 changes to the government's documents, they still do not fit or read like an authentic record of events. In a 10 May message to the government, for example, the republicans state: "We wish now to proceed without delay to the delegation meetings." These "delegation meetings" are mentioned nowhere else in the government's record, which once again seems incomplete. Sinn Féin's explanation for the phrase is that the British offered them two weeks of talks, involving six-strong delegations from each side, in which the British would seek to persuade them that the IRA campaign of violence was unnecessary. Sinn Féin says the IRA offered to stage a two-week ceasefire to facilitate this, but that the idea was not followed through.

The problem for the government is that such an exercise, while an intriguing notion, would clearly have violated its stated point of high principle of not negotiating until the campaign had stopped, not just temporarily, but permanently. The government's position is that the republicans were proposing a complete cessation of violence, while Sinn Féin say a ceasefire of only two weeks was on offer, and that the government excised the phrase "even though it may be of a short duration" from its document.

The government documents tend to support Sinn Féin's version, for the republican message talks of the IRA making "a gesture" to facilitate delegation meetings "so that we can both explore the potential for developing a real peace process". The republicans were hardly likely to describe such a momentous development as the permanent ending of their campaign as "a gesture"; and if they had ended the violence before the delegation meetings, there would have been no need to speak of developing a peace process.

Three weeks after this message, the government says it received another repeating that the IRA had placed on the table the offer of a total cessation. The republicans say this message is a British fabrication intended to bolster Sir Patrick's point that he would not contemplate negotiations during a temporary ceasefire. Yet the next British message in the sequence actually contains the phrase: "The reasons for not talking about a permanent cessation are understood."

In just over a week the government has been forced to reverse its position and admit contacts, and forced to change its documents. If even half of what the republicans claim is correct, a truly appalling vista is being revealed: ministers lied to parliament and public about their contacts, and are lying still about their real extent and nature; they passed information on the Irish government to terrorists; and they have published concocted documents as part of a continuing cover-up.

At the moment the government's mood seems to be one of relief that the immediate storm has been weathered without ministerial casualties. Efforts are being made to get back to business as usual.

In Ireland the criticism has been relatively muted, but the authorities should not delude themselves that things can ever be as they were. The fact that a mixture of politeness and tactics is holding back a storm of protest does not mean that the British government's credibility has not taken a severe blow. The old Sir Patrick has gone.

Political activity intensified into a period of close negotiations between the two governments. Dublin argued that a substantial joint statement on Northern Ireland's future, which addressed itself to republican concerns such as self-determination, could hold the potential for bringing about an eventual IRA cessation of violence.

Drafts of the statement winged their way back and forward across the Irish Sea as the two governments sought agreement. Both wondered what might prove acceptable to the IRA, but John Major had an extra concern: what would be acceptable to James Molyneaux? Since Mr Major needed his support in the lobbies, the Ulster Unionist party leader found himself in a pivotal position.

Unionism's dogged, low-decibel leader

James Molyneaux

One of the key figures who will help determine whether Northern Ireland may at last be on a road leading to peace is a quiet, reserved 73-year-old figure hardly known to the British public. James Molyneaux, an MP for 23 years, has for 14 been leader of Northern Ireland's largest political party, the Ulster Unionists. Yet he is a politician so low-key that after all this time many of his own supporters are uncertain how to pronounce his name. Some sound the final syllable as an "O" and some as a "U", while some mealy-mouthed compromisers attempt a slightly muffled halfway house between the two. It is typical of the man's reticence and modesty that he never bothers to correct anyone's pronunciation.

James Molyneaux's 23 years on the Commons benches have been ones of quietly industrious effort, but even his closest supporters admit that he rarely shines in public. He is not a telling debater, not a fiery orator, not a persuasive advocate for Unionism, not an inspiring ambassador for his cause. But he is head of a nine-strong group of Ulster Unionist MPs whose lobby support is desperately desired by the Prime Minister. To John Major, those nine MPs might, in tight votes, mean the difference between survival and the defeat of his administration. Because of this, the belief in Ireland is that John Major, as he attempts to put together a plan for peace in Northern Ireland, is unlikely to be approaching the question on a completely detached empirical basis. As Mr Major's increasingly extravagant assurances to Unionists have shown, the shadow of Mr Molyneaux is very much on his mind.

The government has been making it known that it has proved impossible to do business with Mr Molyneaux's Unionist rival, the Rev Ian Paisley. Part of the purpose of this exercise is to suggest by inference that Mr Molyneaux is a much more flexible and reasonable person. It is certainly true that, decibel-wise, Mr Molyneaux cannot compete with Mr Paisley. He is unfailingly courteous rather than boorish, businesslike rather than blustering, not given to temper tantrums. But if the government thinks he is likely to approve for one moment of pacific gestures towards republicans, a glance at his background should be enough to dispel any such illusions.

There are many more extreme Unionist politicians than James Molyneaux, who, unlike some colleagues, is not noted for rabid anti-Catholic statements. But he is one of the leaders of the Orange Order and sovereign grand master of its Royal Black Preceptory. His party, a strictly tribal grouping, has no known Catholic members. He has been a member of Ballynadrenta Loyal Orange Lodge for over 40 years, and his father and grandfather were Orangemen before him. His entry into politics came by accident when, one night not long after the war, he was round at the Orange hall helping to fix the heating system. Some Unionist ladies gave him a cup of tea and prevailed on him to join the party, a membership which has lasted almost half a century.

James Henry Molyneaux was born in 1920, the son of poultry farmers who lived at Crumlin, Co Antrim, not far from Belfast. He left school at the age of 15, helping with the hens and turkeys before joining the RAF in 1941. He landed in France on D-Day, as a leading aircraftsman. He suffered from nightmares for years after arriving at a concentration camp three days after its liberation. After the war he became a partner in his uncle's printing business while working his way through the Unionist grass roots. His progress was not

318

exactly meteoric: politics moved at a glacial pace in the days before the Troubles, and it was 24 years before he reached Westminster.

His seat, South Antrim, was what might be called a plum. The story goes that before the 1979 election a Tory backbencher asked Mr Molyneaux the size of his majority. He replied, "38", whereupon the Tory, thinking the constituency was a marginal, replied: "Oh, well, fingers crossed, eh?" At this point Mr Molyneaux explained gently that he meant his majority was 38,000. It was the largest majority in the UK.

Since 1970 Westminster has been Mr Molyneaux's life. A bachelor with few interests outside politics, he spends most of the week there. Unlike most Unionists of his generation, he was never a member of the Stormont parliament, and he has no interest in re-establishing such a body.

After a series of Unionist leaders toppled in the 1970s, the party leadership fell to him in 1979. The party, and Unionism in general, had suffered serious setbacks over the previous decade, and was in bad shape. It was, and still is, a party with various disparate factions and personalities, and his first priority was to provide a sense of unity and reverse its decline. He went about this task in what seemed at the time an almost leisurely way, but within a few years it became apparent that he was achieving results. In particular, he had considerable success in fending off the attacks of the Rev Ian Paisley and his Democratic Unionist party, which for more than a decade had been eating into Ulster Unionist support with its more strident brand of loyalism. The 1981 district council election was a photo finish between the two parties, but the story ever since has been one of gradual DUP decline and steady UUP consolidation.

Mr Molyneaux and Mr Paisley, who have been unkindly described as the Laurel and Hardy of Unionism, are deadly rivals. Yet at times they have formed tactical alliances and during one period in the mid-1980s they stood back to back, helping each other ward off assaults from Young Turks in their parties. Mr Paisley appears to be the dominant partner in the relationship, always first to the microphone and always the louder of the two. Mr Molyneaux's detractors complain that he is colourless and unimaginative, yet he is the undisputed winner of the perpetual power struggle between the two parties.

This is all the more intriguing because no one is quite sure how he does it. He has never mastered the art of the soundbite, and his speeches are often Delphic and puzzling rather than inspiring. Some of his judgements seem so eccentric that he appears capable of a high degree of self-delusion: in 1985, for example, he convinced himself that the Anglo-Irish agreement would not happen, and was personally shattered when it did. A veteran political correspondent said: "Covering Molyneaux is about as exciting as watching grass grow. Half the time he's not entirely coherent, difficult to pin down, he talks in riddles. I've written him off many times, but then he has this hidden tenacity, this ability to survive and to do down Paisley."

But although Mr Paisley wins hands down on drama, threats and histrionics, few close observers of Northern Ireland politics believe that Mr Molyneaux is very much more accommodating than his larger and louder rival. As a convinced integrationist, his basic position is that political activity should as much as possible be confined to Westminster, and that if this were done with sufficient determination, nationalists and republicans would eventually give up and settle down in a British context. He believes that devolution to some new Belfast institution would be dangerous for the union. He has described the idea of powersharing as unnatural and abnormal. He once asked: "Why the insistence that talking is the most important function of elected representatives?"

None of this augurs well for the government's hopes of restarting meaningful inter-party talks, for Mr Molyneaux does not want to go down that road. The concessions he hopes to extract from Mr Major, such as a Commons select committee and legislative changes [the government later granted Mr Molyneaux both concessions], are designed to concentrate activity in London rather than Belfast.

For tactical reasons, however, he has not joined Mr Paisley in declaring that he will not attend any talks, for this would both offend the devolutionists within his party and embarrass Mr Major. His restraint on this point means the government can continue to claim the inter-party talks avenue has some prospect of success.

Among Irish nationalists Mr Molyneaux does not have the status of a hate figure. But his penchant for doing business via Westminster, preferably with a weak Prime Minister, is seen as a mechanism to avoid having to do serious political business with Catholics and nationalists. One nationalist politician complained in frustration: "He's so dead. He has elevated inertia to an art form. There's no give there, no jizz – he just won't engage with us." To Irish nationalists he offers British citizenship and no special recognition for the Irish Republic, characterising the south as a foreign country. His is an essentially defensive position: he once likened his job to that of "a general with an army that isn't making anything much in terms of territorial gains but has the satisfaction of repulsing all attacks on the citadel". His principal political characteristic, in fact, is that of immobility. "He remains inert," a British official complained some years ago. This blocking game has clearly served him well within his party and within Unionism, but it has won few new friends for his cause.

One Tory who knows and likes him said: "Watching him with other Conservatives can be a bit embarrassing. He tends to mutter and to talk very obliquely and circuitously. MPs tend to think he's probably a good egg, but he doesn't connect very well." A close associate says that he is markedly more cheerful since he reached his understanding with the Tories — "he's got the smiling face now, he's in very happy form".

Mr Major's recent enthusiasm for the union clearly arises not from Mr Molyneaux's powers of persuasion, but from parliamentary weakness. Mr Molyneaux has been a lifetime opponent both of nationalism and of boldness. His advice to Mr Major on the Irish peace process will undoubtedly be to have nothing to do with it, for he will regard it as a foolhardy and dangerous exercise.

Mr Major may well, empirically, reach a similar conclusion. But if he does turn down the peace process as proferred by the Irish government and the SDLP, Irish nationalists will be angry. This will especially be the case, if they conclude he has done so not on the merits of the case but because he finds himself obligated to a 73-year-old member of Ballynadrenta Loyal Orange Lodge.

Against the expectations of many, the two governments put together the Downing Street declaration, launching it on 15 December 1993. The document, which contained statements designed to reassure both Unionists and nationalists, made a complicated statement on self-determination. This read: "The British government agrees that it is for the people of the island of Ireland alone, by agreement between the two parts respectively, to exercise their right of self-determination on the basis of consent, freely and concurrently given, north and south, to bring about a united Ireland, if that is their wish." This was, on one reading, an attempt to address republican concerns, though it specified that the concepts of self-determination and consent were inextricably intertwined. Many hailed it as a historic development.

Change of strategy opened door to deal

With the publication of the joint declaration with Dublin, the British government has made a highly significant and possibly irreversible shift in its basic approach to the problem of Northern Ireland. For more than two decades most Prime Ministers and Northern Ireland Secretaries have worked on the theory of finding some middle ground, establishing a devolved administration there, and patiently building up a consensus from the centre out. In this theory the extremes were to become gradually more and more isolated, and would finally wither away. This approach had many drawbacks, not the least of which was that it never worked. In 1974, the only time that the first hurdle was overcome and a powersharing executive was created, the whole experiment fell apart under extremist pressure in less than six months. All other attempts to set up a centrist institution did not reach first base.

One very obvious problem all along was the Rev Ian Paisley, whose anti-establishment instincts generally ensured that he would attack any agreement among the Northern Ireland parties. Another problem lay in the fact that there are actually two middle grounds, one Unionist and one nationalist. Even moderate nationalist politicians insist that their Irishness should be recognised in some form of Irish dimension and link with Dublin. But even moderate Unionist politicians are uneasy about this, worrying that it would weaken their link with Britain.

A further blow to the theory came with the emergence of Sinn Féin as a significant political presence in the early 1980s. Until then, part of the standard rhetoric of government ministers was to declare that only a tiny minority supported violence. Sinn Féin's achievement of winning the support of three out of every ten nationalist voters put an end to that line of argument.

Another problem was that as the years passed, and the various attempts failed, fewer and fewer people maintained any belief that this course might lead to peace. But lack of success did not deter Northern Ireland Office ministers and officials from persevering with it. Sir Patrick Mayhew recently complained that people accused him of whistling in the dark in his efforts to restart inter-party talks, declaring only a few weeks ago: "While the talks retain so much potential, the priority must be to carry them forward, not cut across or duplicate them."

The joint declaration represents a dramatic departure from that traditional approach. The concept of building incrementally from the middle out is, for the moment at least, taking second place to the new idea of attempting to draw the extremists into the political processes. The new approach has received such widespread support in London and Dublin (if not in all parts of Belfast) that it is easy to forget just how controversial a move it seemed a short time ago.

When it emerged in the spring that SDLP leader John Hume was engaged in dialogue with Gerry Adams of Sinn Féin, there were strong responses. The *Independent* reported at the time: "Reaction has ranged from furious Unionist denunciation to warm endorsement of his actions, but between these two poles there is considerable bewilderment about the significance of it all." At that point the idea of talking to, or even addressing, terrorists or those associated with them was one of the most delicate and dangerous issues in Irish politics. When Mr Hume announced that he and Mr Adams had reached a measure of agreement and said he was presenting this to the Irish government, some Dublin sources made it clear they were furious about having to handle anything bearing Mr Adams's thumbprints.

Dublin's decidedly cool reaction to the Hume–Adams initiative was followed by outright rejection from John Major, who declared in the Commons that the thought of talking to Mr Adams "turned his stomach". At that point the initiative seemed to be dead, but, in fact, a wave of popular nationalist support, north and south, not only revived it but propelled it to centre stage of the Anglo-Irish scene. Albert Reynolds was forced to reverse his original judgement and become the idea's chief proponent. His position was explained by an associate: "The Hume–Adams idea is so big that you can't just leave it on the landscape and walk away and say, 'Very interesting idea but we have something else to try.' It's far too big to do that: you have to resolve it into success or failure."

For some weeks it seemed the Hume–Adams initiative – sanitised, by this stage, into the Reynolds initiative – was going nowhere fast. An Anglo-Irish negotiation opened in which the Taoiseach sought to persuade John Major that the IRA could be induced to lay down its weapons and take a political path.

Hume–Adams has never been published, but it is said to include a draft declaration on self-determination, assurances to Unionists that majority consent would be required for a united Ireland, emphasis on agreement, a reference to a new European context, and assurances that Sinn Féin can enter political life if the IRA abandons terrorism. The Major–Reynolds declaration touches on all these points as well as others, though both governments are playing down its antecedents. For the moment the thumbprints of neither Mr Hume nor Mr Adams are unwelcome.

John Major and Albert Reynolds

The Taoiseach's conversion to the new approach was sudden; the Prime Minister's change of tack came more gradually, and was effected rather more elegantly. His problem was that he was anxious to retain the parliamentary support of James Molyneaux and his nine Ulster Unionist votes; and Mr Molyneaux clearly thought the new approach was not worth trying. But he has stopped short of denouncing it, which means that Mr Major has pulled off a considerable political feat: the production of a document which stood some chance of being acceptable to the IRA, and which at the same time appeared to have the acquiescence of the largest Unionist party.

While it has the potential to do both, there is no guarantee that it will do either. The considered reactions of the IRA, and the Unionist community, will take some time to emerge, but it is quite possible that the coming days and weeks could bring heightened dangers – at worst, no IRA cessation, coupled with a rise in loyalist violence. But even such a disastrous short-term outcome is unlikely to kill off completely the notion that addressing the terrorists directly could bring eventual peace. Even if the approach does not work immediately, there will be continuing efforts to bridge the gap between the IRA and the political system.

A fundamental change has been made to the political agenda, for the tantalising prospect that peace could be achieved by this path is simply too

324

big to be ignored. There is more and more hope that it is an idea whose time has come.

THE NATIONALISTS

The verdict of Sinn Féin and the IRA on the joint declaration will indicate whether or not the recently raised hopes for peace have a solid foundation.

In the declaration both governments addressed themselves to the key republican concerns of Irish self-determination and the entry of Sinn Féin into political life in the event of the ending of IRA violence. What is unclear is whether the declaration goes far enough to generate a cessation.

Outright rejection would be difficult, since the two governments will be judged to have made genuine efforts to tackle the issues which matter most to the republicans. The fact that the Irish government was involved in producing the document, which has been approved by SDLP leader John Hume, means rejection would leave Sinn Féin and the IRA isolated. Republicans are no strangers to isolation, but the future would hold little prospect of an end to their ostracism. The Republic, in particular, is showing ever-greater degrees of hostility to IRA methods, and joint British-Irish security initiatives could not be ruled out. The 70 per cent of nationalists represented by the SDLP are heartily sick of the violence, and want only to see it ended.

It seems too easy, on the other hand, to imagine that the IRA will, in the next few days, announce that the declaration has done the trick and that its campaign of violence has ended for ever. The republican movement has been characterised by splits, and few want a messy feud which would result in the emergence of a substantial group of diehards determined to fight to the death. There have been some doubts that some of the further-flung IRA units, such as south Armagh, would be ready to defy any order to lay down their arms. At the same time, there are other signs that even the hard men approve of the course undertaken by Gerry Adams.

One distinct possibility is for the republicans to announce, after due deliberation, that the declaration goes some way to meeting their demands but does not in itself suffice. They could then seek to draw one or both governments into dialogue, either in private or publicly, designed to win concessions before a cessation.

The paradox is that although some republicans are clearly willing to contemplate ending violence, they possess enough sinews of war to continue their campaign indefinitely. Stopping the violence would not be a surrender, for, as security sources readily attest, the guns, the explosives and the recruits are there for many more years of killing.

A cessation, if it happened, would come not because of military weakness but because of a genuine belief that the aims of republicanism could as effectively be pursued through politics and by negotiation. The IRA and Sinn Féin think of themselves as having a real choice between terrorism and political action; at this moment it cannot be predicted which path they will choose.

THE UNIONISTS

The Unionist community is such an insecure entity, nervous of all novelty, that even the prospect of peace can be enough to set alarm bells ringing.

When a community holds the belief, as it does, that the proper way to bring an end to IRA violence is by inflicting military defeat on the terrorists, attempts to bring Sinn Féin to the conference table can seem not only futile but dangerous. And when those attempts include complicated new elaborations on guarantees, traditional suspicions are awakened. The Major–Reynolds joint declaration is so complex that Unionists will now spend some time scrutinising the text, and searching for what may lie between its lines.

Last night it was too early to say whether the considered response will be relatively relaxed or one of nervousness. The widely differing reactions of the Rev Ian Paisley, who says it is a sellout, and Ulster Unionist leader James Molyneaux, who received it fairly calmly, have caused some confusion. Some Unionists said they were alarmed by the paragraph which deals with the self-determination of the Irish people. But others appeared to find little cause for concern, and so far there is no talk of protest rallies. The loyalist paramilitary groups said they would consider it and give their reaction later.

Mr Paisley has his own reasons for crying sellout. No stranger to the politics of denunciation, he condemned the document without reading it: as they say in Belfast, he got his retaliation in first. The DUP leader has an important European election to fight next year, and believes he does best in times of heightened tension.

Mr Molyneaux, by contrast, has his own reasons for hoping the Protestant population stays calm. Although disapproving of the document, he is hopeful of maintaining the special relationship which he believes he has developed with the Prime Minister. That would be difficult to do if Protestants were on the streets burning John Major in effigy, as they did with Margaret Thatcher. Mr Molyneaux hedged his bets with a Janus-like performance. In one interview he described the declaration as "a comparatively safe document" while in another he said: "It has the makings of a betrayal." In yet another he said it would take days to study and decode it.

The two Unionist leaders, and the loyalist paramilitary groups, have set out

326

their respective stalls. Much will also depend on nationalist response, for it is very common for the two sides to pay as much attention to the reactions of their opponents as they do to those of their own leaders.

The Unionist community, much reviled, has also been much bruised over the years as, in its eyes, the nationalists have made gain after gain. It is now poised on the point of deciding whether this declaration is another nationalist gain, or a genuine chance of peace.

It quickly became clear that the declaration was not enough, in itself, to halt the IRA campaign. But the republicans did not immediately reject it out of hand, opting instead for a long period of consideration and debate before delivering a definitive reply.

22 DECEMBER 1993   THE INDEPENDENT

Nervous IRA loiters at the crossroads

The provisional republican movement, led by the IRA and Sinn Féin, has rarely been under such pressure as it is at this moment. For many years it has, often with considerable tactical skill, managed to combine terrorism and political action in a twin-pronged campaign. But the action of the British and Irish governments, in issuing last week's joint peace declaration, has wrong-footed the republicans and confronted them with the most difficult of dilemmas. They must choose between peace and war.

As Gerry Adams of Sinn Féin made clear in Belfast, they are not yet ready to announce a decision. They want time to think; they want to talk to their people; they want clarification of the declaration; they want dialogue with the two governments. In other words, they are playing for time. They are uncomfortable and nervous, for this is a defining, and possibly historic, moment for the republican movement; and whatever path they choose, it is fraught with difficulties and dangers, political and physical.

The declaration surprised them, for they had thought it unlikely that Albert Reynolds could talk John Major into making an announcement which so directly addressed republican concerns. A month ago a senior republican said privately: "He [Major] just hasn't the balls for it, hasn't the bottle for it. He's the wrong man in place at the wrong time." Having underestimated Mr Major, they have now been presented with a document which drew a near-rapturous welcome from almost all shades of opinion not only in the House of Commons, but also in the Republic of Ireland. The declaration, and the reception it received, has increased the widespread hope that peace might be close.

It has tremendously increased the pressure on the republicans. At his press conference in the Falls Road, Gerry Adams faced a row of eight television cameras, arranged a little like a firing squad, and a roomful of British, Irish and foreign journalists who wanted to hear him say the war was over. He has personally invested a great deal in nudging the republican movement into a negotiating posture, but it is clear enough that the joint declaration is not viewed as the basis for a cessation of the IRA campaign. Mr Adams will now spend weeks, and perhaps months, establishing whether or not the two governments will consider making concessions that could make it acceptable. But at some stage soon it will become evident if the IRA intend to stop or go on.

Carrying on the campaign would present many difficulties. Unless the British and Irish governments make major tactical errors, the blame for the continuing violence will, outside the republican community itself, be placed squarely on the shoulders of the IRA. The IRA and Sinn Féin have coped with isolation before now, but their strategists must wonder about the prospects for success of a terrorist campaign which is only generating more and more hostility in the Republic. Sympathy for its cause in the south has dwindled to near-zero: the populace there want Irish unity some day, but not yet and not brought about by violence.

In the declaration the British and Irish governments subscribed to the principle that the Irish people had self-determination, but agreed that this consent was closely entwined, in a double helix structure, with the principle of Unionist consent to Irish unity. The only way for the IRA to force the British government to resile from that central concept, as expressed in a solemn agreement with the Irish government, is for the IRA to inflict a military defeat on Britain. IRA strategists must see how unlikely it is for two democratic governments to capitulate to terrorist activity in such a way.

328

But the other side of the coin is that the declaration, as it stands, offers little enough to the IRA. The concept of self-determination is addressed, but in practice the consent qualification means that a united Ireland is not on the horizon. The Unionist right to say no, as guaranteed by Britain, is arguably buttressed by the fact that it has been formally endorsed by Dublin.

The IRA would ideally like to end its campaign with a British withdrawal, or declaration of intent to withdraw, neither of which is on offer. Failing that, it would want to end in circumstances which set the scene for the eventual ending of the union. The declaration, on a republican reading, does not do so. The campaign would, therefore, be closing on an uncertain note. The declaration contains much green rhetoric, but the IRA does not trust the British. The section on self-determination has such a ring of finality to it that Sinn Féin, when it did reach the table, could be told that that key issue had already been settled.

Furthermore, the nationalist experience has been that the day-to-day reality of British administration in Northern Ireland is often more unionist than the occasional grand declarations which emanate from Downing Street. There is a fair likelihood, republicans would realise, that after an IRA cessation the British would not be inclined to make concessions in their direction.

There remains the key question of the Unionists. An ending of IRA violence would be welcomed by almost everyone, but republicans – and others – have seen no real signs that peace would bring any new partnership approach from a Unionism which they regard as unreconstructed and not in the business of offering a new accommodation to nationalists.

Few outsiders will have much sympathy, at this defining moment, for a movement which has inflicted so much death and destruction over the last quarter of a century. But it is a moment of real agony for the republican leadership; it is a genuine knife-edge decision; and a great many lives will depend on it.

As the months passed, the momentum of the peace process flagged. The loyalist killing rate went up, while the IRA waged a new, carefully tailored campaign: the big bombs in city and town centres stopped but attacks on the security forces went on unabated. The continuing killings soured the atmosphere.

Sinn Féin said it could make no definitive response to the Downing Street declaration until aspects of it were clarified, but the British government said this was unnecessary.

Then the republicans upped the ante: in March 1994 the IRA caused major disruption in London by staging a series of mortar attacks on Heathrow airport. No one was injured, but it was a clear message that the declaration was not enough to stop the IRA campaign.

12–13 MARCH 1994   THE INDEPENDENT

Mortars from the men sticking to the bunker

In 1990 a senior IRA leader defined the organisation's campaign as "armed propaganda". He defined this as "prosecuting a political struggle through military means – there are armed and unarmed political actions". Almost a year of intense political activity has been based on the premise that the IRA could be brought to contemplate a future in which it pursued its aims through unarmed political actions alone. After the Heathrow attack the stark question is whether all that effort has been futile. It may take some time for a conclusive answer to emerge. A slightly testy Gerry Adams was adamant that a peace process could co-exist with mortar bombs raining down on Heathrow's runways. There would be ups and downs and difficulties, his line ran, but coolness and calmness could overcome these.

It hardly needs saying that a great many people are having difficulties coming to terms with this concept, not just in Britain but in nationalist Ireland also. When the Taoiseach, Albert Reynolds, spoke in late 1993 of the possibility of peace before Christmas, he was seen as an optimist but not a complete Pollyanna. Suddenly there was a glimpse of light at the end of the tunnel.

In the Republic it seemed suddenly almost easy: London and Dublin were specifically offering Sinn Féin a route out of violence and into politics, which the republicans would be mad not to accept. Mr Reynolds and his people remained determinedly confident. This week an Irish government source gave the upbeat assessment: "So far so good." That was three hours before the first mortars fell on the airport.

The full implications will take some time to sink in. Even after the first Heathrow attack, the *Irish Times* said it "represents, it must be hoped, one of the last throws of the bloody dice by that violent organisation". Thus the disappointment at the Heathrow attacks is even more keenly felt in Dublin than in London, where counsels tended to be divided on the republican intentions.

Mr Adams, it should be remembered, has much to lose in the south, for he has made great presentational gains there of late. These gains were almost entirely contingent on his proving himself to be a man of peace. This new image has taken a battering with the Heathrow attacks and his use of the word "spectaculars" on an Irish radio interview. He is now in the business of selling a new vision, that of a protracted peace process during which the war will continue. The idea of quick fixes and short cuts to peace has been shattered.

So was the IRA serious in the first place, or was it all a con? Was all the talk of peace nothing more than a cynical device to make short-term propaganda gains? Or did Gerry Adams and his associates fail to persuade the republican movement to abandon violence? And will he keep trying?

Before the British government committed itself to the declaration, teams of military, security and political analysts made thorough examinations of Adams's character, his intentions, and the extent of his control over the movement. According to one government source: "Some pretty careful assessments were made before we took things to where they are now. There is confidence that Adams is serious, but he doesn't yet speak for the whole movement by any means. The odds seem to be slightly tipped against him being able to deliver the republican movement in the short term. But the movement can't ignore the declaration and maybe at some stage, if Adams could deliver Tyrone and Fermanagh and south Armagh, or felt he could marginalise them, then we might be taking things forward." Another government source reported that opinions differed within departments, but added: "The consensus seems to be that if he could carry them he would go for it, but he's not prepared to do it unless he's certain that they'd nearly all fall in behind him. My guess is that his main preoccupation is to maintain the unity of the movement."

Many will now conclude that Mr Adams never was serious, or that if he was, his pacific tendencies have been overruled by militants in his movement. Others may, after some thought, consider that there is still enough hope of peace left to justify not slamming the door in his face. Either way, the hard, brutal fact is that there are to be more killings. Snubbing Mr Adams means Northern Ireland goes back to square one, enduring continuing violence. Taking him at his word means continuing to invest in his credibility, and hoping that somewhere down the line the IRA can be persuaded to abandon armed propaganda. It is a bitter choice for the two governments, and everyone else, to have to make.

August 1994 brought the 25th anniversary of the arrival of British troops, and a reassessment of whether better days might lie ahead.

13 AUGUST 1994   THE INDEPENDENT

Catholics sense the chance to win the peace

After 25 years and more than 3,500 funerals, what remains uppermost in the memory is not the dead but the bereaved. The quiet but inconsolable grief of the widows; the bitter, hatred-soaked stare of a brother whose sister was gunned down; the 10-year-old girl who asked her mother for a kitchen knife "because I want to put it in my heart and go and see Daddy in heaven".

The political profit and loss accounts can be drawn up, with conclusions drawn on how the Catholics have fared, how Protestant fortunes stand, what the British government has achieved. But the essence of the Troubles lies in those little homes which now lack a father or a son; where even if peace comes it will bring no real respite from sorrow.

Six years ago, at the time of another anniversary, the *Independent* concluded: "There is no great ground swell of opinion in favour of accommodation in either community; no perceptible desire for compromise. The maiming and killing

332

will continue. Peace is not in prospect." That bleak assessment proved unhappily accurate. This time, however, there are realistic grounds for hoping that the beginning of the end may be in sight, and that a continuation of the conflict cannot be so confidently and coldly predicted.

Today the republican movement may be in the process of moving, however slowly and fearfully, away from IRA violence and towards political activity. If that happens, loyalist paramilitaries might follow suit. This time, therefore, peace could be in prospect. This is not a confident prediction, for much could go wrong. If it happens, it will not be a quick, clean ending: it is more likely to be a messy business, with many dying kicks and old scores being settled. It could take years, but there is in the air a sense that the conflict has entered a new phase, which is possibly the final phase.

Yet, as six years ago, there is still an absence of a great ground swell for accommodation between the two communities. The IRA, if and when it lays down its arms, will be doing so because it believes it is moving towards new understandings with the rest of Irish nationalism, and with the British government. It is not about to stop because it thinks it is about to find new common ground with Unionists. Far from it, in fact: one of its persistent demands now is for Britain to "break the Unionist veto", which is to say, to reduce Protestant power and influence. In other words, the onset of peace would be a spectacular step forward, but it would still leave a land disfigured by deep and bitter divisions. Some of the scars will never heal. In that sense peace would not be the end of the matter, but rather the first real step in a long and painful rebuilding process.

The Catholic community is in better shape to meet such a future. Both its republican component and its much larger nonviolent section display a confidence unimaginable 25 years ago. It is growing in numbers and rapidly climbing the social and economic ladders. It has redefined and reinterpreted its beliefs and its goals, junked much redundant ideological baggage, and modernised itself in a new flexible European pragmatism. Its people are already running large sections of the Northern Ireland public sector. It has powerful friends in Washington, Boston and Brussels. The future seems to hold either a united Ireland or a fairer Northern Ireland; either way it wins.

Unionism, by contrast, is facing into a fearful future. The two governments are looking ahead and so are the Catholics, even the IRA; but the Ulster Protestant has not moved with the times. The 25 years began with a historic defeat for Unionism, which found itself unable to justify, defend or even acknowledge its discriminatory system. In a sense it has never really recovered from that, playing a defensive game that has won it few outside friends over the years. Its lack of influence has to some extent been masked by the violence of the IRA, which brought as its incidental corollary a certain sympathy for its Protestant victims.

But for Protestants now the closing of the IRA campaign would be a distinctly dubious blessing. The end of the killings would of course be welcome, but cessation would bring with it the prospects of far-reaching negotiations and debate on how everyone's interests could be accommodated in a new political deal. The problem for Unionists is that their basic tenet – the assertion that Northern Ireland is British and nothing else – is incapable of being reconciled with any settlement acceptable to the nationalists, north and south, who would be at future conference tables. Thus an IRA cessation could spell increased political trouble for the Protestants, since in the new situation many elements will be arguing that republican aspirations have to be given due account.

It has been a terrible 25 years, with all those people being dispatched to premature graves. With luck, we may be at a juncture where the conflicting currents can, finally, be drawn together in a new synthesis; when belief in politics overcomes belief in the gun; when assassins no longer sledgehammer down doors and shoot people in their beds.

A great many people have learnt lessons during the last quarter of a century, often the hard way. Hopefully, if the Troubles really do end, the most lasting lesson is that Northern Ireland has more than its fair share of widows and orphans, and needs no more of them.

INDEX

Military Intelligence, 164–71
Mill, John Stuart, 62
Molyneaux, James, 6–7, 88, 208
  career of, 317–21
  and Downing Street declaration, 324, 326
  and Major, 287–8
  and talks process, 90, 197–205, 308
Moore, Gordon, 42
Moore, John, 114–15
Morrison, Danny, 121, 226
Murphy, Liam, 174
Murray, Lord Justice, 248–9, 250
Murray, Father Raymond, 182

nationalism, 19
nationalists
  aims of, 221–2
  relations with Unionists, 7–8, 334
  and the Republic, 60, 306–7
Neave, Airey, 89–90
Nelson, Brian, 137, 163–71
New Ireland Forum, 61
North Howard Street barracks (Belfast),
  192–5
Northern Ireland Civil Service, 14–15, 25
Northern Ireland Executive, 4–5, 60–1
Northern Ireland Office (NIO), 48, 88, 180
  and Brooke talks, 199
  and business community, 217–18
  compensation payments, 111, 112
  and Mayhew–Sinn Féin talks, 313–14
  on UDA, 137
Northern Ireland Parliament see Stormont

Ó Brádaigh, Ruairí, 225–6
Ó Conaill, Dáithí, 253–4
Ó Muilleoir, Máirtín, 249
O'Brien, Dr Conor Cruise, 8
O'Connell, Daniel, 208, 266
O'Donnell, Joe, 243
O'Donnell, Kevin Barry, 98, 100
O'Dwyer, Michael, 263
O'Farrell, John, 100
Official IRA, 119–20, 286
O'Hagan, Bernard, 241, 263
O'Hagan, Fiona, 241
O'Higgins, Thomas, 64, 65, 67
O'Malley, Des, 72
O'Neill, Captain Terence, 13
Orange Order, 318
Ormeau Road shootings (Belfast), 132–4,
  140

Paisley, Rev Ian, 6–7, 34, 58, 102, 181, 322
  assassination fears, 253

and Downing Street declaration, 326–7
and Dr John Dunlop, 209
and Mayhew–Sinn Féin talks, 312, 314
and Molyneaux, 318, 319–20
and talks process, 197–205, 308
Palace barracks (Holywood, Co Down), 195
Parnell, Charles Stewart, 208, 266
Paxman, Jeremy, 307
Phoenix Trust, 25
population movement, 38–9
Portadown, Co Armagh, 129–32
post office robberies, 103–6
Powell, Enoch, 88, 208
Presbyterians, 209–12
  meet UDA, 252–4
Prior, James, 88–9
prison system
  costs of, 49
  parole, 189–91
Progressive Democrats, 54, 72
proportional representation, 72–3
Protestants; see also unemployment
  emigration, 14, 38, 210, 261
  fear of British withdrawal, 216–19,
    333–4
  numbers of, 36–9
  sectarian assassinations, 147–8,
    149–52
public sector employment, 14–15, 25, 33,
  47–8

Queen's University Belfast, 13
  discrimination in, 26–31
Quinn, John, 65, 67–8

racketeering, 93, 125, 302
Relate, 108–13
religious segregation, 40–6
Reynolds, Albert, 77, 306, 307, 314, 331;
  see also Downing Street declaration
  (1993)
  election (1992), 69, 71–3
Robinson, Mary, 59, 75–6, 306
  in Belfast, 274–5
  election of, 52–7
Robinson, Nick, 56
Robinson, Peter, 201, 202, 205
Rocke, Lawrence, 141–2
Rose and Crown bar (Belfast), 134–5
Rough Justice (BBC), 188
Royal Ulster Constabulary (RUC), 16, 64,
  99–101, 132, 147, 194, 232, 296
  and attacks on Sinn Féin members, 262,
  263
  Casement Park inquiry, 184, 187–8